BRITISH AIRWAYS

BRITISH AIRWAYS
Its History, Aircraft and Liveries

KEITH GASKELL

Airlife
England

ACKNOWLEDGEMENTS

A project such as this can only be tackled successfully with a great deal of help and encouragement and my thanks go to the many people from British Airways and its partner airlines who have given me every possible support. In fact so many people have willingly shared their knowledge and experience that it is an impossible task to list them all individually, but I would like to use this opportunity to thank them for their contributions.

Mentioned here are several people without whom the book could not have been published. Samantha Gregory and Geoff Want of Operations Control who showed such unwavering faith in my ideas. Michael Blunt and Andy Patsalides for their media and marketing input and Fred Huntley from the Archive and Museum Collection. I am also indebted to Richard Church for his many long hours of proof-reading and expert critique.

All photographs were taken by the author unless otherwise credited.

Finally thanks to my most loyal and long suffering supporters Maria, Christopher and Peter.

Copyright © 1999 Keith Gaskell

First published in the UK in 1999
by Airlife Publishing Ltd

British Library Cataloguing-in-Publication Data
A catalogue record for this book
is available from the British Library

ISBN 1 84037 142 0

Printed in Spain

Airlife Publishing Ltd
101 Longden Road, Shrewsbury, SY3 9EB, England
E-mail: airlife@airlifebooks.com
Website: www.airlifebooks.com

CONTENTS

INTRODUCTION

My aim with this book has been to produce a pictorial record of British Airways' aircraft and their colour schemes as seen during the last twenty-five years. Whilst the airline can trace its ancestry back much further to the very earliest days of civil aviation in 1919, it is British Airways as we know it today, an airline created by merging the two great State-owned corporations BEA and BOAC in 1974, which is illustrated here. The photographs are accompanied by a narrative which describes the development and operational use of each of the many varied aircraft types to have served the airline, its partners and subsidiaries.

British Airways' fleet has of course changed out of all recognition since the early post-merger days. The patriotic red, white and blue airliners of the 1970s gave way to new and much more efficient Boeings along with a classic business-style livery for the 1980s. That identity has in turn been superseded as the airline now promotes its 'global' image, and many, even more capable airliners are now arriving from both Airbus and Boeing. This evolution has occurred against a background of unprecedented growth in air travel and structural changes in the airline industry. Governmental influence and control has diminished, deregulation has emerged gradually throughout the world and competition as well as co-operation between airlines is now widespread. One outcome of this process has been franchising, a relatively recent phenomenon pioneered by British Airways which, together with the ownership of various subsidiaries, has greatly increased the number of aircraft to have displayed the airline's identity. The operations of these various partner airlines and their fleets are also described in some detail.

After completing the merger in 1974, British Airways set about the difficult and sometimes painful transition from an inefficient state-owned enterprise into a privately owned and highly profitable world airline. Part of that process involved sweeping away almost all of its inherited fleets with just a handful of the original 218 aircraft still in service twenty-five years later. These survivors were some of BOAC's Boeing 747-136s, but even this final link to the pre-merger days has now been severed by their recent retirement. Sadly, the last great fleets of British-built airliners have all disappeared, some to exciting and new careers such as the VC-10s which became tankers with the RAF, whilst others like the Trident simply faded away into history. Lockheed TriStars arrived after the merger and, having made their contribution to the airline, have also moved on. The first Airbus A320s and a small fleet of DC-10s unexpectedly joined the airline through the merger with British Caledonian, and Concorde of course became the ultimate example of fleet development and innovation following its introduction in 1976. Several other types have made brief appearances; aircraft such as a Boeing 727-100, the McDonnell Douglas MD-80 and British Aerospace 146 operated on short-term leases, and additional examples of established fleet types have also been used to boost capacity or to cover for aircraft undergoing maintenance.

The aircraft types which now dominate British Airways' fleet are vastly more capable than their predecessors in terms of range, payload, operating economics and passenger comfort as well as being much more acceptable to airport neighbourhoods through their lower noise characteristics. The fleet is made up largely of Boeing's family of twin-jet airliners, 747-200s, 747-400s, a rapidly growing fleet of narrow-body Airbus A319/320s and of course Concorde. The route network served by these airliners has also evolved to accommodate the relentless growth in commercial demand. Many new destinations have been introduced, often to parts of the world which were previously inaccessible, and frequencies have increased on established routes. Operational constraints have also played their part, with congestion at Heathrow forcing the introduction of larger aircraft and to some extent encouraging the tremendous growth of operations from Gatwick. Regional services have evolved from a large and diverse fleet of Viscounts and One-Elevens operating throughout the British Isles to a network based on Birmingham and Manchester which includes flights across the Atlantic as well as to many European destinations.

As a result of these many changes, over 900 airliners have flown the flag for British Airways during the last 25 years, encompassing most airliner types built by western manufacturers. There have in fact been very few types which have not been used,

the obvious exceptions until recently being most of the Airbus range. However, the recent consolidation of large airliner manufacturing into just two groups, Boeing and Airbus, was followed in 1998 by British Airways' first ever order for Airbus airliners, as well as more Boeings. This decision to buy from both manufacturers has probably set a trend which will lead to many more European airliners displaying the airline's livery alongside their American rivals.

The public image of British Airways as seen on its aircraft has also evolved and changed with three distinct corporate identities used, each linked to a particular phase of the airline's development. The initial red, white and blue flag-based design took the new airline through its troubled post-merger consolidation phase and on to 1984, when the Landor-designed scheme was introduced during a period of steady growth leading towards privatisation. This in turn has now been swept away as British Airways enters the new Millennium, transforming itself into a truly 'global' airline with a dramatic and innovative 'World Image' livery to match. This exciting development introduced over thirty different artistic tail designs and has certainly provoked much comment and interest in the airline. Apart from these three main identities, there have been many partial, temporary and hybrid schemes as aircraft have been leased or transferred between subsidiaries. Special occasion designs have also become increasingly common in recent years.

Formed in 1946 BEA took over the operation of most UK domestic routes in 1947 with a fleet of wartime transports such as the DC-3 (top) or the Vickers Viking (bottom) which was an interim design derived from the Wellington bomber. BEA had to make do with such small and uncomfortable types until new designs in the form of the pressurised Airspeed Ambassador (centre) and turboprop Vickers Viscount entered service in 1952/3. (BRITISH AIRWAYS ARCHIVE)

CHAPTER ONE

BEA AND BOAC
Forerunners of British Airways

The new British Airways born in 1974 resulted from the combination of two long established and quite unique airlines, British European Airways (BEA) and British Overseas Airways Corporation (BOAC). Both of these State-owned airlines had evolved during the post-war years under conditions of considerable political control and interference which had greatly influenced their aircraft purchases and ultimately determined which types were brought together in the merger. The history of both airlines has been well documented elsewhere, but a brief historical overview of some of the political circumstances and corporate policies prevalent during the years leading up to the merger now follows, setting the scene for the development of the two very diverse fleets which British Airways inherited.

BEA – British European Airways

BEA's contribution to the new British Airways consisted of a large fleet of almost entirely British-built airliners (BEA Airtours and Helicopters fleets being the exceptions), ranging from 1950s-vintage Vickers Viscounts to the recently delivered Trident 3Bs. A large Heathrow-based Mainline fleet of Tridents plus a few remaining Vanguards operated domestic trunk routes and supported the most extensive European network of any airline, justifying the advertising slogan 'Number One In Europe'. New BAC One-Eleven-510s flew schedules from their 'Super One-Eleven Division' base at Manchester and maintained the Internal German Services from West Berlin. Domestic and international routes from UK regional airports were the domain of BEA's Channel Islands and Scottish Airways Divisions and subsidiary British Air Services which operated as Cambrian Airways and Northeast Airlines, utilising an extensive fleet of Viscounts, Trident 1Es, One-Eleven 400s and Shorts Skyliners from several bases around the country. A fleet of nine Merchantman freighters flew scheduled cargo services from Heathrow to several European destinations. Gatwick was the base for charter subsidiary BEA Airtours with its fleet of ex-BOAC Boeing 707-436s and was also the headquarters of BEA Helicopters, although most of its fleet was based elsewhere in the United Kingdom.

The origins of this impressive network and extensive fleet date back to 1946, when the UK government formed BEA to operate European services, followed in 1947 by the transfer of most UK domestic routes from the unfortunate independent airlines as part of the nationalisation policy of the time. BEA began operations with a fleet of outdated and hopelessly uneconomic derivatives of wartime types, such as the Rapide, Ju-52, DC-3, Avro 19 and Viking, which resulted in very heavy losses. British manufacturers soon designed more modern types and the first to reach BEA was the pressurised Airspeed Ambassador in 1952. Although this was an excellent airliner it was soon superseded by Vickers' revolutionary turboprop Viscount, which entered scheduled service as a forty-seven-seater in April 1953. The Viscount fleet rapidly grew, with longer fuselage Series 802s carrying up to sixty-five passengers entering service in 1957. By the end of that year over fifty Viscounts were in service, contributing enormously to an improvement in BEA's results with the airline making profits from 1955 for the first time. Thirty-three of the BEA Viscount 800s were eventually destined to fly for British Airways many years later.

A larger and faster follow-up to the Viscount, designed to satisfy BEA's need for an aircraft to carry 100 passengers on European trunk routes, was the Vickers Vanguard and twenty of these splendid airliners entered service from March 1961. Sadly for its manufacturer, by that time the jet revolution had taken hold and the Vanguard only ever sold to two airlines. Despite this BEA employed its fleet profitably and reliably for many years, in particular on domestic routes as well as to popular European destinations such as Gibraltar, Malta and Palma. Three passenger Vanguards plus nine of the very capable Merchantman freighter conversions remained in service at the time of the merger, the passenger aircraft being withdrawn soon after, but the freighters serving British Airways until December 1979.

With the race to join the jet age underway, BEA introduced a stop-gap fleet of fourteen Comet 4Bs from April 1960. Ten of these were later used to form BEA Airtours, which flew Mediterranean charters with them until 1971. It was, however, the Hawker Siddeley Trident which was destined to establish BEA firmly in the jet age, a type which became synonymous with the airline through the 1960s and which eventually became the most numerous of any aircraft type with the new British Airways in 1974. The Trident introduced many new technologies and resulted from a lengthy evaluation of BEA's very

G-AOJB wearing the 1960s 'red square' colour scheme of BEA was one of 33 Viscount 800s transferred to British Airways in 1974. Although the type went on to serve until 1981, OJB's career was somewhat shorter as it was retired in 1976. (MAP)

specific requirements for a 600 mph jet capable of carrying up to 100 passengers in six-abreast seating, economically and in all weathers. These requirements were eventually met, although just how economical the aircraft was is still open to debate, but such a narrow set of specifications from just one airline hampered sales of the Trident to other customers. With BEA, however, the Trident 1C became an instant success after entering service in 1964 on prime European routes and was soon followed by the longer-range Series-2E, ordered to operate non-stop services to distant cities such as Nicosia and Tel Aviv.

By that time the political influence which played a major part in BEA's aircraft purchase decisions had become an important factor in determining which types would be handed over to British Airways in the not too distant future. Instead of more Tridents BEA wanted to order Boeing's 727-200 or the proposed BAC-211, but its choice was overruled by the government which insisted upon another Trident order for domestic economic reasons. An order duly followed for the third and final variant, the 140-seat Trident 3B, twenty-six of which were delivered between 1971–2. This was a prime example of how interference for short-term political gains was to have a long-term affect on the new British Airways, as sixty-five of the airline's initial short-haul fleet consisted of an assortment of increasingly inefficient and noisy Tridents, all of which would have to be replaced within a few years. Similar circumstances surrounded the 1967 order for eighteen One-Eleven-510s for Manchester and the Internal German Services where permission to order BEA's chosen aircraft, the Boeing 737-200, was denied. British Airways would eventually order both the 737-200 and the 727-200's successor, the 757, to replace its Tridents some ten years later.

The final example of such political control over investment decisions came during BEA's selection during the early 1970s of a new high capacity wide-bodied airliner. Although destined never to be flown by BEA, being delivered after the merger, the Lockheed TriStar with its British RB-211 engines was ordered when H.M. Government once again refused to support BEA's choice, in this case the BAC-Three-Eleven. The government had hoped that the proposed European Airbus A300B would be ordered but eventually the TriStar was bought, an aircraft which was much too big and which struggled for many years to find its place within British Airways.

These decisions settled BEA's fleet plans for the final run-up to the merger and a re-organisation in April 1971 established profit centres to operate the various types. BEA's final year of 1973–4 saw a total of 8.74m passengers carried and the airline also produced its best ever result, making a £6.7m profit, excluding the loss-making Scottish and Channel Islands Divisions. At the end of March 1974 the fleet of what had once been BEA was divided up as follows:

* Mainline Division flew sixty-one Tridents plus three remaining Vanguards from Heathrow.
* The Super One-Eleven Division based at Manchester flew eighteen of the type, which was proving to be an ideal complement to the Trident on European scheduled services.
* British Air Services operated as Cambrian Airways (four One-Eleven-400s, eight Viscount 806s) and Northeast Airlines (four Tridents-1Es, six Viscount 806s).
* BEA's Channel Islands Division flew twelve Viscount 802s and a newly delivered One-Eleven-400.
* The Scottish Airways Division operated seven Viscount 802s and two Shorts Skyliners.
* Other types were nine Merchantman freighters of the Cargo Division, seven Boeing 707-436s of BEA Airtours and the rotary-winged fleet of BEA Helicopters.

From 1964 to 1974 up to 70 examples of Hawker Siddeley's Trident dominated BEA's unrivalled network of European routes. Three main versions of this sleek, high-tech airliner were developed to meet BEA's exacting requirements and whilst initially giving the airline what it wanted, such narrow specifications restricted the aircraft's appeal elsewhere. (BRITISH AIRWAYS ARCHIVE)

BEA took delivery of 26 stretched Trident 3Bs between 1971 and 1973 and transferred them all to British Airways in 1974. G-AWZA, photographed here in BEA's final livery, was the second Trident Three to be built, flying for the first time in March 1970. However, its career was brief and in October 1982 it became the first Trident Three to be retired. (MAP)

BOAC – British Overseas Airways Corporation

Throughout its final decade as a separate and purely long-haul carrier BOAC operated a fleet of modern, high-speed airliners, primarily the VC-10 and Boeing 707, and from 1970 onwards the new 747. Surprising exceptions to this all-jet fleet were two twenty-year-old examples of the ubiquitous Viscount which began operating in their own 'long-haul' niche from 1972, of which more later. The sixty-four-strong jet fleet of March 1974 bore absolutely no resemblance to the slow, lumbering piston-engined types which were in service just fifteen years earlier. Jets had indeed brought a sweeping revolution to long-haul travel.

After World War Two BOAC set about re-building its network of Empire routes and expanding into other parts of the world using wartime bomber and transport designs hastily converted for airline use, aircraft such as the Avro Lancastrian, Avro York and the Handley Page Halton. Converted Shorts Sunderlands and new Solents were also in use but the large flying boat with its leisurely and luxurious style of long-haul travel belonged to another era and they were all retired by the end of 1950. Early British attempts to design new long-haul airliners produced aircraft which were either disastrous, such as the Avro Tudor, or, like the Handley Page Hermes, hopelessly outclassed by their American rivals. BOAC was therefore forced to buy a series of expensive American airliners, particularly to operate on the prestigious North Atlantic routes. Eight Lockheed 049 Constellations acquired in 1946 were followed by another seventeen improved L-749s and in 1950 the first of ten Boeing Stratocruisers arrived. Twenty-two Canadair C-4 Argonauts were also bought to operate the Commonwealth routes.

Meanwhile the British aircraft industry produced a range of innovative designs throughout the early 1950s in an attempt to regain the lead. Exciting new technologies in the form of the turboprop Bristol Britannia and pioneering turbojet de Havilland Comet promised great things for both BOAC and Great Britain, but sadly, technical

Following the end of World War Two, BOAC began to rebuild and expand its network with a selection of obsolete designs which were soon supplemented by new and much more capable Lockheed Constellations such as the three magnificent specimens in this nostalgic photograph. (BRITISH AIRWAYS ARCHIVE)

BOAC and the British aircraft industry bravely pioneered many new technologies during the 1950s in an attempt to regain the lead in airliner design and production. The de Havilland Comet entered service with BOAC as the world's first jet airliner in May 1952 but a tragic series of crashes led to its withdrawal for a complete redesign. A rare early Comet survivor is G-APAS which is preserved at RAF Cosford in BOAC colours.

problems delayed their entry into service and brought tragic consequences in the form of three early Comet crashes. BOAC was once again forced to import American airliners in order to remain competitive. Seven second-hand Statocruisers were bought and Her Majesty's Government reluctantly sanctioned the acquisition of a stop-gap fleet of ten Douglas DC-7Cs, aircraft which gave excellent service while the Britannia's problems were resolved and the Comet was redesigned. Ultimately both types emerged from their difficulties and flew for many years, but for BOAC they had arrived too late and were soon superseded by newer long-haul jets. Inevitably the end result for BOAC was many unprofitable years which lasted until 1963–4 when a small profit of £1m was made. This, however, was the beginning of a very profitable period which was to continue, apart from

one year, until the merger with BEA in 1974.

By the end of the 1950s jet airliner technology had begun to mature and new designs for the 1960s emerged for fast, productive and reliable long-haul aircraft which would soon replace their propeller-driven predecessors and begin a new era of unprecedented growth in air travel. BOAC took full advantage of these new airliners to operate what was the largest international network of any airline in the world.

The first scheduled jet services across the Atlantic were flown by BOAC Comet 4s during 1958, just weeks before Pan-Am introduced the Boeing 707. For the 1960s, however, a new fleet of jets for two very different missions was needed. To operate BOAC's traditional Empire routes to East Africa and the Far East, an airliner which could operate from short runways at hot and high airfields was required.

During the 1950s, as BOAC waited for new British airliners to arrive, seven additional Boeing Stratocruisers (top) were acquired from airlines in America followed by a fleet of ten new Douglas DC-7Cs (middle and bottom), all of which were needed to operate the airline's highly competitive North Atlantic routes. (BRITISH AIRWAYS ARCHIVE)

The Vickers VC-10 was specifically designed with a very large wing and an excess of engine power to cope with such conditions, but those same features meant that it was totally unsuited to the North Atlantic routes which needed airliners such as the 707 with their longer-range and better payloads. These conflicting requirements set the scene for many years of confrontation with successive governments, as the airline fought to have its way and purchase Boeing 707s rather than more of the home-grown VC-10s. The

end result for BOAC, and later for British Airways, was a mixed fleet of the two types.

Twelve Standard VC-10s were delivered, along with another seventeen Super VC-10s with stretched fuselages and longer-range to make them more suitable for North Atlantic routes. These elegant airliners were always very popular with passengers and excellent performers on the routes for which they were originally designed, but could never compete on equal terms with their American rivals on longer

Unfortunately for the British aircraft industry and the airlines which had ordered its products, several promising airliner designs from the 1950s failed to live up to expectations until it was too late. One such aircraft was the Bristol Britannia which first flew in 1952 but had been overtaken by the new generation of jets by the time it entered service with BOAC in 1957. Despite this the Britannia matured into a reliable and economic airliner which served the airline until the mid-1960s. (BRITISH AIRWAYS ARCHIVE)

BOAC's last major airliner acquisition was the Boeing 747, the first of which entered service across the North Atlantic in April 1971. By 1974 the 747 had taken over many routes from the 707/VC-10s and fifteen were handed over to British Airways, most of which were still in service 25 years later, including this example, G-AWNE, which was finally retired in 1999. (MAP)

routes. Throughout the 1960s BOAC fought continually to be allowed to order more 707s and in total took delivery of twenty Rolls-Royce Conway-powered 707-436s, followed by eleven of the later turbofan-powered 707-320B/Cs, several of which operated as freighters.

The next type to be bought by BOAC was destined to have the biggest impact on long-haul travel of any airliner ever built, and was the only aircraft operated by either BOAC or BEA to see service with British Airways throughout its first twenty-five years. Boeing's 747 came into being through the vision and determination of Pan-American's leader Juan Trippe, and once purchased by the American airline it soon became an essential part of all other major international carriers' fleets. The first 747s entered service with Pan-Am in January 1970 and deliveries to BOAC commenced soon afterwards, but because of a dispute with the pilots they did not enter service until April 1971. The fleet soon grew so that by the time of the merger in 1974 fifteen were in service and had taken over many of the airline's prime routes. Some of the displaced 707-436s transferred to BEA Airtours from 1971, to

replace their Comets, and others were converted to an all-economy seat configuration to serve with British Overseas Air Charter on North Atlantic charter work.

So by 1974 BOAC was operating the world's most extensive long-haul network which included such globe-spanning routes as that which crossed North America and the Pacific to Australia, another from Hong Kong via the Indian Ocean to South Africa, and the Trans-Polar route via Moscow to Tokyo. This network was maintained by the fleet of VC-10/707/747s which stood at eleven Standard VC-10s, sixteen Super VC-10s, eleven 707-436s, eleven 707-336B/Cs and fifteen 747-136s. Finally the two remaining aircraft operated at that time in BOAC's dark-blue and gold colours were the Viscount 700s mentioned earlier. Proudly named 'Scottish Prince' and 'Scottish Princess' they were the last Viscounts still flying from BEA's original turboprop fleet of 1953 and were operated by Cambrian Airways on domestic feeder services from Prestwick for BOAC. Also on order following many years of development were five Concordes which BOAC had agreed to buy in July 1972 but would never actually operate as the first one did not enter service until January 1976 with British Airways.

CHAPTER TWO

THE CREATION OF BRITISH AIRWAYS IN 1974

Lead-up to the merger

Throughout the 1960s rumours concerning the joining together of BEA and BOAC into a single airline were often heard, rumours which began to take on substance in 1967 when Her Majesty's Government set up an enquiry to look into the organisation of the British airline industry. The Edwards Committee Report was published in May 1969 and made several important recommendations. One of these was that a 'second force' airline be established in order to provide the two State-owned airlines with effective competition. This came about in 1970 through the takeover of British United Airways by Caledonian Airways to form British Caledonian. Of much greater significance however, was its recommendation that BEA and BOAC should be looked after by a single holding board with a view to increasing co-operation between them and reducing wasteful duplication of resources and facilities. To implement this the British Airways Board was established on 1 April 1972 to take control over the operating divisions of BEA, BOAC and their associated subsidiaries, bringing them together as the British Airways Group on 1 September 1972. Task forces were set up to study ways of integrating their operations and led to a British Airways Board recommendation, duly accepted by the government, to implement a full merger from 1 April 1974, although the trading name of British Airways was adopted from 1 September 1973.

And so a new British Airways emerged as the world's biggest international airline, flying to 200 destinations in 84 countries with a fleet of 218 aircraft. At the same time, however, an important chapter in the story of British airlines closed and the charismatic names of British European Airways and British Overseas Airways Corporation were consigned to history.

The progression from BEA and BOAC into a combined British Airways is illustrated in this line of tails. A BOAC Super VC-10, BEA Trident and ex-BEA Super One-Eleven, all of which had served British Airways before their retirement, are now preserved at Duxford.

British Airways – initial operations, organisation and corporate identity

From an operational point of view BEA and BOAC disappeared quietly and without fanfare, and flight operations initially carried on much as before. British Airways, however, had come into being at a difficult time with fuel supplies restricted and the price spiralling upwards following a Middle East war, and the UK economy was suffering from high inflation and industrial unrest. The airline industry, and the country as a whole, was shocked by the spectacular collapse of holiday airline Court Line in August 1974, a victim of such problems. British Airways soon found itself with too much capacity (this was graphically described as being equivalent to several empty 747s crossing the Atlantic every day), and a fleet of new TriStars was about to be delivered which would only make the situation worse. The expensive-to-run Standard VC-10s became early casualties, withdrawn along with the remaining Vanguards, but this was not enough to prevent the airline from descending rapidly into a period of instability and unprofitability.

The initial organisational structure comprised seven autonomous operating divisions. These were basically unchanged from pre-merger days and it was to take many years of difficult and gradual change before the airline could claim to be fully integrated into a single operating unit.

The four aircraft-operating divisions were:

British Airways European Division (BA ED)	previously BEA Mainline, plus the Super One-Eleven Division, Cargo and Airtours.
British Airways Overseas Division (BA OD)	previously BOAC.
British Airways Regional Division (BA RD)	previously British Air Services (Cambrian, Northeast), BEA Scottish Airways and Channel Islands Divisions.
British Airways Helicopters	previously BEA Helicopters.

The other three divisions were all non-aircraft operating and comprised:

British Airways Associated Companies
British Airways Engine Overhaul
International Aeradio.

ABOVE: *A fresh new livery for British Airways appeared in September 1973 as illustrated by Viscount 806 G-AOYG. Whilst certain elements could be traced back to the final BEA and BOAC colour schemes, it was designed to project the image of a single unified British flag carrier.*

BELOW: *A lengthy period of consolidation and change followed the merger of BEA and BOAC which was fully implemented on 1 April 1974. Evidence of previous ownership was visible for some time after that date as illustrated by VC-10 G-ARVM, which is in a hybrid BOAC/BA livery alongside a Super VC-10 fully painted in the new livery.*

Another example of the transitional liveries can be seen here on Trident Three G-AWZH, photographed at Heathrow in August 1977 with a basic BEA scheme modified by the addition of British Airways titles.

British Airways fleet – April 1974

BA European Divn	BA Overseas Divn	BA Regional Divn	BA Helicopters	
18 One-Eleven-510	11 Standard VC-10	33 Viscount 800	10	
20 Trident 1C	16 Super VC-10	5 One-Eleven-400		
15 Trident 2E	11 B707-436	4 Trident 1E		
26 Trident 3B	11 B707-336B/C	2 Shorts Skyliner		
3 Vanguard	15 B747-136			
9 Merchantman	2 Viscount 700			
7 B707-436 (Airtours)				
98	**66**	**44**	**10**	**218 total**

The new airline of course needed a new identity. More than just a new livery for its aircraft, it required a completely new and unifying corporate identity which would be acceptable to the two very different organisations being brought together, each of which was fiercely proud of its own heritage. Every aspect of the airline from baggage tags and tickets through to the vehicles and uniforms, as well as aircraft, would need to incorporate the new identity and be instantly recognisable as part of the new British Airways. In order to achieve these aims the airlines settled on a design in July 1973 which included recognisable elements from both the BEA and BOAC liveries and which was based on the United Kingdom's national colours and flag. The first aircraft to carry it, a Boeing 707-336B, appeared during September 1973 and although many others from right across the airline had been repainted by April 1974, completion of the fleet was a long-drawn-out process with examples of previous liveries still visible in hybrid schemes as late as 1981. The identity achieved its aims and was soon widely credited with being innovative, modern and ideally suited to its purposes. Full details of this and the other British Airways identities and their implementation throughout the fleet can be found in Chapter Six.

The last BOAC tail finally disappeared in February 1977 when 747-136 G-AWNC was stripped and repainted in British Airways colours.

CHAPTER THREE

TWENTY-FIVE YEARS: 1974–1999

Following from the initial post-merger period described earlier a great many changes have occurred. Some of these were specific to British Airways, such as privatisation and the freedom to stand or fall by its own decisions, whereas others have resulted from outside influences such as fuel shortages, economic recessions and even wars. Worldwide deregulation and political changes have greatly increased competition and opened up new market opportunities. Barriers to foreign ownership have fallen, allowing airlines to link up and co-operate as never before and new technologies have been introduced of which Concorde is of course the most dramatic example. Many other advances, however, have contributed to a steady but continuous improvement in the efficiency and environmental acceptability of new airliners, with the introduction of a completely new generation of extremely reliable, powerful and very quiet engines of particular importance. The result is that when a typical Trident of 1974 is compared to a new A320, or a long-haul Boeing 707 with the same manufacturer's ultra-efficient 777-236ER – there really is no comparison!

The list of changes is extensive and if each was examined in detail would probably fill several books. What follows in this section is a brief summary of significant events which have occurred during the twenty-five years since 1974, events which have had a direct effect upon the operation of British Airways and its aircraft.

1974

* Two British Aerospace 748s ordered shortly after the merger for delivery in 1975 for use in Scotland, partly to begin replacing the ageing Viscounts and also to support North Sea oil exploration.
* The Standard VC-10 fleet and three remaining Vanguards were retired due to over-capacity.
* The first Lockheed TriStar arrived in October but did not enter service until January 1975 because of industrial problems.

1975

* Domestic Shuttle services introduced during January, initially to Glasgow, after many years of study.
* During May an agreement with Air New Zealand (ANZ) enabled ANZ DC-10s flown by BA crews to operate the LHR–Los Angeles route in place of 707s.
* The Rolls-Royce-powered 747-200 was launched with a BA order for four.
* The years 1974–5 and 1975–6 were both loss-making. The 1975–6 loss was £16.3m.
* Thirteen Viscounts were withdrawn during 1975–6 to reduce some of Regional Division's losses.

1976

* Concorde finally entered commercial service, from Heathrow to Bahrain on 21 January. Services to

The first major new type of aircraft to be delivered to British Airways was the Lockheed TriStar which had been ordered by BEA in August 1972 and entered service in January 1975 on the airline's prime European routes. G-BBAJ, the sixth TriStar, is seen here at Heathrow in October 1978 after its conversion for long-haul use.

Washington began on 24 May, but services to New York JFK were held up by legal battles in US courts.

* An agreement to form a common BA pilot force allowed TriStars to be used on flights to India and the Middle East from April, initially using range-limited TriStar-1s in a long-haul configuration. This, however, sparked off industrial unrest in various parts of the airline. The requirement for longer-range aircraft led to an order for six short-fuselage TriStar-500s in August.

* The first two 747-236s arrived during June.

* A profit of £35m was made in 1976–7.

1977

* During April 1977 a major reorganisation saw the airline adopt a single functional-based operating structure with departments set up to oversee Flight Operations, Engineering, Planning etc. for the whole airline. Commercial operations were split into geographical route groups: UK & Ireland, North and East Europe, West and South Europe, and for the long-haul network, Eastern, Southern and Western Routes.

* The search for new short-haul airliners to replace Tridents began.

* Concorde began scheduled services to New York JFK on 22 November and to Singapore in December, but this route was suspended after only three services until January 1979.

1978

* Orders for nineteen Boeing 737-200s and three BAe One-Eleven-539s were placed in July.

* 1978–9 produced a £110m profit.

1979

* Concorde began operating between Washington and Dallas under a lease agreement with Braniff International in January. Three services per week operated until June 1980.

* Two TriStar-200s were ordered in January followed by six in September, BA's final TriStar order.

Deliveries took place between March 1980 and May 1981.

* The new Boeing 757 was launched during March with orders for nineteen from British Airways and twenty-one from Eastern Airlines in America.

* The first of six long-range TriStar-500s entered service between Heathrow and Abu Dhabi in May.

* A Conservative government was elected in May, which declared that BA would no longer receive any State support or interference in its commercial decision making. In July the government's intention to go ahead with privatisation was announced but this was soon delayed by a forthcoming recession which plunged BA into massive losses.

* By this time BA was substantially over-staffed and awaiting delivery of £1bn worth of new 737/747/757s and TriStars, aircraft which in addition to being more efficient would also be considerably bigger than those being replaced. BA decided to use these resources to expand into the leisure travel market which was expected to continue growing rapidly. However, competition from domestic carriers such as British Caledonian, British Midland, Dan-Air and Laker was also increasing and BA was not aware that a devastating recession was about to strike.

* The last Merchantman service was flown on 2 December from Stockholm and Gothenburg to Heathrow.

1980

* By the end of March twenty-six domestic regional routes including all of those from Cardiff, Bristol, Leeds, Liverpool, the Isle of Man and most of those from Newcastle were dropped because a viable economic replacement for the Viscounts could not be found. Only seven Viscounts remained in service on Scottish routes, but these were soon replaced by the acquisition of more 748s, and all had gone by May 1982.

* British Airtours began replacing its 707-436s with new 737-236s during March.

The last one of 20 Concordes to be built arrives at Heathrow on delivery to British Airways in June 1980. At the time it carried the registration G-N94AF but entered service as G-BOAF because an agreement to jointly operate the Concorde fleet with the American airline Braniff had just ended.

* A small change to the livery was introduced during June. 'British airways' titles were replaced by the single word 'British' in large letters on the upper fuselages.

* The seventh and final Concorde was delivered in June.

* BA's first 747 freighter, G-KILO, entered service during October but soon fell victim to the developing economic problems and was sold to Cathay Pacific in March 1982. The only freighters operated since then have been wet-leased from other airlines.

* As new 737-236s entered service BA also saw fuel prices rising at the alarming rate of 70% per year. Immediate action came in the form of a survival plan which called for unprofitable routes to be dropped, staff number reductions and the early retirement of older aircraft. Many Trident Ones had already gone and these were followed by some Trident Twos, the 707s and the Super VC-10s, all of which were withdrawn by March 1981.

1981

* The recession continued to deepen, resulting in a deficit of £544m for the year.

* Several new 747-236s were delivered directly into storage in the USA and offered for sale. Two 747-136s were sold to TWA during March.

1982

* The first signs of of recovery began to appear, but the airline was deep in debt and continued to implement its survival plan.

* Highlands Division was established as an autonomous unit in a successful attempt to reverse many years of losses on Scottish routes. Three additional HS-748s were acquired on lease to replace the airline's final Viscounts.

* A reorganisation into business centres took place during May, creating an Intercontinental Division to administer long-haul routes, European Division for short-haul and domestics and the Gatwick Division for all operations from Gatwick, including British Airtours.

1983

* Boeing 757s introduced during February, initially on Shuttle followed by European routes during the summer.

TOP: *A desperately needed new short-haul fleet of 737-236s began to enter service in February 1980, allowing the airline to begin replacing its substantial fleet of noisy and expensive to operate Tridents.*

ABOVE: *The severe economic recession which struck during the early 1980s came at a time when many new airliners were being delivered to British Airways. A 'survival plan' was implemented which led to the retirement of several older fleets including the long-haul Super VC-10s and 707s. Two redundant 707 freighters spent a year in storage at Heathrow awaiting sale.*

Two 747-136s were sold to TWA as part of the airline's early-1980s survival plan. G-AWNI was seen shortly before leaving Heathrow for its new owners in March 1981.

A surprising casualty of poor economic conditions was the TriStar 500 fleet, sold to the RAF in 1983 after only four years in service. Two of the TriStars were then flown on RAF passenger flights prior to their tanker conversion and one of these, previously G-BFCA, displays the full markings of 216 Squadron which were applied for the inauguration of services to Mount Pleasant Airport in the Falklands.

A welcome addition to the short-haul fleet came with the first of nineteen 757s in February 1983, acquired along with additional 737-236s to replace the airline's extensive Trident fleet.

*   The urgent need for survival cash led to the TriStar-500 fleet sale to the RAF during March.

*   Sixteen additional 737-236s were ordered as Trident replacements ahead of the 1986 noise deadline.

*   An operating surplus of £268m for the year along with some progress towards reducing the debt was the result of the many changes and cutbacks.

1984

*   Concorde's future was secured through an agreement whereby BA took over responsibility for all support costs. BA actually acquired an eighth Concorde, the first production aircraft at Filton, which was retained as a source of spares.

*   Concorde services to Washington were extended to Miami, three per week from March.

*   BA retired its final Boeing 707, which had operated with British Airtours until March.

*   The airline became British Airways plc on 1 April.

*   A Civil Aviation Authority review in July led to the publication of a White Paper which recommended a reduction in the size of BA and the transfer of many routes to British competitors. After much pressure from the airline and its employees the final result was a transfer during April 1985 of the Saudi Arabian routes to British Caledonian (BCAL) in exchange for their South American rights.

*   In December a new corporate identity designed by the Californian company Landor was unveiled.

*   By 1984–5 the airline's strength had been built up to such an extent that it could claim to be the world's most profitable airline.

1986

*   The largest single aircraft order ever placed came from BA during August, for sixteen 747-436s plus another twelve on option worth $4.3bn and destined, at that time, to replace the 747-136s.

*   BA Helicopters was sold to the Mirror Group of Companies in September.

1987

*   BA was finally privatised during February in a hugely oversubscribed flotation.

*   A merger with financially troubled British Caledonian was announced in July and implemented in December after agreement to drop some of BCAL's route licences and Gatwick slots had been reached. BA acquired a fleet of eight DC-10s, five miscellaneous 747s, thirteen One-Eleven-500s and an order for ten Airbus A320s. The DC-10s were the first to be owned by BA and remained based at Gatwick for another eleven years.

*   Eleven Boeing 767-336ERs plus another fifteen options were contracted for in August.

1988

*   Airbus A320s began to enter service in April, operated initially from Gatwick's new North Terminal which had opened the previous month. The A320s transferred to Heathrow in November and have been based there ever since. Gatwick operations began to see a significant increase in European schedules with a growing fleet of 737-236s. Other changes, which established a pattern for subsequent years, were the transfer of Bermuda, Islamabad and Nassau services to

With British Airways recovering strongly from recession by 1984 and preparing for privatisation, a new corporate image was unveiled in December as illustrated by 747-236 G-BDXD, pictured alongside G-BDXL in the previous 'British' livery.

1985

*   Two Air Lanka TriStar-500s were leased in April to operate the ex-BCAL South American services.

*   Two Middle East Airlines 747 Combis were leased to provide extra capacity.

*   On 31 December the last two Tridents were retired.

Gatwick, and Saudi services from Gatwick to Heathrow.

*   As part of the changes associated with the BCAL merger, British Airtours was re-named Caledonian Airways and adopted a lion-tailed livery from February and tartan uniforms similar to those of BCAL.

*   Eight British Aerospace ATPs were ordered in July for UK domestic and Internal German Services use from January 1989.

During December 1987 a merger with British Caledonian Airways was implemented. This began a period of rapid expansion for British Airways' operations at Gatwick from the airport's new North Terminal.

January 1989 saw the first of an eventual fleet of 14 British Aerospace ATPs enter service with Highlands Division, primarily as replacements for the HS-748 fleet.

British Airways' eagerly awaited fleet of 747-436s began arriving in June 1989 and by December of the following year G-BNLP, the last aircraft from its initial sixteen-strong order, had been delivered.

*   During October an order for twenty-four 737-300/400/500s was placed, along with another for six 767-336s and a 757. The new 737s were all delivered from 1991 as Series-436s. Meanwhile four 737-300s were leased from Maersk Air.

1989

*   The first 747-436s entered service in July.

1990

*   Boeing 767s entered service during February on European routes, predominantly to Paris CDG.

*   Twenty-one 747-436s were ordered and twelve options placed during July. The airline's total order for the type was forty-two.

1991

*   The Gulf War during February caused a significant loss of traffic, resulting in job losses and the deferral of several aircraft deliveries.

*   Concorde services to Miami ended in March.

*   Orders for fifteen Boeing 777-236s plus a similar number of options were placed in August. Also included were twenty-four more 747-436s and eleven ATPs, with a total order value of £4.3bn.

British Airways' rapid expansion continued with the Boeing 767-300 entering service on European schedules during February 1990. Any remaining short-haul TriStars were soon withdrawn and in later years the process was repeated with 767s replacing the last TriStars from long-haul routes. (ADRIAN MEREDITH PHOTOGRAPHY)

Twenty-seven stretched 737-436s began to enter service from Heathrow during October 1991, displacing 737-236s which moved to Birmingham and Manchester to replace the airline's final One-Elevens.

* The first 737-436s arrived in October and the last TriStars were withdrawn from scheduled services.

1992

* British Airways Regional was established in March as a separate business to operate services from Birmingham, Manchester and throughout Scotland. ATPs replaced the last HS-748s during April.

* German regional airline Delta Air was purchased by BA and several German banks during March and renamed Deutsche BA during May.

* BA was obliged to withdraw from the Internal German Services in October following the reunification of Germany. The remaining routes were transferred to Deutsche BA to be flown by a fleet of leased 737-300s.

* The assets of Davies and Newman, owners of long established but virtually bankrupt Dan-Air, were acquired by BA for a nominal £1.00 in November. The charter side of Dan-Air was closed down but its Gatwick scheduled service routes and fleet of 737-300/400s were retained with a view to creating a low-cost BA operation at Gatwick to operate a much enlarged network of European services.

1993

* A further overseas purchase was made in January when 49.9% of French airline TAT European Airlines was acquired.

* An alliance with US Air was agreed in January. BA invested an initial £198m which was later increased to give it a 24.6% shareholding in the American airline. Code-sharing on US Air services began and three transatlantic routes were introduced for BA using US Air 767s and crews. These were the only 767-200s to have carried BA livery and were flown from Gatwick to Pittsburgh, Baltimore and Charlotte.

* In March 25% of Qantas was purchased.

* 747-436 G-BNLZ entered service in March with British Asia Airlines titles and a Chinese tail logo for services to Taipei. Two other 747-436s, G-CIVA and G-CIVE have since carried this livery.

British Airways Regional Division was established as a business unit with its own fleet of aircraft in March 1992. G-BKYF 737-236 taxies from the airline's Eurohub terminal at Birmingham, complete with appropriate titles.

Financially-exhausted Dan-Air was purchased in November 1992 and its extensive Gatwick-based scheduled service network retained. Twelve 737-300/400s came with the deal and soon received British Airways titles prior to a full repaint or disposal.

With the acquisition of an initial 49.9% shareholding in French TAT European Airlines during January 1993, British Airways began to take advantage of the gradual deregulation of European air transport. Airliners such as this Fokker 100 soon adopted British Airways' identity and several new international routes from France were opened.

* BA Regional began to operate two-class services with three 767-336s during March from Birmingham, Manchester and Glasgow to New York and from Manchester to Los Angeles.

* BA and Danish carrier Maersk Air agreed in May to purchase Brymon European Airways with BA becoming the owner of Brymon Airways and its Plymouth City Airport base.

* BA's final One-Elevens were retired at Birmingham during July.

* In what would become the first of many similar deals BA announced a marketing agreement whereby Gatwick-based independent airline CityFlyer Express would operate all of its scheduled services as British Airways Express flights, repaint its fleet into BA colours and operate to exacting BA standards. The

A 25% shareholding in Australian flag-carrier Qantas was acquired in March 1993.

British Airways' first four-engined propeller-driven airliners since the Viscounts were five de Havilland Canada Dash-7s, acquired along with Brymon Airways in May 1993. Also during 1993 BA signed franchise agreements with Cityflyer Express and Maersk Air Limited, the first of many such partnerships.

five-year franchise agreement was implemented from 1 August and soon resulted in Shorts 360s and ATR-42s appearing in BA Express colours.

* Agreements for Brymon Airways' services and those of Birmingham-based Maersk Air Ltd to fly in British Airways colours were also announced in August, leading to the appearance of Brymon's de Havilland Canada Dash-7s and -8s and Maersk's One-Eleven-400/500s and Jetstream 31 in BA livery.

* The final four ordered 737-436s were placed directly into storage because of BA's attempt to improve the utilisation of its existing fleet.

1994

* During July Loganair became the latest BA franchise carrier. The company's Islanders, Shorts 360s and later a Twin Otter soon began to appear in BA Express colours.

* Concorde services to Washington were withdrawn in November after eighteen years of operation.

1995

* With effect from January Manx Airlines (Europe) became the fifth franchise carrier, which resulted in many UK and Irish additions to the BA network, operated by a large and growing fleet of ATPs and Jetstream 41s in BA Express colours.

* From February GB Airways began operating its scheduled services under a franchise agreement and its 737s were repainted into BA colours.

* Caledonian Airways along with the remaining ex-BA TriStars were sold to Inspirations PLC in March.

* The forty-second and final new 757 then on order arrived in March.

TOP: *GB Airways confirmed its long-standing ties with British Airways through a franchise agreement in February 1995.*

MIDDLE: *Charter subsidiary Caledonian Airways took full advantage of the Boeing 757's excellent long-range capabilities through the operation of long-haul charters to Africa, the Far East and across the North Atlantic during the early 1990s. British Airways sold Caledonian in 1995 and the 757s were replaced with Airbus A320s.* (ADRIAN MEREDITH PHOTOGRAPHY)

ABOVE: *The first Boeing 777, G-ZZZC, entered service from Heathrow to Dubai and Muscat on 17 November 1995.*

TOP: *A major expansion of services from Gatwick took place during 1996 with the transfer from Heathrow of long-haul flights to parts of Africa and the addition of many new short-haul destinations. Longer-term plans were drawn up to replace the ageing 'Classic' 747-236s at Gatwick with 747-436s and new 777s.*

ABOVE: *A code-sharing agreement with Canadian Airlines was implemented in June 1996.*

BELOW: *British Regional Airlines was established in October 1996 to operate the British Airways franchise services of Manx Airlines (Europe) and Loganair.*

* The first 777 was delivered in November and entered service from Heathrow to Dubai and Muscat.

1996

* Three 767s transferred to Gatwick in January, beginning to take over from the US Air 767s.

* In February a major expansion of Gatwick services was announced. This began during March with the transfer from Heathrow of the airline's East and Central African services along with another four 747-236s. Major changes to the Gatwick fleet were announced with plans for 757s, 767s, 747-400s and ultimately 777s to be based there over the following two years. New destinations to be introduced included Edinburgh, Kano, Kiev, Phoenix-San Diego, Stockholm and Zürich, taking the total served from Gatwick to eighty-seven.

* Bids for up to sixty new Regional Jets were invited in April as replacements for 737-236s and for Deutsche BA. Many European airports were restricting the use of 737-200s on noise grounds, making their replacement ever more urgent.

* Code-sharing agreements were initiated with Canadian Airlines International from June and America West from July.

* The first overseas franchise agreement came into effect on 1 August with Danish regional airline Sun-Air becoming the seventh such carrier. Its Jetstream fleet soon appeared in BA Express colours, feeding traffic to BA's Scandinavian services.

* A major alliance with American Airlines was announced in June, designed around the co-ordination of both airlines' extensive North Atlantic networks and with code-sharing on each others' services. This was expected to come into effect from

April 1997, but regulatory approval from both sides of the Atlantic was not forthcoming.

* The remaining shares in TAT were acquired in August, giving BA full control over the French airline. At the same time the final package of EC legislation to complete the deregulation of European air travel came into effect.

* Additional orders for four 747-436s, plus the confirmation of orders for ten others and for three 777-236IGWs and three 757s, were announced at the Farnborough Airshow in September.

* Rumours about an identity change for BA began to spread during September.

* South African airline Comair began flying as the eighth franchise partner in October, the first such agreement to be signed by an airline outside Europe. This resulted in Comair's fleet, which includes Boeing 727-200s, appearing in BA colours.

* British Regional Airlines was established during October to operate the BA Express services of Manx Airlines (Europe) and Loganair.

* Air Liberté, a struggling French airline, was acquired in December.

1997

* An interim livery introduced during January tended to confirm the new identity rumours.

* A record number of six wide-bodied airliners was handed over by Boeing during February, three 777-236IGWs, two 747-436s and a 767, together valued at £0.5bn.

* All agreements, including code-sharing, with US Air were terminated during March and BA's shareholding was sold two months later.

* South American and Mexico services, along

Maersk Air Jetstream 41 G-MSKJ illustrates the revised 'interim' livery which began to appear in January 1997. This was accompanied by the spread of rumours about the development of a radical new corporate identity for British Airways.

with 747-436s to operate them, transferred from Heathrow to Gatwick during March.

* The operation of DC-10 G-NIUK on BA leisure routes to the USA and Caribbean was taken over from Caledonian by Airline Management Limited on 30 March.

* British Mediterranean Airways became a franchise partner in March.

* For summer route expansion Gatwick's fleet of 737s increased from twenty-seven to thirty-three aircraft. This was made possible through the build-up of bigger aircraft at Heathrow. The long-haul fleet at Gatwick stood at three 747-436s, eleven 747-236s, five 767s and eight DC-10s. BA and its partners were serving more destinations from Gatwick, over 100, than from Heathrow.

* Air Liberté and TAT, BA's two French subsidiaries, became jointly managed from April in the run-up to a complete merger as Air Liberté later in the year. Together they controlled 22% of the French domestic market.

* After much media speculation a dramatic revision to the airline's corporate identity, code named project 'Utopia', was unveiled at various locations around the world at 1200 GMT on 10 June.

* An associated programme to introduce new services, products, aircraft, facilities and training at a cost of £6bn was announced for implementation over a three-year period. This was designed to strengthen BA's leading position amongst world airlines.

* Six 777-236IGWs and three more 767-300s were ordered in June. The 777s were confirmed options and were bought for use from Gatwick from February 1998. These orders brought the total of new aircraft on order for delivery during the next four years to forty-five: twenty-eight 747-436s, ten 777s, four 757s and three 767s.

* British Regional introduced Britain's first

Embraer EMB-145 regional jets during August.

* Fourteen of the fifteen remaining 747-136s were finally sold in September to AAR Corporation, probably for spares use. The remaining aircraft would also be leaving the fleet, returning to its leasing company owner.

* A new low-cost airline owned by BA was announced during November under the project code name 'Operation Blue Sky'. The airline was later named 'go', to be based at Stansted using eight ex-Philippine Airlines 737-300s on lease.

* The 737-236 fleet began to decrease in size with two aircraft returned to their owners for onward lease to LAN Chile. Another seven were withdrawn by June 1998, leaving twenty-six of the original forty-four 737-236s in service.

1998

* During January, European Aviation at Bournemouth announced that it had purchased two of the 747-136s previously destined for AAR.

* BA Regional acquired seven 737-300s on lease from January to begin replacing their noisy 737-236s. Other BA Regional changes during 1998 were the transfer of its Aberdeen to Birmingham and Manchester services to Brymon, and withdrawal of the ATP fleet.

* Brymon ordered an additional eight DHC Dash-8-300s for growth and route expansion.

* A severe financial crisis in several Far Eastern countries led to the suspension of flights to Seoul, Nagoya and Osaka, together with a much reduced service to Jakarta.

* Boeing 777s began operations from Gatwick during February with five based there at the beginning of the summer season. A new route for the aircraft was Gatwick to Denver, due to be inaugurated in June but delayed by the withholding of US operating approval.

Showing its age just three months before standing-down, veteran 747-136 G-AWNB taxies out for another transatlantic crossing. The 15-strong 747-136 fleet began to retire in August 1998, beginning with this aircraft which achieved a remarkable 102,480 flying hours and 22,150 landings during its 29-year career with BOAC/BA. Retirement of the early 'Classics' finally severed the last remaining link to the pre-merger fleets of the early 1970s.

Many other airlines have signed code-share agreements with British Airways including LOT of Poland and Japan Airlines.

Overall Gatwick's capacity rose by 25%, with a total of 120 cities in 71 countries served. £12m was invested in customer service improvements to keep up with this growth.

* AML increased its fleet from one to three DC-10s for BA services from Gatwick during April.

* Deutsche BA became fully-owned by BA during April. With a fleet consisting entirely of eighteen 737-300s, DBA was concentrating on increasing its share of German domestic traffic.

* An order for five 777-236ERs replaced an order for four 747-436s. Six 757s were also ordered in April. Two of the 777s and six 767s from Heathrow were to replace the DC-10 fleet by March 1999.

* 'Go' began operating in May from Stansted to Rome and Milan, followed by Copenhagen in June.

* During May a dedicated BA terminal opened at Manchester, Britain's third busiest airport. Manchester also has BA's third largest network of schedules with thirty-three services per day to London's airports plus flights to many European destinations, Islamabad and New York.

* More 747-436s were based at Gatwick. By June the entire fleet of thirty-one 'Classic' 747s as well as thirty-three 747-436s were based at Heathrow.

* Maersk Air introduced Britain's first Canadair Regional Jets during June and retired its final One-Elevens, which were the last to wear BA colours, during August.

* Japan Airlines, LOT and Finnair began code-sharing with BA during the summer of 1998.

* Atlas Air replaced its 747-200 freighters with new 747-400 freighters during August on the wet-lease scheduled services flown three times per week between Stansted and Hong Kong.

* BA announced its largest ever package of new aircraft orders during August:

  * Fifty-nine firm orders for Airbus A319/320s plus 129 options. Initial deliveries of A319s for BA Regional, followed by Euro Gatwick, Deutsche BA and Air Liberté.

  * Sixteen firm orders and sixteen options for extended-range 777-236ERs. Rolls-Royce Trent engines were selected to power these latest 777s.

  * Significantly five 747-436 orders were cancelled and the airline announced that it would not take any more 747s once its existing orders were fulfilled.

* A new alliance of five airlines was announced

Although the long drawn-out attempts to gain regulatory approval for a major alliance with American Airlines were put on hold in October 1998, a new **one**world alliance of major carriers was announced. The initial members comprised American Airlines, British Airways, Canadian Airlines, Cathay Pacific and Qantas which were soon joined by Finnair, Iberia and LAN Chile.

during September to be called **one**world. The airlines are American, BA, Canadian, Cathay Pacific and Qantas.

* 'Go' announced further expansion during October with the lease of another eight 737-300s.

* The full strategic alliance with American Airlines which had been waiting for approval from British, E.C. and U.S. authorities for over two years was finally postponed in October. An E.C. demand that 267 Heathrow and Gatwick slots be given up as a condition of approval was felt to be unacceptable.

* GB Airways ordered nine Airbus A320/321s in November and took out options on another five. An agreement was announced, subject to approval, for BA to acquire Cityflyer Express. Like Brymon Airways it would become a wholly-owned but independently managed subsidiary. Cityflyer operated five Avro RJ-100s plus eleven ATR-42/72 turboprops and had another two RJ-100s on order.

* During December Finnair announced that it would join the **one**world alliance.

1999

* The **one**world alliance became effective on 1 February.

* An agreement was announced in February whereby British Airways would acquire a 9% shareholding in Iberia as part of the Spanish airline's privatisation later in the year. American Airlines would purchase another 1%. Iberia also announced

plans to join the **one**world alliance.

* AML's three DC-10s returned to BA during February and March, replaced with three new 777-236IGWs in a two-class configuration. All eight DC-10s were retired by the end of March and the first of three destined for Gemini Air Cargo was undergoing its freighter conversion.

* BASE Airlines of the Netherlands became the tenth franchise partner in March and inaugurated twice-daily services from its Eindhoven headquarters to Heathrow.

* The 57th and final 747-436 arrived in April.

2000 and beyond

British Airways enters the new century at a challenging time for the airline industry, which finds itself influenced more than ever by global events and trends. A lengthy process of structural change is underway as the regulatory frameworks which govern air travel are progressively dismantled. The industry is also suffering from a cyclical business downturn triggered off by an economic slowdown in many parts of the world. These factors are reshaping the whole industry and British Airways' strategy has been revised to ensure that it maintains its position at the forefront of the changes which are necessary to survive.

The current economic slowdown began with a crash in the financial markets of a series of Far Eastern countries during 1997 and subsequently spread to

The thirtieth anniversary of Concorde's first flight was celebrated during March 1999. Structural analysis of the seven Concordes has confirmed their excellent condition and cleared them for many more years of service in their unique and exciting role. (JOHN M. DIBBS)

other emerging markets, including Russia, in 1998. Just how far the downturn eventually spreads and how long it will last remains to be seen, but a slowdown has already occurred in the economic growth of the UK and many of the airline's markets. So far passenger numbers have continued to grow, but the all-important premium traffic has weakened. British Airways weathered the previous downturn and emerged in much better shape than most airlines and has used this experience to prepare for the current one by implementing a range of cost-cutting measures. These have been followed by major strategy changes to adapt to the changing circumstances and which are now having a significant impact on the airline and its fleet plans.

These plans and strategies are also being shaped by the removal of barriers to world trade through deregulation, and increasing access to new markets. The airline industry is by the very nature of its product one of the most global of industries; one where competition is intense and where single airlines now cannot hope to survive in isolation. For this reason airlines are consolidating into several large groups, but because many countries still maintain limits on the level of foreign ownership, co-operation rather than mergers is presently the only way to achieve this. Hence the current trend towards international partnerships and alliances.

These factors have brought about the strategies which are now shaping British Airways for the years ahead. Firstly, a major cost saving Business Efficiency Programme has been underway for some time, which has enabled the airline to remain profitable by delivering savings that are targeted to reach £1bn per year by 2000. Secondly, product improvements have included the World Traveller re-launch in 1998 followed by a Club World upgrade including fully flat beds, and improvements to first class and Concorde, plus an on-going drive to improve the basic service standards which passengers expect, such as good punctuality and baggage delivery performance. The airline is also concentrating on attracting more high-yielding premium-fare passengers and operating the routes which maximise profitability. Other significant strategies include a major revision of the airline's fleet plans and the further development of its partnerships and alliances.

Fleet plans

Recent new aircraft orders have signalled the airline's intention to reduce the rate of seat growth, by taking delivery of smaller airliners which are more efficient and cheaper to operate. More twin-engined Boeing 777s are being acquired instead of 747-400s, to replace older airliners such as the Classic 747s and DC-10s. Although the new 777s will each have considerably fewer seats, the number of premium-fare passengers that can be accommodated will remain the

same and it will only be the much less profitable low-fare seating which will be reduced. This will enable the airline to concentrate on operating the most efficient, modern airliners on the more profitable routes, at increased frequencies and with a higher-yielding mix of passengers. For short-haul use a new fleet of up to 188 narrow-body Airbus airliners is being acquired through a flexible agreement with the manufacturer that allows the airline to accurately match its future capacity to demand. Delivery rates can be varied by confirming or deferring options and decisions about exactly which models will be delivered need not be taken many years in advance.

The 747-236s are now expected to have been retired from service by 2002. Once this has occurred the fleet will comprise a selection of modern and very efficient airliners from Airbus and Boeing with capacities ranging from the A319's 126 seats up to the 747-436's 409 seats. The one obvious exception is of course Concorde which is expected to continue operating in its own unique niche for the foreseeable future.

The airline's fleet will soon comprise:

Long-haul:	Boeing 747-436
	Boeing 767-336
	Boeing 777-236
	Concorde
Short-haul:	Airbus A319/320
	Boeing 737-436
	Boeing 757-236
	Boeing 767-336

Alliances and partnerships

British Airways will maintain its efforts to secure a wide-ranging strategic alliance with American Airlines as soon as conditions allow. This is seen as an essential step towards countering other similar alliances which are already in operation such as the Lufthansa/United-led Star Alliance, Alitalia/KLM/Northwest and the newly-formed Air France/Delta grouping. Such alliances give the participants access to much larger markets and enable them to offer higher and more consistent standards of customer service across their linked networks. Participants also benefit through a range of operating and marketing efficiencies. In the meantime the **one**world alliance with American Airlines, Canadian Airlines, Cathay Pacific, Finnair, Iberia, LAN Chile and Qantas will be developed and additional airlines are expected to join. Other relationships from code-sharing and franchise partnerships to the operation of subsidiary companies will also continue and will probably be expanded into parts of the world which are not presently served. This will result in many more aircraft carrying British Airways colours.

CHAPTER FOUR

CURRENT AIRCRAFT TYPES

This chapter examines the aircraft types currently operated by British Airways. Background information sets the scene for the airline's purchase decision, followed by details of the aircraft's role and how that may have changed as performance improvements were introduced and fleet sizes increased.

Current British Airways aircraft types:

Boeing 737
Boeing 747
Boeing 757
Boeing 767
Boeing 777
Airbus A319/320
Concorde

Note: Details of each individual aircraft's history can be found in Appendix One.

Boeing 737

Following from an initial purchase of nineteen 737-200s in 1978, Boeing's smallest jet quickly established itself as British Airways' prime European airliner at the lower end of the capacity scale and demonstrated such a degree of acceptance that, by the end of 1998, a total of 155 Boeing 737s had served throughout the airline's various operating divisions. Such widespread acceptance reflects the worldwide popularity of an aircraft type that first entered service in 1968, and which has recently undergone a major redesign to enable a third family of 'Next Generation' 737s to enter service. In all, of its nine versions over 4,250 737s have been sold, more than any other jet airliner, with the 3,250th rolling off Boeing's Renton production line during 1998.

British Airways' selection of the 737 came over ten years after the first production aircraft had entered service with Lufthansa and began the first stage of a modernisation plan to replace the airline's large fleet of obsolescent Tridents and One-Elevens. Implementation of this plan actually began during November 1977 with the lease of 737-200s and DC-9-51s to provide extra capacity and to enable an evaluation of each type to take place. Finnair DC-9s were wet-leased for the Heathrow to Helsinki route and several Transavia 737s operated in hybrid Transavia/BA liveries on routes to Amsterdam, Brussels, Frankfurt, Hamburg, Helsinki, Istanbul, Stavanger and Stockholm between November 1978 and March 1980. Alternative types evaluated for this major order also included the Boeing 7N7 (which subsequently developed into the 757) and various Airbus proposals. Boeing won with its popular 737-200, receiving an initial order for nineteen in July 1978. The model purchased was an updated Series-200 Advanced, designed to meet British Airways' requirement for 'CAT 3A' autoland certification by upgrading the flight deck layout and avionics to

With the exception of G-BGDA which was retained by Boeing for systems development, all of British Airways' initial order for nineteen 737-236s entered service during 1980. This welcome addition to the airline's fleet allowed several leased aircraft to return to their owners as well as the retirement of the Trident 1E fleet. A total of 44 737-236s were eventually acquired new from Boeing.

Twenty-seven second-generation 737-436s, powered by CFM-56 engines and capable of accommodating 35 more passengers than a 737-236, were delivered to British Airways between 1991–93. G-DOCX is seen arriving at Heathrow on a scheduled service from Newcastle in January 1995.

incorporate a new digital Automatic Flight Control System. To placate UK industry, as British Aerospace One-Eleven developments were not seriously considered for the order, three One-Eleven-539s were also bought. The first 737-236s entered service during February 1980, allowing the leased aircraft to return to Transavia.

Coinciding with the arrival of its 737 fleet British Airways found that fuel prices were soaring by a devastating 70%, so the economic benefits derived from operating the new airliner, which burned 25% less fuel per passenger than the Trident as well as needing one less crew member on the flight deck, were very timely. A second order was placed for nine 737-236s, to be delivered to British Airtours as 707-436 replacements during 1980–81. This was followed by a further order for fourteen, later increased to sixteen, placed during 1983, aircraft which, along with 757s, were to replace all of the remaining Tridents ahead of a 1986 noise deadline. These latest 737s were acquired after a fierce competition against the McDonnell Douglas MD-80 and the brand-new, but at that time unflown, Airbus A320.

Throughout the 1980s with the 737 firmly established as Britain's prime Inclusive Tour charter aircraft, British Airtours regularly boosted its own fleet of nine 737-236s by leasing-in others. Seasonal transfers between British Airways and British Airtours also took place to cover operational peaks and maintenance requirements. Leased 737s came from a variety of sources, including competitor airlines Air Europe and Britannia as well as leasing companies GPA and ILFC. Some British Airtours 737-236s transferred to the newly-formed Caledonian Airways during March 1988, but were soon superseded by 757s, which by then had begun to take over the 737's role of British charter airline workhorse. GB Airways, once part-owned by British Airways and now a franchisee, began using leased 737-200s in 1979 and has subsequently used several BA aircraft in the lead-up to acquiring its own fleet of

modern 737-300/400s by 1998.

Second-generation CFM56-powered 737s joined British Airways from September 1988, beginning with four Series-300s leased from Maersk Air to bridge the gap until the delivery of a new fleet of 737-436s from Boeing began. Three of the Maersk aircraft were delivered new and initially two were wet-leased, retaining their Danish (OY–) registrations. All four transferred to Berlin during March 1990 to operate on the Internal German Service network and returned to Maersk by May 1992. Meanwhile, during October 1988, an agreement was reached with Boeing for the acquisition of twenty-four 737-300/400/500s, plus eleven more on option, as part of a larger deal including 757/767s. The 737 was chosen once again over the competing A320 and MD-80 because of the flexibility offered in terms of aircraft size, especially as a final decision regarding how many of each model would be taken could be left until a later date. For example, using typical two-class configurations, seat capacity ranged from 105 in the 737-500 through to 145 in the 737-400. BA eventually took delivery of a total of twenty-seven aircraft, all of them the larger Series-400s.

Delivery of the 737-436s began during October 1991, allowing many 737-236s to transfer to British Airways Regional as replacements for the airline's remaining One-Elevens at Manchester and Birmingham. Four others transferred to GB Airways at Gatwick during March 1992. Heathrow-based 737-236 numbers reduced rapidly to just four aircraft for use on UK domestic services to Inverness, Jersey and Newcastle and for Shuttle back-up work until March 1997.

During November 1992, as the 737-436s were arriving from Boeing, British Airways somewhat unexpectedly acquired a motley collection of 737-200/300/400s as part of its purchase of Dan-Air, and initially retained the leases on three -300s and nine -400s to operate scheduled services from Gatwick. This influx of new and used 737s, plus a major growth in European scheduled services at the low-cost

European Operations at Gatwick (EOG) unit, led to a period of great change for the 737 fleet. Attempts were made to rationalise some of the many 737 sub-fleets and to begin the gradual phase-out of the Series-200s. First of all the three 737-300s inherited from Dan-Air were disposed of and, having been declared surplus to requirements, the final four new -436s were not delivered but flown directly to Mojave, California, for storage. One of these (G-GBTA) later entered service and the others were leased-out for several years before finally joining the BA fleet. During 1994–95 eight 737-236s were sold, three going to Transaero in Moscow, two to LAN Chile, one to Cayman Airways and two to Comair of South Africa. Additional 737s arrived at Gatwick during the

summer 1995 season with the transfer of five -436s to expand the European operation.

Franchise partner airlines, in addition to the previously mentioned GB Airways, have made extensive use of the versatile 737. Deutsche BA now operates exclusively with 737-300s, and Maersk took delivery of three 737-500s in December 1996 to replace its One-Eleven-400 fleet, the first 737-500s to fly in British Airways colours. Comair became a franchise partner in October 1996 and brought with it a fleet of six 737-200s, two of which had been purchased from BA just one year earlier. TAT also became a 737 user when it took delivery of two leased 737-300s in March 1996.

During January 1997 exploratory talks began

ABOVE: *Twelve 737s arrived with the acquisition of Dan-Air in November 1992 and although they soon received British Airways titles, the three Series-300s were soon disposed of. G-BOWR, seen in the company of another three ex-Dan-Air 737s at Gatwick in December 1992, left to join Southwest Airlines in America six months later.*

BELOW: *During December 1994 a 737-236 appeared with the winning designs from a children's Christmas competition decorating each side of its fuselage. G-BKYK is seen here about to leave Heathrow for a celebratory pre-Christmas flight for the winners and runners-up from the 17,000 entries which were submitted.*

with manufacturers with a view to acquiring replacements for the eighteen 737-236s and ten ATPs operated by British Airways Regional from Birmingham, Glasgow and Manchester. Boeing 737-200s were becoming increasingly unwelcome throughout Europe because of their inability to meet the forthcoming 'Chapter Three' noise limitations. Airports in Germany, the Netherlands and Switzerland imposed curfews and fines, making their continued operation very difficult. Candidate aircraft for the order were the Airbus A319, 737-600, Avro RJ-85/100 and MD-95, and the possibility of hush-kitting the 737s remained. Although these discussions ended later in the year as sufficiently attractive terms could not be reached, negotiations reopened again early in 1998, this time with a view to acquiring a substantial number of aircraft to provide a standardised type for BA Regional, EuroGatwick and some of the partner airlines.

Meanwhile many more complicated changes were taking place within the fleet as 737-236 retirements began again, and new and used Series-300/400/500s arrived to join British Airways' thriving partners. As mentioned earlier, restrictions in Europe were making efficient scheduling of 737-236s increasingly difficult, even though the Chapter Three noise deadline would not be reached until the year 2002. Because of both this and the declining passenger appeal of the aircraft an accelerated retirement programme commenced in November 1997. Firstly, at Heathrow, the use of larger aircraft (mainly 767s) on European routes allowed more 737-436s to transfer to Gatwick which in turn released 737-236s. By midsummer 1999 there were no 737s left at Heathrow. Secondly, BA Regional took delivery of seven leased 737-300s during 1998 as an interim measure whilst its longer term fleet replacement

plan was examined, and these rendered several more 737-236s surplus to requirements. Additionally GB Airways continued to update its fleet taking leases on an ex-BMA 737-400, an ex-Deutsche BA -300 as well as two new -300s, thereby allowing its last 737-236 to return to BA in March 1998. Surplus 737-236s were returned to their owners as their leases expired, beginning with G-BGJI and 'GDP in November 1997 and by December 1998 many more had gone, leaving just twenty-three of the original forty-four aircraft delivered still in service. Most have found new homes in the Americas with Aerolineas Argentinas, Aero Peru, LAN Chile and Winair of the USA.

Other major changes saw Deutsche BA standardise on the 737 with eighteen in service by November 1997. Maersk Air's fourth 737-500 arrived in February 1998 and one of the two TAT 737-300s continued to fly in British Airways colours but operated by Air Liberté from November 1997. New low-cost subsidiary 'go' began flying with eight leased 737-300s in April 1998.

Boeing has further improved the world's best selling airliner by introducing the 'Next Generation' 737-600 to 900 series, basically giving the aircraft a new, bigger wing and more efficient engines to increase its range and cruising speed. The Series-600 seats 108 in two-classes and this increases in the larger -700 and -800 to 177 on the 737-900. A major milestone reached during May 1998 was an order by Delta Airlines which took the total number of 737s sold to 4000.

With over one hundred 737s flying for British Airways and its partners during 1998, the future of the type looked secure. But when the airline finally announced the results of its long drawn out selection process for a new airliner in August 1998, it broke a long tradition by choosing Airbus! This substantial

Boeing 737-236 disposals began during 1994 with the sale of eight aircraft. Three went to Transaero, one of which was photographed arriving at Lasham for the installation of new galleys prior to its delivery to Russia. As noise restrictions began to limit operations throughout Europe many more were retired from late 1997 and by mid-1999 just 18 of the original 44 Boeing 737-236s remained in service.

Although the fleet was about to begin a steady rundown in numbers many 737-236s received the new 'Utopia' livery during 1997, such as G-BGDE photographed departing Gatwick with a German Bauhaus 'Fairy Tale' tail!

commitment to 59 firm orders and 129 options for A319/320s will see many 737s replaced; initially the remaining Series-236s of BA Regional and EuroGatwick, followed by the Deutsche BA and Air Liberté aircraft. GB Airways has also opted for Airbuses and it therefore appears that the Boeing 737's dominance at British Airways will gradually erode during the early years of the twenty-first century. It is however very difficult to envisage a time without a substantial number of 737s in the airline's colours given the large numbers in service today and the fact that Boeing continues to build the type at a rate of almost one per day!

During December 1998 the number of 737s with British Airways and its associated airlines stood at 110, operated as follows:

December 1998 737 Fleet	
737-236	23 (9 at LGW, 14 at BHX+MAN with BA Regional)
737-436	27 (18 at LGW, 9 at LHR)
737-400 (ex-Dan-Air, LGW)	7
737-300 (BA Regional)	7
737-200 (Comair)	6
737-300 (DBA)	20
737-300/400 (GB A/w)	8
737-300 ('go')	8
737-500 (Maersk)	4
737 Total	**110**

Boeing 747

Any study into the developments which have taken place in world air transport since the early 1970s will clearly demonstrate that an unprecedented rate of growth has occurred, particularly in long-haul travel which has changed out of all recognition. If any aircraft can claim credit for this transformation, Boeing's 747 would undoubtedly be the one, having

reigned virtually unchallenged for most of that time. The basic design has proved to be correct and also capable of accepting significant upgrades as engine and systems technologies have advanced, further increasing the aircraft's capabilities and improving its operating economics. Over 1200 have now been built, handsomely rewarding Boeing for taking one of the biggest commercial gambles of all time, one which could so easily have been lost and bankrupted the company. British Airways has been one of the biggest users of the 747, second only to Japan Airlines, having operated 101 since the original Series-136s entered service with BOAC in 1970. Further developments may soon be under way that could result in even-more capable 747s appearing early in the twenty-first century, guaranteeing production for the foreseeable future.

The 747 came into being through the ideas of two very powerful Americans. Juan Trippe, the head of Pan-American, wanted a new large-capacity transatlantic airliner and persuaded Boeing's President Bill Allen to build one. Boeing had undertaken many large transport aircraft studies during a competition to design a new strategic airlifter for the United States Air Force (a competition won by Lockheed's C-5A Galaxy design) and used these as a base for its new airliner. Similarly, Pratt & Whitney had lost out to General Electric in the C-5A engine competition and was left with a suitable design for a new large-airliner powerplant. In April 1966 and after much secrecy, Pan-Am ordered twenty-five Boeing 747-100s at a cost of $18m each, to be powered by the Pratt & Whitney JT-9D high-bypass turbofan. This agreement restricted delivery of the first five, and many subsequent, 747s to Pan-Am and it was only after the order had been signed that full details of the aircraft were released. Orders soon followed from the world's major airlines and by November 1968 BOAC had signed up for twelve and taken options on another four.

The first flight took place on 9 February 1969 and Pan-Am introduced 747s between New York JFK and Heathrow on 21 January 1970. BOAC had planned to inaugurate services in April of that year, but a pilots' dispute delayed crew training and the initial aircraft remained firmly on the ground at Heathrow. One benefit from this unfortunate delay was that some of the JT-9D engine's teething troubles had been overcome by the time BOAC finally began 747 services in April 1971 (the engine suffered from many early failures causing severe flight disruptions). The initial route flown was from Heathrow to JFK and frequencies quickly built up to daily. Six of the new 'Jumbos' were in service by the end of the summer season, and another six had arrived by the following spring. The final 747 to be delivered in BOAC's livery was the thirteenth aircraft, G-AWNM in May 1973. Subsequent aircraft, beginning with G-AWNN in November 1973, arrived in British Airways' new scheme in anticipation of the merger consummation in April 1974, by which time fifteen were in service. Repainting the entire fleet into the new livery took some time however, and 747s could be seen with hybrid schemes for many years. The final aircraft in the British Airways fleet to fly with a BOAC tail was 747 G-AWNC which was not repainted until February 1977. Conversely, this same 747 became the first aircraft to appear with the large – and thankfully short-lived – 'British' titles in July 1980.

The eighteenth and final 747-136 entered service in April 1976, by which time all Australian services were being flown by the type. Development of the heavier and longer-range 747-236 was also well under way following British Airways' 1975 launch order for four at a cost of £85m. Financial assistance from the British Government enabled Rolls-Royce to build an uprated version of its TriStar engine, the 50,000 lb thrust RB-211-524B2, allowing the 747-236 to uplift over thirty tonnes more than a Series-136.

The prototype, G-BDXA, flew for the first time in September 1976 and during the course of flight testing achieved a new world record by taking off at a gross weight of 381,251 kg, more than any other aircraft at that time. The first two -236s arrived at Heathrow during June 1976 and soon proved their worth on such demanding sectors as Heathrow to Los Angeles, and Nairobi to Heathrow. One other world record was achieved in an unexpected and very dramatic way by G-BDXH which, on 24 June 1982, flying at night and without warning, flew through a volcanic ash cloud over Indonesia from erupting Mount Galunggung. As a result all engine power was lost and 'DXH flew on as 'the world's largest glider' for the next twelve minutes, until it descended beneath the ash cloud where the crew were able to restart three engines and make a difficult but successful emergency landing at Jakarta.

Following the completion of 747-136 deliveries an Aer Lingus 747-100 (G-BDPZ) was leased to provide extra capacity and operated the daily Chicago service from April 1976. After disappearing during the winter of 1978 for a lease to British Caledonian, 'Paddy Zulu' returned to British Airways between April 1979 and May 1981, this time heading east to Dhahran each day. Following this second lease the aircraft was overhauled and repainted into full Aer Lingus colours as EI-ASJ. Rumour has it that when an Irish crew came aboard for the ferry flight home, they were none too pleased to discover a new plaque on the flight deck instructing them to 'fly green side up'!

Orders for -236s continued to be placed during the late 1970s, including one for the airline's first freighter 747 which was delivered in October 1980 as G-KILO, looking splendid in British Airways' familiar red, white and blue livery but with large 'British Cargo' titles. Services to New York JFK and Hong Kong were flown with the 'British Trader' but a deteriorating economic climate meant that it could not be operated profitably and the aircraft was sold to Cathay Pacific in March 1982. Since then only wet-leased freighters have been used.

Boeing 747-236 G-BDXH completes an approach to land with all four engines turning just two years after achieving fame by becoming the world's largest ever glider! In June 1982 'DXH unknowingly flew through a volcanic ash cloud over Indonesia and lost all engine-power for a frightening twelve minutes. After a successful landing at Jakarta the 747 received a new set of engines followed by a thorough overhaul at London and has served the airline reliably ever since.

The only 747 freighter ever to be acquired by British Airways was G-KILO, which was delivered new from Boeing in October 1980. Unfortunately a rapidly deteriorating economic climate soon led to its sale to Cathay Pacific and since then only wet-leased freighters have been used. 'British Trader' was perhaps the best looking aircraft to carry the extra-large 'British' titles of the early 1980s.

Other 747s became victims of the early 1980s recession, as British Airways urgently needed to reduce its fleet size and costs. Two -136s were sold to TWA in March 1981 and four new -236s which were due for delivery that year were placed into storage. Two of these were sold the following year to Malaysian Airlines and the others entered service with BA in 1983–84.

The airline's final purchase of 747-236s came later in the decade and these four aircraft were delivered during 1987–88. Three were built as Combis, with a stronger floor and large fuselage-side cargo door to enable the carriage of a mix of passengers and freight on the main deck. They were bought to replace two other Combis, G-BLVE/VF, which had operated on lease from Middle East Airlines (MEA) since 1985. British Airways carries large volumes of cargo and found it worthwhile to lease and then purchase Combis to serve destinations such as Chicago, Tokyo and Hong Kong after its own 707/747 freighter fleet had been sold. Following delivery of the new Combis, BA further extended the lease on the MEA aircraft through to April 1990 and converted them to operate in an all-passenger role.

This was to maintain capacity levels in a market which had entered a period of rapid growth, until the next 747s arrived – the eagerly anticipated fleet of new Series-436s. By May 1991 the three -236 Combis had also converted to operate as all-passenger aircraft and have not been used in the Combi role since.

British Airways' charter subsidiary British Airtours used a total of three 747s at various times to operate its long-haul charters from Gatwick. The first of these was new 747-236 G-BDXL, delivered from storage in the USA during March 1984 and operated until October of that year. Next an ex-SAS (Scandinavian, not Hereford!) 747, registered G-BMGS, was delivered to Hong Kong for modifications in March 1986, and flew for Airtours from May 1986 until October 1987. 'MGS then flew for both BA and British Airtours before returning to its owners in January 1990. Finally, one of the MEA 747s mentioned previously (G-BLVE) was sub-leased to British Airtours from October 1987.

Although no other 747s were due to enter service with British Airways until the arrival of new-generation Series-400s in 1989, five assorted -200s unexpectedly joined the fleet in April 1988 from

During April 1988 a selection of used 747s joined British Airways from BCAL, aircraft with totally different engines and equipment from the airline's existing 747s which meant that they were not retained for long. G-CITB, departing from Gatwick's North Terminal during July 1989, left the fleet to join All Nippon Airlines of Japan in November 1990.

Having first been stripped of its paint at Heathrow this 747-236 was about to leave for a major overhaul with British Airways Maintenance Cardiff. Several weeks later the 747 returned for a repaint before re-entering service looking as good as new.

British Caledonian (BCAL). Unfortunately these 747s, which BCAL had picked up second- or third-hand from Braniff, Wardair and Royal Jordanian, were completely incompatible with the -136/236s in terms of their engines, interior layouts and equipment, and therefore had to be confined to specific routes. To make matters worse they were not even compatible with each other in their cockpit instrumentation, so careful scheduling and crew control was needed to ensure that a type-qualified crew was always available (something which was not always achieved!). Along with the ex-BCAL DC-10s, four of these 747s were powered by GE CF-6-50 engines, the first of their type with British Airways. With this latest addition the airline found itself operating forty 747s of various models with engines from three different manufacturers and with bases at Heathrow and Gatwick. Rationalisation was obviously needed.

747-136	16
747-236	16
747-200 (ex-BCAL)	5
747-200 (MEA lease)	2
747-200 (G-BMGS lease)	1
Total	**40**

Many more 747s were required by the late 1980s for two main reasons:

(a) To release the oddball 747s for return to their owners, thereby reducing the number of sub-fleets with different engine and airframe combinations.
(b) For fleet expansion, in particular to operate new, very long-range routes.

The original -136s, by then re-equipped with more powerful 46,300 lb thrust JT9D-7 engines, had a useful range of 4500 miles, making them ideal aircraft for USA/Canada routes. The -236s had also received uprated engines, RB211-524D4s of 53,000 lb thrust, making them suitable for sectors up to 6500 miles such as Heathrow to Los Angeles. By that time, however, the airline's commercial department was demanding aircraft which could operate much longer non-stop routes such as between Heathrow and Bangkok, Hong Kong, Singapore, and Tokyo, year-round with a full passenger load. Boeing therefore took the opportunity presented by the availability of even more powerful engines capable of delivering up to 60,000 lb of thrust to completely update the 747 airframe and systems to produce a superb ultra-long-haul version, the Series-400, which would satisfy the airline's requirement.

Improvements included a completely re-designed flight deck with six CRT screens in place of the previous banks of dials to enable two-pilot operations, increased wingspan with winglets for aerodynamic efficiency, extra fuel in a new stabiliser tank and a major reduction in airframe weight through the use of new materials. The 747-300's extended upper deck was incorporated to increase passenger accommodation, and additional crew rest facilities were provided in a previously unused space above the rear passenger cabin. British Airways placed its first order for the new version in August 1986, contracting for sixteen aircraft plus twelve options in what was the largest individual aircraft order ever placed. Rolls-Royce's latest RB211-524G engines of 58,000 lb thrust were chosen as powerplants. At the time it was confidently predicted that these new 747s would also replace the ageing 747-136s, but as will be seen later, the early 'Classics' were to survive all attempts to displace them for another decade.

Deliveries commenced in June 1989 and progressed at a rapid rate so that within the first year thirteen 747-436s were in service and by March 1991, just twenty months after the first delivery, nineteen were flying. Initially they operated relatively short sectors from Heathrow to Philadelphia/Pittsburgh, Montreal/Detroit, and San Francisco to maximise the number of landings for crew training purposes but by the summer of 1991 747-436s flew non-stop to Singapore and Bangkok en route to Australia as well as daily to Hong Kong and to South America.

Another large order was announced in July 1990 for twenty-one 747-436s plus options for another twelve, taking British Airways' commitment to a total of forty-two. All of these, plus two from a December 1989 order, were acquired with uprated RB211-524H engines of 60,600 lb thrust, and all previously delivered aircraft have had similar engines retrofitted, allowing them to carry more payload on some of the very long sectors. Surprisingly, given the capability of the aircraft, four -436s from this order were delivered as 'lites', with a reduced take-off weight (381,000 instead of 396,890 kg), a deactivated stabiliser fuel tank and with fewer crew rest and galley facilities. G-CIVF/G/H/I are flown on sectors which do not need the full range capability of a standard aircraft and, as they operate at lower weights, incur lower landing fees. They were later modified to have crew rest facilities fitted to restore some of their long-range capabilities.

Meanwhile the 747-136/236s, christened the 'Classic' fleet by their pilot community, continued to give excellent service, defying all attempts to replace them despite their advancing age and increasing maintenance costs. With their cabin fittings and seats continuously upgraded the -136s could match new 747 standards of comfort and customer service and they continued to be very productive vehicles on the relatively undemanding North Atlantic routes. As a result, justifying the huge investment needed to replace them with brand-new aircraft continued to prove very difficult. Sadly one of their number, G-AWND, was destroyed in well publicised circumstances by the Iraqi Army on the ground at Kuwait in February 1991 during the Gulf War, reducing the fleet to fifteen. From May 1990 onwards 747-236s began to appear at Gatwick as replacements for the leased and ex-BCAL aircraft, which were all withdrawn by February 1991. More -236s followed with the transfer of several long-haul routes to operate Gatwick's rapidly growing network of flights to Africa, the Caribbean and Islamabad. From March 1996, when some Southern and East African services transferred, ten of the sixteen -236 fleet were Gatwick-based, four of them operating in a high-density two-class configuration for the leisure routes.

At Farnborough '96 an order for four 747-436s was announced, plus a decision to bring forward the delivery of ten more. Between 1991 and 1996 deliveries had fallen to an average of three per year, but accelerated again from 1997 when six new 747s arrived. As an example of this increased rate, during the month of February 1997 two new 747-436s (G-CIVJ/VK) were accepted along with three 777s and a 767, together representing an investment of £0.5bn

With 57 in service British Airways now operates the largest fleet of Boeing 747-400s of any airline. Two examples were photographed whilst under tow from the airline's Heathrow Engineering Base to Terminal 4 to be prepared for their evening departures to South Africa and Australia.

A surprising sight at both Heathrow and Cardiff during early November 1998 was that of a 'BOAC' 747! It was actually British Airways' oldest aircraft and BOAC's first 747, G-AWNA, which had retired from service after operating flight BA068 from Philadelphia to Heathrow on 30 October. Before leaving Heathrow for the last time 'November Alpha' received BOAC decals for a nostalgic send-off. This historic airliner's last flight was from Cardiff to Bruntingthorpe near Leicester, where sadly it has been scrapped.

– a record for both British Airways and Boeing. Another eleven -436s arrived during 1998, a figure which represented about 20% of Boeing's entire 747 production for the year. Firm orders were held for another fifteen to bring the airline's fleet total to sixty-six, plus seven more on option. However, during 1998 traffic growth faltered, in particular on many Far Eastern routes, so the decision was taken to acquire additional extended-range 777s at the expense of some 747-436 orders. Four of these were cancelled during May 1998, followed in August by another five and the seven options, leaving just seven more to be delivered. These had arrived by mid-1999, bringing the 747-436 fleet to a grand total of fifty-seven.

How has the airline absorbed such a large number of new 747s into its fleet? Gatwick began to receive 747-436s from March 1997 with an initial fleet of three, operating Central and South American services transferred from Heathrow. More soon followed to begin replacing 747-236s, a process completed by June 1998 by which time fourteen -436s were Gatwick-based. These aircraft also contributed to Gatwick's 25% capacity increase during the summer of 1998, operating to the Caribbean, South America, Southern USA, Southern Africa, the Indian Ocean islands, Islamabad and to Phoenix/San Diego in place of DC-10s. At Heathrow the trend towards using larger aircraft continued and absorbed much of the new capacity.

For a few months during the 1998 summer season the complete 747-136/236 'Classic' fleet was together once again at Heathrow before the long-awaited -136 withdrawals finally began at the end of August. The thirty-year lifespan of the pioneering 747-136s has been truly remarkable and a testimony to the excellence of Boeing's original design, but age finally caught up in September 1997 when British Airways announced that AAR Sales and Leasing had agreed to purchase all but one of them for delivery between September 1998 and 2000. The fifteenth aircraft, G-AWNF, will return to its leasing company

owner during that period. Although fully serviceable, it was expected that the age of the aircraft and their noise characteristics would almost certainly condemn most of them to be broken up after any useful spares had been recovered. First to go was G-AWNB which landed at Heathrow for the final time, appropriately from New York JFK, on 31 August 1998. After decommissioning at Cardiff 'WNB ferried to Roswell, New Mexico, on 28 September, arriving with a remarkable 102,580 flying hours and 22,163 landings to its credit. By December 1998 six had retired, including BOAC's original 747 G-AWNA which nostalgically displayed its early BOAC livery for a few days before departing to Bruntingthorpe. A welcome reprieve for two of the old 'Classics' came with their acquisition by European Aviation, the enterprising Bournemouth-based company which has achieved great success with the ex-BA One-Eleven fleet. 'WNC was delivered to European in November 1998 followed by G-BBPU in 1999.

By the time the airline's fifty-seventh and final 747-436 G-BYGG arrived on delivery in the spring of 1999 the 747-136 retirement programme was well under way and only eight remained. At that time the 747 fleet peaked at an impressive eighty-one aircraft in service and the total number to have served in the airline's colours had reached 101.

	Operational 747 fleet as at May 1999	Total of 747s operated by BA up to May 1999
747-136	8	18
747-236	16	16
747-236F	—	1
Ex-BCAL 747s	—	5
Leased 747s (Aer Lingus, MEA, SAS)	—	4
747 'Classic' Total	24	44
747-436	57	57
747 Fleet Total	**81**	**101**

The number of 747s in service has now started to diminish and will continue to do so as the 747-136s retire and no further Series-400 orders are held. Time will also reveal the fate of the Series-236s which still have many useful years of life remaining, but with the current trend towards the increased use of large twin-jets, their long-term future with the airline is now much less secure.

As for the 747-436, British Airways took delivery of the final seven aircraft with a new version of Rolls-Royce's engine, the RB-211-524G/H-T (!), which incorporates the Trent 700's high pressure system and is expected to deliver a 2% fuel burn improvement plus a useful 365 kg. weight saving. This allows the removal of payload restrictions at certain times of the year on some of the longest routes flown and is also more economical to operate. The engine will also be retrofitted to twenty-five other 747-436s in the fleet from September 1999.

Boeing 747-436s, which can expect to achieve at least as long a life as the 747-136s, are now set to dominate the airline's long-haul routes for the medium-term along with an increasing number of 777s. Looking further ahead, Boeing has for some years been working towards the launch of larger and longer-range 747s in response to requests from airlines who see a need to maximise the number of passengers carried per flight in this slot-restricted era. Despite rumours of an imminent launch for the longer-range re-winged 747-500 and the larger 747-600

at Farnborough '96, nothing happened and Boeing has retreated from an early commitment to such a huge investment whilst the size of the market remains uncertain. A longer-range 747-400IGW with uprated weights and tankage has so far been the only positive development. Airbus shows no such nerves and plans to launch a direct challenge to the 747 in the form of its brand-new A3XX for entry into service by around the year 2005, direct competition at last for the 747!

Colour Schemes

The 101 747s operated by British Airways since 1974 have displayed several different liveries in addition to the three main corporate schemes. There have been the early hybrid BOAC/BA variations, G-BDPZ in its adapted ex-Aer Lingus schemes, two British Airtours and a one-off livery carried by 'IVB in 1995 to promote British Airways' backing of The International Children's Conference. 'NLR was first to appear in the 'interim' livery of 1997 and 'NLO was one of the aircraft used to unveil the new corporate identity at the 'Utopia' launch on 10 June 1997. For the last ten years a 747-136, usually 'WNN, has carried large 'Dreamflight' stickers for its operation of the annual flight to Orlando for sick and disabled children paid for by British Airways' staff. British Asia Airways, which is a wholly-owned operating division for flights to Taipei, has had its titles and Chinese tail markings applied to three 747-436s since 1993, 'NLZ initially and currently 'IVA and 'IVE.

Six new 747-436s were handed over by Boeing during 1997 including G-CIVO, the airline's fortieth, seen here on its delivery flight. By April 1999 seventeen more had arrived to complete British Airways' outstanding 747 orders. (JOHN M. DIBBS)

Classic Flower Power! With a 'Chelsea-Rose' decorating its fin G-BDXK taxies past the Swedish 'Flower Field' of sistership 'DXG. Only four of the 747-236s have received the airline's current livery as revised plans have brought forward the expected retirement date for the whole fleet by several years.

Boeing 757

Designed primarily as a replacement for its best-selling 727, Boeing's 757 has matured into a flexible, economical airliner, popular with passengers and operators alike and suited to a wide variety of airline tasks. Over 850 Boeing 757s are now in use and operating comfortably on routes which vary from short-haul Manchester to London services through to long-haul 'ETOPS' Manchester to Orlando charters. The first stretched 757-300s have recently entered service and, apart from more efficient engines, represent the only major change to Boeing's original design. This success came despite the 757 achieving poor sales during the early years when worldwide economic conditions were rapidly deteriorating, but its entry into service was perfectly timed to satisfy British Airways' urgent need for a modern airliner to take over its prime European services.

When Boeing finally launched its new 757 design at the end of the 1970s after years of studies, prospective airline customers began to encounter a severe recession with fuel costs soaring and traffic levels falling steeply, leading most of them to retain their existing fleets of second-generation jets and defer the acquisition of expensive replacements. British Airways, however, found itself in a much worse situation with a large fleet of hopelessly uneconomical Trident 2s and 3s, aircraft which would be grounded at the end of 1986 by stringent

Two early production Boeing 757s which were originally destined to join British Airways were sold before delivery to Air Europe. As part of that deal various Air Europe aircraft were leased to British Airways including 757 G-BKRM which appeared on Shuttle services in this modified Air Europe colour scheme.

British Airways was one of two launch customers for Boeing's new 757 and took delivery of its first aircraft, G-BIKB, the tenth 757 to be built, in January 1983.

One of British Airways' most important aims during the first half of the 1980s was to completely update its short-haul fleet. This was achieved through the acquisition of more 737-200s and by taking delivery of 20 Boeing 757s between 1983 and 1985. The 757 soon proved itself to be a much more efficient and productive aircraft than the three-engined, three-crew Trident which it replaced.

noise limitations. The airline carefully examined all available alternatives for a new mid-capacity, medium-range airliner to fit between its 737 and TriStar fleets. These alternatives included new Airbus proposals and various British Aerospace derivative designs considered during the recently completed 737 selection process. Boeing's lengthy studies into 727 replacements throughout the 1970s were at that time crystallising into two new designs: the larger 7X7 – which finally emerged as the 767, and the 7N7, a narrow-bodied 180-seat twin based on the 727 fuselage but with new wings, tail, engines and flight deck. This design, re-designated 757, always appeared to be the airline's favourite and was duly selected in 1978. British Airways and Eastern Airlines provided Boeing with the necessary orders for nineteen and twenty-one aircraft respectively, and the aircraft was launched in March 1979. These were the only sales for some considerable time.

The first flight of a 757 took place on 19 February 1982, followed by the first British Airways aircraft in October of that year. CAA certification was obtained in January 1983 allowing services to begin on 9 February from Heathrow to Belfast, with other Shuttle services to Edinburgh, Glasgow, and Manchester soon following. Prime European routes to Copenhagen, Milan, Paris CDG, and Rome received a welcome boost from 757s during the

summer 1983 season and as deliveries picked up the type was introduced to Amsterdam, Athens, Frankfurt, Geneva, Nice, and Zürich during the following winter. The new two-pilot 757's excellent economics soon became apparent with its two Rolls-Royce RB-211-535C engines contributing to a reduction of 30% in the amount of fuel consumed per passenger compared to the Trident 3 with its three thirsty Speys. New 757s continued to arrive at a rapid rate throughout 1984-85 and, together with a second batch of sixteen 737-236s, displaced Tridents from many routes. When the end of Trident operations finally came in December 1985 British Airways had taken delivery of twenty 757s, completing a huge investment and training programme.

Sales of the 757 eventually picked up during the second half of the 1980s with major US carriers Delta and Northwest, followed by American and United, taking large fleets as originally expected, to replace 727s. What had not been apparent early in the 757 programme was the extent to which the aircraft would become accepted as a long-haul, primarily charter, airliner. Demand for cheaper long-haul travel and package holidays to ever more exotic destinations coincided with the introduction of the ETOPS concept of using twin-jet airliners on long-range services. UK holiday travellers in particular wanted direct flights to Florida, the Caribbean, Canada, Africa and the Far East and they also wanted to fly from their local airports such as Newcastle, Glasgow and Bristol. British Airways' newly reconstituted charter subsidiary Caledonian Airways was quick to exploit this new market by acquiring a fleet of 757s beginning with an order for two in February 1988, aircraft which would also replace its 737-236s on more traditional European charter work. In order to gain CAA approval for long-haul operations with twin-jet airliners under ETOPS rules, a very high level of in-service engine and systems reliability had to be demonstrated. The key factor for the 757 was the development of Rolls-Royce's advanced RB211-535E4B engine, which delivered an impressive 10% fuel burn improvement thereby providing the necessary range and lower still seat/mile costs. Caledonian eventually operated seven 757s on lease from its parent British Airways, including two ex-Air Europe aircraft acquired in 1992, and continued to operate the type until 1995 when the airline was sold to Inspirations. The final three 757s were returned to BA in October 1995 after Caledonian's new owners had replaced them with A320s.

In the USA, Eastern Airlines undertook an expensive programme to retrofit its entire 757 fleet of twenty-seven aircraft with the more efficient E4 version of the RB211-535, obviously believing that this significant investment would be repaid through lower operating costs. In contrast British Airways retained the original Series-535C engines on its

European 757 fleet and for some time purchased used -535Cs from re-engined Eastern aircraft to power new 757s after Rolls-Royce had stopped building this older version. From G-BPEA onwards, however, all BA 757s have been delivered with the E4 engine, many of which are ETOPS-capable.

During January 1995 British Airways Regional began to take advantage of the 757's long-haul attributes and unmatched low operating costs through the introduction of two examples on transatlantic services from Birmingham and Glasgow, replacing 767s which had proved to be too large for such routes. By summer 1997 one aircraft was flying a daily Glasgow–New York JFK–Boston service, the other Birmingham–JFK–Toronto in a spacious two-class (18J 138M) configuration. By the end of October 1998, however, BAR's services to JFK from Birmingham and Glasgow were withdrawn and the 757s returned to short-haul use.

Boeing 757s have comprised the major part of British Airways' Heathrow short-haul fleet for many years now and have operated in several different configurations to suit the commercial requirements of particular markets. One such configuration was the 201 seats fitted to G-BPED and G-CPEP for the operation of up to eight sectors per day on UK domestic services, contrasting vividly with the transatlantic lifestyle of the BA Regional 757s in their 156-seat two-class layout. Most of the 757s are now configured to carry 180 passengers in a flexible two-class layout but seven operate with 195 seats for use primarily on domestic services. From the end of

The 757 has proven itself to be a remarkably versatile design, an airliner which is equally at home on long charter flights and short domestic and European sectors as flown by this example G-BIKZ.

The first 757 to arrive with improved 'E4' engines and ETOPS clearance was Caledonian Airways' G-BPEA 'Loch of the Clans', seen here about to line-up and depart along Gatwick's runway 08-Right in May 1989. These features enabled charter airlines to make full use of the 757's excellent range capabilities to open up many new long-haul holiday markets.

March 1998 757s began to appear once again at Gatwick, where the continuing rapid growth of traffic on the existing European network and the opening of many more new routes led to a requirement for a larger aircraft with longer-range than the 737-400. A fleet of five 757s transferred from Heathrow for the summer 1998 season and operated to Edinburgh, Frankfurt, Manchester, Moscow, St Petersburg and Tel Aviv.

During 1995 British Airways took delivery of the last 757 from its outstanding orders. G-BPEK, which entered service from Heathrow to Copenhagen on 28 March, was the forty-second 757 to have been delivered from Boeing since 1983. Two other 757s (G-BPEF and G-CPEL) had been acquired second-hand and completed the mid-1990s fleet total of forty-four aircraft. This was not the end of the story, however, as BA subsequently placed three additional orders for 757s. An August 1996 agreement to acquire £600m worth of new Boeings included three 757s on firm order plus three options. Another three were ordered in 1997 for delivery by April 1998 and finally, in May 1998, six more 757s were ordered for the Heathrow fleet to release 767s for Gatwick, where they in turn would replace DC-10s. All of these 757s have been built as standard -236s which, apart from upgraded engines, are the same as the initial 757s delivered sixteen years earlier – a testimony to the soundness of the original design.

Somewhat surprisingly a leased 757 entered service with British Airways during July 1997. G-CPEP arrived at Heathrow in basic Air Transat colours as C-GTSU during April and after a period of storage and lengthy maintenance, 'PEP began its five-year lease to operate domestic Shuttle services.

Four other 757s have served British Airways and Caledonian on various medium-term leases. Air Europe agreed to buy two 757s from BA's original order in July 1982, a deal which also included the lease of various Air Europe aircraft to BA. Some of Air Europe's 737s subsequently flew for British Airtours and its 757, G-BKRM, operated Shuttle services for several seasons whilst BA's own aircraft were undergoing maintenance. After this arrangement had ended, an Air 2000 757 was leased during the winter 1987 season followed by a Monarch aircraft from April 1988 for a year, both for Shuttle use. The fourth leased aircraft was operated by Caledonian, on behalf of a new airline based at Newcastle called Ambassador Airlines. Whilst awaiting its own AOC, Ambassador contracted Caledonian to operate 757 G-BUDX, which was delivered new in May 1992 in Ambassador colours but with Caledonian titles. Apart from these leased aircraft, non-standard liveries were not seen on 757s in pre-'Utopia' days, with the exception of G-BIKC which displayed a large red poppy on its fin and 'Pause to Remember' titles to mark the Royal British Legion's 75th Anniversary Appeal at the end of 1996.

The 757 fleet status at December 1998 was:

LHR European (180 seats)	39
LHR Shuttle (195 seats)	7
BA EuroGatwick (180 seats)	5
Total 757s in service	**51**
BA/Caledonian 757s no longer used:	5 (G-BPEH, 'BKRM, BUDX, DRJC, OOOB)
Total 757s ever operated	**56**

As at December 1998, another six 757s remained to be delivered between April and July 1999, which would have increased the in-service total to fifty-seven. However, because of a downturn in traffic and

Deliveries of 757s continued from 1983 through to the completion of all outstanding orders in 1999 by which time 53 were in service. The only significant change which was incorporated throughout that 16-year period involved the fitting of improved engines from 1989, proving just how correct Boeing was with its original design for the aircraft.

the return of BA Regional's two 757s to the European fleet, these aircraft were sold before delivery and only two have entered service, bringing the fleet total to 53.

During August 1998 the first, and so far only, major new 757 variant took to the air and entered service with German charter carrier Condor in January 1999. The 757-300 incorporates a twenty-three feet fuselage stretch and can carry 243 passengers over distances of up to 4000 miles at seat/mile costs which are 10% lower than those of the 757-200. Whether this formidable new airliner, or indeed any more examples of its shorter cousins, joins British Airways remains to be seen, but with so many new narrow-body Airbus aircraft on order, the 757 fleet size may now have peaked.

Boeing 767-336

The 767 resulted from long-drawn-out studies undertaken by Boeing during the 1970s with the aim of producing a replacement for the highly successful 727, which although still achieving significant sales was obviously approaching the end of its production life. By 1977 the company had concluded that two different aircraft types would be needed and began to seek the necessary launch orders. As a direct 727-200 replacement Boeing finally opted for a twin-engined 757 design based on the existing 727's fuselage cross-section, but for the larger aircraft the company came up with a new wider fuselage incorporating a seven- or eight-abreast seat layout and twin-aisles. The 767-200 was, in fact, a completely new design that shared little with the 757 except for the flight deck and related systems, which were designed to enable the operation of either type by common-rated two-pilot crews. Two 747-size engines were selected and a new large wing was designed, paving the way for the development of larger and heavier versions and leading to many more sales as the concept of long-

range 'ETOPS' operations became widely accepted ten years later.

United Airlines was first to place an order, for thirty 767-200s in July 1978, followed by American Airlines, both of which saw the aircraft as an ideal DC-10 replacement for US domestic routes. Scheduled services commenced with United on 8 September 1982 from Chicago to Denver. As with the smaller 757, sales of the 767 were slow for many years as airlines in general struggled through a deep recession. Boeing however continued to look towards a future upturn and pressed ahead with new variants – the 767-200ER with extra centre-wing tanks and heavier operating weights in 1984, the 767-300 with a twenty-one feet fuselage stretch in 1986 and the 767-300ER which combined the extra capacity with additional tankage. This has proved to be the most popular version and the one bought by British Airways.

Much of this popularity resulted from certification authorities accepting from the mid-1980s that modern turbofan engines had reached such a level of reliability that airlines could be permitted to operate long-range over-water services with airliners powered by just two of these engines. This opened up many new route opportunities where DC-10/TriStar/747s were just too big or could only be operated at a very low frequency. The 'ETOPS' (Extended Range Twin Engine Operations) concept was initially pioneered by El Al between Tel Aviv and Montreal during 1984 and by Air Canada to the Caribbean and Europe from 1985, both airlines flying 767s. These initial flights were flown so that the aircraft was at all times within sixty minutes of single-engined flying time from the nearest, acceptable diversion airfield. As experience grew, approval was gradually obtained to increase this to 120 minutes and eventually to 180 minutes – sufficient for operations virtually anywhere in the world. By 1986 airlines such as American and TWA were flying ETOPS 767s across the Atlantic, and

Following a period of desert storage in the USA during the post-Gulf War downturn G-BNWL entered service with British Airways in October 1991 and has operated short-haul services from Heathrow ever since. It was photographed about to touch down on Runway 27-Left at Heathrow in September 1995.

Boeing 767-336 G-BNWK promotes the introduction of British Airways' new Club Europe product during 1994 whilst a reminder of Heathrow's past can be seen touching down in the background!

Qantas across the Pacific. Boeing's big twin-jet subsequently went on to displace the 747 from its position as the most popular North Atlantic airliner (with the airlines; passengers may not necessarily agree!) and by mid-1998 it was estimated that over 1.2 million ETOPS flights had been flown by Boeing twins and that 767s were operating 13,000 ETOPS flights every month.

British Airways purchased 767s with a view to taking full advantage of this increasing flexibility, placing an order for eleven 767-336ERs plus options for another fifteen during August 1987, valued at $500m. They would be the first 767s equipped with Rolls-Royce engines – RB211-524Hs producing 60,600 lb

of thrust and almost identical to the engines powering the airline's new 747-436 fleet. Another six were ordered and six options taken out during October 1988 as part of a package which included 737-436s and 757s, taking the total number of 767s on order to seventeen well before the first flight date of 23 May 1989. Initial deliveries and entry into service took place during February 1990 and, by the end of April, five were operating European scheduled services, predominantly to Paris CDG. The 767-336 offered 247 seats in a typical two-class European layout and was the ideal size for routes requiring larger aircraft than the 180-seat 757. Any remaining short-haul TriStars were quickly displaced, the 767

G-BZHC was the 28th and final 767 to be delivered, arriving in June 1998 with Japanese 'Waves and Cranes' artwork decorating its fin.

G-BZHA climbs rapidly under the power of its two Rolls-Royce engines. All 28 of British Airways' 767s have RB211-524H engines which are fully interchangeable with those fitted to many of the airline's 747-436 fleet. Only one other airline, China Yunnan Airlines, operates 767s with these engines.

being far more economical to operate.

The next batch of four 767s was delivered between June and December 1990, but this time in a long-haul three-class configuration of 9F/44J/141M. Whether used for short- or long-haul flying the basic 767-336ER airframe and engines are identical, with seat type and layout and other passenger amenities being the only differences. This has allowed the airline to be flexible in its use of 767s and has led to aircraft transferring frequently between short- and long-haul flying.

During 1990–91 767s replaced the final TriStars on routes to the Middle East – initially to Abu Dhabi, Bahrain and Riyadh, then to Doha, Jeddah and Khartoum, although at that time schedules were severely disrupted by conflict in the Gulf area. An

order for five placed in January 1991 was followed by another for three in December, taking the total to twenty-five, neatly fitting into the alphabetical range G-BNWA–Z. Plans for the next batch of 767 deliveries were upset by a marked downturn in global traffic levels as a consequence of the Gulf War, and led to two new aircraft being delivered directly into desert storage at Mojave for six months during 1991. Otherwise the build up of this new fleet continued, with the delivery of five in 1991, three in '92, four in '93, two in '94 and the remaining two in '96 and '97.

British Airways Regional began using three 767s ('NWN,WO,WU) from March 1993, operating two-class scheduled services from Manchester and Birmingham to New York JFK (some via Glasgow), and Manchester to Los Angeles. Although traffic

Whilst all of British Airways' 26 Boeing 767-300s are the 'ER' extended-range version, currently just six are configured for long-haul use from bases at Gatwick and Manchester. The remainder such as G-BNWJ, seen arriving at a Terminal One Europier stand, are Heathrow-based for domestic and European use.

levels were promising, the Los Angeles route was dropped at the end of the summer 1994 season because the fare yields were unacceptably low. Similarly, as the aircraft had proved to be too large for profitable year-round use on most BA Regional services, the fleet was changed in January 1995 to just one 767 (initially 'NWU, later swapped for 'NWH) and two 757s. This 767 now reliably maintains a daily year-round service between Manchester and JFK.

Boeing 767s have proven to be ideal aircraft for developing new routes and maintaining others which would be economically disastrous if flown by larger airliners, such as those to Beirut, Amman and Damascus which were restored from 1994 to 1995. Second-daily frequencies to some North American destinations to backup existing 747 services were introduced with the 767, for example to Philadelphia from summer 1995. Other long-haul destinations served from Heathrow at that time were Seattle, Vancouver, Newark and Cairo.

Change has continued to be a constant feature of the 767 fleet. During the 1995 summer operating season the long-haul 767 fleet, which had peaked at twelve aircraft, began to reduce with the progressive implementation of a long-term plan to maximise slot utilisation at Heathrow through the increased use of larger aircraft. Boeing 767s were replaced by a combination of upgrading some services to 747s and, from November 1995, the new 777s. Boeing 767s released from long-haul flying replaced 757s on many prime European services, the 757s in turn displacing all 737-236s from Heathrow. The run-down of long-haul flying continued until the last service from Teheran and Larnaca arrived back on 7 July 1997 and all Heathrow-based 767s then became dedicated to

short-haul flying. The type has continued to maintain a long-haul presence flying with BA Regional and from Gatwick, which began to see British Airways' own 767s in January 1996 (as opposed to US Air 767s in BA colours – see later). By midsummer 1996, five 767s had transferred to Gatwick to operate as 30J/183M two-class aircraft on daily Baltimore, Charlotte, JFK and Pittsburgh services plus three per week to Baku, capital city of oil-rich Azerbaijan.

The twenty-fifth delivery to complete the airline's full 767 order occurred early in 1997. This final aircraft, G-BNWZ, was one of six new wide-bodied airliners handed over by Boeing during February 1997 (the others being three 777s and two 747-436s), although it did not arrive at Heathrow until 25 March after cabin work at Dothan, Alabama, and began earning its keep by flying to Moscow on the 26th. However, not long after 'NWZ entered service, during June 1997, British Airways launched its new corporate identity and announced that, as part of an associated £6bn investment plan, an additional three 767-236s would be ordered for delivery during April–May 1998, taking the fleet to twenty-eight aircraft.

Boeing, meanwhile, had not finished with 767 developments and launched a further stretched version, the 767-400ER, to satisfy a Delta Airlines TriStar replacement requirement during April 1997. Measuring over twenty-one feet longer than a 767-300 and accommodating 20% more passengers, the Series-400 also has a longer wingspan, heavier operating weights and a stronger undercarriage, and has been sized to fit between the 767-300 and 777. Whether this new version will ever carry a British Airways livery remains to be seen.

Further mention must also be made of the three other 767s to have carried a British Airways livery, 767s which were also the only short-fuselage Series-200s to have been used. British Airways took a shareholding in US Air during January 1993 and entered into an agreement whereby US Air would open three new transatlantic routes using 767-200s in BA livery and flown by US Air crews wearing BA uniforms. Flights from Gatwick to Pittsburgh began in June 1993 followed by Baltimore in October and Charlotte in January 1994. They operated successfully until British Airways' own 767-336s took over, the final US Air-operated services being flown by N655US during March 1996.

Boeing 777

Often mistakenly thought of as merely a scaled-up 767 during the early project definition days, the remarkable Boeing 777 ('Triple Seven') emerged as a completely new aircraft, the biggest twin in existence with the most powerful engines ever built and which in due course may well achieve the same level of sales success as the 747. In its stretched form the 777 is actually longer than a 747, making it the longest commercial airliner ever built, and if Boeing should ever launch an extended-range version of the 777-300 it will match the current 747-400 in both size and

G-ZZZC was the first of British Airways' Boeing 777s to enter service, flying from Heathrow to Dubai and Muscat on 17 November 1995. The five 'A-Market' 777s are used predominantly on Middle Eastern services in a spacious low-density seating layout.

To lift such a large twin-engined airliner into the air brand new purpose-built General Electric GE90 engines capable of producing up to 84,700 lb of thrust were installed on the A-market 777s. To put this figure into context a typical 757 engine produces just 40,100 lb or a 747-400 Trent 60,600 lb.

range. British Airways looks set to take full advantage of the 777's impressive abilities with a total of twenty-nine in service at the turn of the century, followed by sixteen extended-range variants by 2002.

The initial design studies were in fact based upon the 767, as Boeing began to explore ways of filling a gap in its product range between the 767-300 and 747. Various '767X' derivatives were examined including stretched and three-engined versions, but by 1988 the major US airlines wanted a DC-10/TriStar replacement which would offer a wider fuselage than the 767. British Airways' somewhat more urgent requirement also specified a 250–300-seat TriStar replacement for short routes such as London to Paris, but more importantly, the airline looked upon the new aircraft as a potential replacement for its early 'Classic' 747s, particularly on long-haul routes to the USA/Canada and Middle East. Boeing had also realised that a new market opportunity was opening up following the 767's growing success on long-range ETOPS operations. The company foresaw a larger twin taking over from the long-haul tri-jets and ultimately replacing some of the early 747s, many of which were twenty-five years old, increasingly expensive to operate and showing their age.

During December 1988 Boeing invited eight major airlines, all of which were potential customers and including British Airways, to become closely involved in defining the new airliner's characteristics. What emerged was a detailed specification which led Boeing finally to abandon its ideas for 767 derivatives, largely because the narrow fuselage would have been uncompetitive against the new Airbus A330/340 and McDonnell Douglas's DC-10 derivative, the MD-11. The airlines wanted a wide-bodied fuselage with flexible interior layouts, modern technology throughout and ETOPS clearance from service entry, something that United Airlines in particular wanted.

By late 1990 Boeing was offering a brand-new airliner called the 777-200 which although similar in appearance to the 767 was actually much closer in size to the 747, just twenty feet shorter, with a similar wingspan and a fuselage width only one foot less. The 777 was officially launched with a United Airlines order for thirty-four, plus options for another thirty-four in October of that year, the design incorporating most of the features requested by the airline teams. To achieve the desired fast cruising speeds of up to Mach 0.84, long, aerodynamically efficient wings were needed, but a potential airport handling and parking problem was foreseen with such a wingspan, which would be thirty-five feet greater than that of a DC-10. To overcome this Boeing offered to incorporate folding wing-tips, but as yet no airline has taken up this rather heavy option. Nine per cent of the airframe was to be built from composite materials to reduce weight and the 777 would become Boeing's first fully 'fly-by-wire' airliner, controlled from a brand new glass cockpit equipped with flat-screen LCD displays. As for powerplants, the decision to fit only two engines to such a massive aircraft coupled with the requirement for long-range performance dictated the need for a new generation of engines, the most powerful ever built, delivering an initial 75,000 lb of thrust for the

In October 1996 G-VIIA became the first 777-IGW to fly and was delivered to British Airways after certification work with Boeing in July 1997. ETOPS clearance was soon confirmed and by the following summer 14 Boeing 777s were in service and had completely replaced 767s on long-haul services from Heathrow.

basic 777, much more powerful than a typical 56,000 lb 747 engine. All three major manufacturers decided to produce suitable engines; General Electric opting for an entirely new design, Pratt & Whitney and Rolls-Royce building derivatives of existing engines. Boeing also agreed to United's request for ETOPS clearance upon service entry, a challenging decision given the combination of a brand-new aircraft and engine, which would require many extra hours of reliability testing before certification.

Two basic models of the 777 emerged, identical in dimensions but with different operating weights and range capabilities, each capable of accommodating 440 passengers or 320 in a more typical two-class layout, and with a massive underfloor cargo capacity for thirty-two standard LD-3 containers. The A-market 777 has a range of 5,300 nm, more than sufficient for US domestic routes and capable of transatlantic flying. The B-market aircraft, known as the Increased Gross Weight (IGW) by Boeing, has structurally strengthened wings to take a higher maximum take-off weight of 286,900 kg v the A-market 242,670 kg. It incorporates more fuel in a new centre-wing tank and requires engines of up to 90,000 lb thrust to make full use of its 7,600 nm range capability to fly such sectors as London to Los Angeles or Peking. This model was launched in June 1991 with an order from Euralair.

British Airways' initial purchase of the 'Triple-Seven' soon followed. During August 1991, an order for five A-market and ten IGW 777s was placed, along with options for another ten, worth £2.2bn and part of a massive package worth £4.3bn which also included twenty-four 747-436 orders/options (and eleven ATPs)! Deliveries would take place between September 1995 and May 2002, all to be powered by the new GE90 engine. This decision not to select Rolls-Royce's Trent engine, a development of the 747-436's RB211-524 powerplant, came as something of a shock to many people – especially at Rolls-Royce. General Electric had chosen to build a totally new engine to obtain better fuel efficiency, lower noise characteristics and to allow for future growth versions, and British Airways became its launch customer. This was viewed as a surprising decision for many reasons, one of which was that the combination of a brand new airframe and engine is a challenge at any time, but particularly so for a twin which must demonstrate very high levels of reliability to qualify for ETOPS clearance. The GE90 is an enormous engine, the largest of the three competing engines, with a 10 ft 3 in diameter front fan which equates roughly to the size of a 737 fuselage. The GE90-85B engines for the A-market aircraft were certificated at 84,700 lb thrust but operate at a reduced 76,000 lb. For the IGW an uprated GE90-92B version can produce 92,000 lb but generally operates at up to 90,000 lb. To put these figures into context, a 757's RB211-535E4 engine generates 40,100 lb.

The first flight of a 'Triple Seven' took place on 12 June 1994, with a Pratt & Whitney-powered aircraft

G-VIIE taxies out for a flight to the Middle East whilst in the background sistership 'IIC climbs away. By the end of 1999, 29 Boeing 777s were in service: 5 A-Market based at Heathrow and 24 IGW split between Gatwick and Heathrow.

During 1998 many 747-436 orders were replaced with a commitment to acquire additional long-range 777s as British Airways began to refocus on the carriage of high-yield traffic on smaller more economical airliners. The total number of 777s in service will reach 45 once deliveries of the latest Series-236ER (extended range) version powered by Rolls-Royce Trent engines are complete.

destined eventually for United Airlines. The first GE90-powered aircraft, which later became G-ZZZA, flew on 2 February 1995 and was one of two British Airways aircraft used for flight testing. This was intended to include a 1000 hour ETOPS validation programme, 100 hours of which would be flown by the airline, with the aim of gaining 180 minutes ETOPS clearance by the time of the aircraft's type certification. However, development problems with the new GE engine delayed flight testing so the aircraft initially entered service without ETOPS clearance and worked towards building up the necessary hours by flying non-ETOPS routes.

Type certification was obtained on 19 April 1995 and the Pratt & Whitney-powered 777 entered service with United on 7 June flying from Heathrow to Washington with a full 180 minutes ETOPS clearance, as originally promised by Boeing. The first visit to London by a 777 destined for British Airways came when N77779, which ultimately became G-ZZZA, visited Heathrow on 20 April for an overnight stay. Deliveries were slightly delayed by engine problems and Boeing retained 'ZZB for ETOPS reliability testing. G-ZZZC entered service on 17 November 1995, flying from Heathrow to Dubai and Muscat, and for the rest of the winter 1995 season three 777s, 'ZZC/D/E, served on Paris CDG and Cairo services in addition to Dubai–Muscat. Service introduction was exceptionally smooth and overall reliability was much better than for other new types such as the 747-436 at a similar stage. The engines were particularly notable for their exceptional quietness and efficiency.

Another three IGW 777s were ordered in September 1996, taking the total to five 777-200As

and thirteen IGWs, all due for delivery by March 1998, plus options for seventeen more IGWs to be delivered after September 1998.

Approval for 120 minutes ETOPS flying was finally obtained during October 1996 and daily Heathrow to Boston services began immediately. By the end of the month 138 minutes ETOPS was approved but the full unrestricted 180 minutes had to wait until more service experience was obtained. By winter 1996 the four 777As were flying to Boston, Riyadh, Jeddah, Dubai–Muscat and three per day to Paris CDG for crew training purposes. This pattern was the beginning of a significant increase in capacity for Middle Eastern destinations and released 767s for services to Amman, Beirut and Kuwait. However, plans to use the 777 to Philadelphia, Abu Dhabi and Bahrain were delayed by late deliveries.

The first of any IGW 'Triple Seven' to fly was G-VIIA, which flew on 7 October 1996 and was then used for type certification flying. First to arrive at Heathrow was 'IIC during February 1997, one of six new Boeing wide-body airliners, including three 777-IGWs, handed over to British Airways during that month. These aircraft immediately began services to Philadelphia, but gearbox problems soon resulted in the withdrawal of ETOPS clearance, necessitating the substitution of A-models for some weeks.

At the end of March 1997 four A and four IGWs were in service. The A-models were primarily allocated to Middle Eastern routes in a low-density 17F/70J/148M (235-seat) configuration whereas the IGWs flew mainly North Atlantic services in 14F/56J/197M (267-seat). Five IGW options were confirmed during June for delivery between September 1998 and April 1999, primarily for operation from Gatwick as part of the airline's plan to standardise operations there on the 777, 747-436 and 767.

By midsummer 1997, 777s had completely replaced the 767 on long-haul routes from Heathrow. The 767s transferred to short-haul routes, allowing 757s to replace 737s, thereby providing an overall increase in capacity for the same number of frequencies. The eighth IGW arrived on delivery on 14 June 1997 fully painted up in *Delftblue Daybreak* colours, ready for its appearance the next day at the Paris Airshow as part of the airline's 'Utopia' launch. This aircraft was also notable for its out of sequence registration, G-RAES, in recognition of the Royal Aeronautical Society. The development IGW, G-VIIA, arrived on delivery on 4 July, completing the summer 1997 fleet of nine aircraft.

G-VIIH inaugurated twice-weekly services to Almaty, capital of Kazakhstan in Central Asia on 10 November 1997, the 777's most difficult route to date. Winter weather forecasts regularly predict less than 100 metres of visibility and a cloudbase at ground level, sometimes also with snow. If such conditions persist a diversion to the nearest suitable alternate airfield will be necessary, probably many hundreds of miles away in another country. The selection of such airfields must be very carefully made because handling an aircraft of this size will be a problem if suitable equipment is not available. For example, just starting the engines in the event of an APU (Auxiliary Power Unit) failure requires the use of three fully serviceable ground start units.

Gatwick operations with the 777 began with G-VIIA flying to Bermuda on 3 February 1998, followed by services to Atlanta, Dallas and Accra. G-VIIL arrived at Gatwick on its delivery flight on 14 March as part of the fleet build-up to seven aircraft for the summer 1998 programme, which saw the type scheduled to operate additionally to Dhahran (transferred from Heathrow) and Denver. Services to Denver should have commenced on 1 June, but were delayed until later in the year because US approval to operate the route was not forthcoming. Summer operations from Denver are providing the 'Triple Seven' with another operational challenge. With the airfield 5,341 feet above sea level and high summer temperatures, the only way to achieve a useful payload is by using the full 90,000 lb thrust capability of the 777's GE90 engines.

The fleet deployment for summer 1998 was:

'A'	LHR	Middle East destinations	5
IGW	LHR	Almaty, Boston, Cairo, Detroit, Jeddah, Newark, JFK, Tel Aviv, Teheran	7
IGW	LGW	Atlanta, Bermuda, Dallas, Dhahran, Denver	7
		Total	**19**

Another five 777-200IGWs were ordered during May 1998, at the expense of four 747-436 options,

taking the total on order to twenty-nine. Three of the ordered aircraft arrived at Gatwick on delivery early in 1999 to take over the AML leisure network from a similarly-sized fleet of DC-10s. G-VIIO entered service from Gatwick to Tampa on 1 February in a high-density two-class configuration (28J/355M), seating a total of 383 passengers. By the end of March all three were in service, flying to many new destinations for this big airliner including Cancun, Grand Cayman, Havana, Kingston, Montego Bay, Nassau, Puerto Plata, San José, San Juan and Tobago.

Boeing have also built and flown a stretched version of the 'Triple Seven' aimed primarily at the 'Classic' 747 replacement market. The 777-300 is 33 feet 3 inches longer than the 777-200 and is actually 10 feet 6 inches longer than a 747, making it the longest ever commercial aircraft and the biggest twin-jet yet built. It can accommodate 370 passengers in a three-class layout, but could take 550 in a high-density all-economy configuration. Using up to one-third less fuel than a 'Classic', and with greatly reduced maintenance and operating costs, the 777-300 should be a formidable 747 replacement. All of the commitments have so far come from Far Eastern airlines; fifty-one aircraft were ordered by All Nippon, Asiana, Cathay Pacific, JAL, Korean, Malaysian and Thai International before the economic crisis hit the region during 1997. The 777-300 was launched during June 1995 and first flew on 16 October 1997. Engines with 90,000 lb thrust are available from all three manufacturers and give the 777-300 similar range to the A-market 777-200.

Further developments which may be launched when Boeing foresees a worthwhile market include an increased-range -200X and the formidable -300X, which would incorporate the stretched fuselage 777-300 with the extended-range of a -200IGW, giving it the capability of matching the payload and range of today's 747-400s. Meanwhile, Boeing continues to increase the take-off weight of the current production aircraft, the maximum take-off weight of 287,000 kg increasing from the 140th aircraft to 294,200 kg and again in 1999 to 297,800 kg.

Following from the financial crisis which began during 1997 in the Far East, airlines everywhere began to limit their plans for future capacity growth. British Airways changed course to concentrate on carrying more high-yield passengers on smaller, more economical aircraft and as a result during 1998 replaced many of its outstanding 747-436 orders with 777s. Nine 747-436 orders were cancelled, as were all outstanding options, and instead during August 1998 the airline ordered sixteen heavyweight 777s and took options for another sixteen. These 777s will be Series-200ERs (Extended Range) with the maximum take-off weight increased to 297,800 kg. Rolls-Royce triumphed over GE to win the engine order, their uprated Trent 895s of 95,000 lb thrust giving the new aircraft sufficient range to fly non-stop to Hong Kong, Singapore, South Africa or South America with a full payload. When all deliveries have been completed in 2002, British Airways will have a total of forty-five 777s in service, comprising:

A-market	5
IGW	24
ER	16
Total – by the year 2002	**45**

Another sixteen options are held and if these aircraft are delivered British Airways will have more 777s in service than 747-436s.

Airbus A320 family

British Airways acquired a small fleet of Airbus A320s almost by accident during the late 1980s. For the next ten years, surrounded somewhat uncomfortably by an ever increasing fleet of Boeing twin-jets, they operated very successfully from Heathrow but with the axe expected to fall on several occasions. This, however, changed dramatically with the airline's decision in 1998 to purchase up to 188 A319/320s, neatly turning the tables on Boeing's 737. Franchise partner British Mediterranean also operates the type and GB Airways is set to follow.

The success of its initial foray into the airliner business with the innovative A300 wide-bodied twin led Airbus Industrie to expand its airliner family through the development of an advanced technology, short/medium-range 150-seater, the A320. The company's aim was to produce a more modern rival for the Boeing 737 and McDonnell Douglas MD-80 ranges which were both derivatives of 1960s designs, and to that end as much new technology as possible was incorporated to give the A320 a commercial advantage. Studies refined the design into two identically sized versions, each with a generous six-abreast fuselage cross-section but with different take-off weights and range capabilities. Fly-by-wire controls were incorporated for the first time on a subsonic airliner (Concorde being the true pioneer), operated by a system of linked computers programmed to ensure that the aircraft can not exceed safe flight parameters. On the flight deck advanced electronic displays are complemented by side-stick controllers instead of the traditional control columns. The extensive use of composite materials is another of the innovations which distinguish the A320 from earlier designs.

Launch orders came during late 1983, the first of which was from British Caledonian (BCAL) for ten A320s to be powered by 25,000 lb thrust CFM-56-5A engines, although these aircraft were destined never to serve BCAL. The first flight of an A320 took place from Toulouse on 22 February 1987 and deliveries to Air France began during March 1988. The first two BCAL A320s flew in their full 'Golden Lion' colours during November and December 1987, but were actually delivered for service with British Airways after a hasty repaint following the merger of BA and BCAL in 1988. Also, before entering service, the originally allocated registrations of G-BRSA etc. were amended to G-BUSB–SK. The first British Airways A320 service was from Gatwick to Geneva on 29 April 1988 and during their first season the A320s operated from Gatwick's new North Terminal on ex-BCAL routes to Geneva, Genoa, Milan and Tunis as well as Inclusive Tour charters to Mediterranean destinations. As deliveries built-up the fleet transferred to Heathrow during November 1988, replaced at Gatwick with a fleet of 737-236s.

Captured seconds before touching down on Heathrow's Runway 27-Left, G-BUSH is one of ten Airbus A320s originally ordered by British Caledonian but flown by British Airways since 1988. Prominent wing tip fences identify it as one of the airline's five longer-range Series-210s.

Two early production Airbus A320-100s, of which only 21 were built, await their next flights. The lack of wing tip fences distinguishes these early models from the later Series-200s. Although there are no other visible differences, the Series-200s have extra fuel tanks to increase their range by 1,000 miles. British Airways' fleet includes five of each type.

The first five deliveries were all A320-110 variants with a maximum take-off weight (MTOW) of 68,000 lb and had all entered service by June 1989. Only twenty-one of this version were built before Airbus standardised production on the heavier Series-200, which incorporated a centre-section fuel tank and an increased MTOW of 73,500 lb, increasing the range by 1000 miles. Five of this type were delivered to British Airways, the last arriving in October 1990. Externally the two types can be differentiated by the wing tip fences fitted to the -210, but internally they are identical with a 149-seat two-class layout.

The A320 has continued to sell exceptionally well to airlines around the world. In Europe most major carriers operate large fleets and in North America, a market which has traditionally been difficult for foreign airliners to break into, Air Canada, Northwest, United and US Airways have all become major users. Airbus's long-term goal of producing a complete family of airliners came two steps closer to fruition with the introduction of the longer fuselage A321, seating 185 passengers, in 1994 and the smaller 124-seat A319 in 1996, derivatives which share a common flight deck and pilot rating with the A320. During January 1995 Airbus delivered the 500th A320, the first time a large European airliner had ever reached that number, and with total sales of the A319/320/321 family exceeding 2000 during 1999, future prospects look excellent.

Meanwhile, British Airways continued to successfully operate its small fleet of ten Airbuses on domestic and European scheduled services from Heathrow alongside an ever-larger Boeing-dominated fleet of twin-jets. The 737/757/767 family with capacities ranging from 108 to 252 seats neatly brackets in size the 149-seat Airbus, leading to speculation over the years about the continued viability of such a small number of A320s, which require a completely separate pilot establishment and different engineering support. However, as the Airbuses performed well and are very popular with passengers and crews alike, they survived.

This uncertainty came to an end during 1998 when British Airways placed its first ever order with Airbus, a huge order which was not only for the largest number of aircraft ever acquired by the airline in a single deal, but was also the largest order Airbus had ever received from a non-US airline. Both Airbus and Boeing had competed to supply new airliners to replace some 737s and after lengthy negotiations Airbus received an order for fifty-nine A319/320s, plus options for an additional 129. Of the firm orders, twenty are for delivery as A320s, thirty-nine as A319s. The initial recipient, BA Regional, is taking a total of twenty-one A319s from September 1999 to replace its 737-236 fleet, followed by deliveries to EuroGatwick. Some of the optioned aircraft, which will all be delivered by 2004 if the orders are confirmed, are expected to go to Air Liberté and Deutsche BA and can be either A319s, A320s or A321s. The International Aero Engines (IAE) consortium's V2500 engines have been chosen to power the new Airbuses.

About to push-back from its parking stand between two other Airbuses, G-BUSI displays 'Britain in a teacup' tail-art, a competition winning design carried for six months from December 1997.

ABOVE: *Airbus has achieved tremendous success with its family of narrow-body airliners and finally persuaded British Airways to place a huge order for up to 188 A319/A320s during 1998 to replace many of the Boeing 737s currently in service with the airline and its partners.*

Partner airlines are also responsible for the appearance of more A320s in British Airways' livery. During April 1997 British Mediterranean Airlines became a franchise partner, operating a range of services to Middle East destinations for British Airways with its original A320-200 plus another two ex-China Airlines examples. These aircraft have V2500 engines and were the first of the type to carry British Airways' new colour scheme. GB Airways placed an order for nine A320-family airliners during November 1998 along with options for another five, all to be powered by IAE V2500s. The first of these will be delivered during the second quarter of 2000 and will be a 159-seat A320. The rest of the order is expected to be a mixture of A320s and A321s and once delivered will replace completely the existing fleet of 737-300/400s. Although they are being acquired separately, the GB Airways Airbuses will be of a similar standard to those of British Airways EuroGatwick.

BAC Aérospatiale Concorde

Concorde! Merely mentioning the name conjures up images of something beautiful, exciting and unique. Intense feelings of pride are felt by those who built and operate it, and for those who admire the elegance of its lines, a longing to be on board as a passenger. No other airliner has the power to generate such emotions or to captivate the imagination in a way which is undiminished even after thirty years in the air.

Concorde today looks as futuristic as it did back in 1969. Remarkably, in a world where increased speed has always counted for so much, it remains totally unchallenged by any other airliner ever built or which is likely to see passenger service within the next twenty years. This has happened because Concorde was built as an era was ending; a time when the thrust for technological advancement at almost any cost was being overtaken by new commercial realities and concerns for the environment. These changes took place during the long and careful development programme and eventually denied Concorde the opportunity to fully exploit its potential, as well as killing off any competitors. The fact that it finally became such a success highlights the incredible achievement of Britain and France in designing and building Concorde and the skill of its two airline operators in maintaining and flying the world's only supersonic commercial airliner. Even now Concorde still achieves with relative ease the sort of performance which the best military fast-jets can only envy. Whilst some of these could just about catch Concorde, none would be able to keep up with it for long and their occupants certainly would not share the comforts and fine cuisine enjoyed by Concorde's passengers!

The story began during the 1950s with separate projects in Britain and France to recapture the lead in long-haul airliner design which had been lost to the American Boeing 707s and Douglas DC-8s. Long-haul piston-engined airliners were being replaced by such jets which reduced transatlantic crossing times from eighteen hours to just eight, and designers felt that the next logical step would be to go for another increase in speed, which of course meant flying supersonically. Military aircraft were achieving such speeds and it was felt that civil airliner design would soon follow. After many studies a design emerged from Bristol Aircraft for an airliner capable of crossing the Atlantic with 100–150 passengers at just over twice the speed of sound (Mach 2.00–2.2), a design which was remarkably similar to that which was eventually built as Concorde. France was undertaking similar studies but favoured a smaller airliner with less range. However, both countries came to realise that the scale of the technical challenges and the finance required to build such aircraft meant that they could not hope to go it alone. This led to a major political agreement, the Anglo-French Supersonic Aircraft Agreement, signed in November 1962 by the British and French Governments, to jointly finance the development and construction of a supersonic airliner to be built by the British Aircraft Corporation and Sud-Aviation (airframe), and Bristol Siddeley and SNECMA (engines).

Evidence of British Airways' attempts to share its Concorde operations with other airlines can be seen in this photograph. The Concorde displays Singapore Airlines' livery on its port side for joint operations to Bahrain/Singapore and carries the dual American/British registration G-N94AD for Braniff Airways' use between Washington and Dallas/Fort Worth.

TOP: *Concorde G-BOAG had a very uncertain start to its flying career and spent several years out of service as a source of spares for other fleet members. Because of this time on the ground 'OAG has accumulated approximately two-thirds of the flying time achieved by the high time aircraft in the fleet. Seen here in October 1984 awaiting parts during a difficult and costly re-build, 'Alpha Golf' re-entered service the following April resplendent in the new 'Landor' livery and has given the airline excellent service ever since.*

ABOVE: *On 21 Januray 1986, ten years to the day after Concorde entered commercial service, G-BOAC performed a special anniversary flight. All seven Concordes are now over twenty years old but recent structural inspections have confirmed their excellent condition and suitability to continue in service for the foreseeable future.*

The specification finally agreed upon was for an airliner capable of carrying up to 126 passengers over transatlantic distances at Mach 2.2, and to achieve this a thin fuselage and slender delta wing design was adopted. The project cost was estimated at £150–170m and the first flight of the newly named Concord/Concorde was planned for 1966, leading to entry into service in 1970. Power would be provided by four extensively redesigned Olympus engines which were then being built for the Avro Vulcan bomber.

To develop such an aircraft meant overcoming many formidable obstacles. The wing needed to be designed for both efficient supersonic cruise and for slow landing speeds, and these conflicting requirements led to the adoption of a highly refined, curved delta shape. Slow speeds with such a wing would only be possible at a very high angle of attack and so a hinged nose was incorporated which could be lowered for take-off and landing to enhance visibility from the flight deck. New materials were needed which could withstand temperatures of up to 120° Celsius for sustained periods. Cabin temperatures had to be kept at comfortable levels for passengers and to achieve this a heat exchanger using fuel to cool the

air was designed. Fuel was also to be used to adjust the centre of gravity of the aircraft during the different phases of flight and to do this a transfer system was installed which could pump fuel between trim tanks near the front and rear of the aircraft.

The engines also needed an extensive redesign to take their thrust from the Vulcan's 20,000 lb to an eventual maximum of 38,050 lb with re-heat on the production Concorde's Olympus 593s. One of the most difficult tasks encountered was to design intakes for the engines, which in order to function properly need to take in air at speeds no greater than Mach 0.5. With the aircraft travelling at up to four times faster than this a variable intake was designed which uses a system of movable ramps and spill doors to regulate the speed and quantity of air received by the engine to suit each phase of flight. Overcoming these challenges was made even more difficult by having widely separated British and French teams which used different languages, working methods, and systems of weights and measures. Perhaps the most significant disagreement was whether to use the letter 'e' in the new airliner's name! This issue was not resolved until the first aircraft rolled-out in December 1967 when the French version 'Concorde' was officially adopted.

TOP: *Heat from four powerful Rolls-Royce Olympus engines distorts the background as G-BOAG taxies out for a Saturday morning departure to Barbados during March 1997. These trips have now become very popular with two Concorde flights from London operating most weekends during the winter months. Similar trips from New York to Barbados began in February 1999.*

ABOVE: *At the 'Utopia' launch on 10 June 1997 a variation of the airline's new identity for the Concorde fleet was unveiled on G-BOAF. The simple but effective 'Union Flag' design has proven to be very popular for an aircraft which spends much of its time in the limelight as a flagship for British Airways and as an ambassador for Britain.*

One by one the various technical challenges were overcome and Concorde moved on to a successful first flight from Toulouse on 2 March 1969. The political path, however, was not so smooth and Concorde came very close to cancellation several times. Commercially the future looked bright, with options to purchase a total of seventy-four Concordes received from many of the world's major airlines by 1971, and estimates of 400 sales by 1980 were confidently being made. BOAC converted its options into a firm order for five in July 1972 and Air France ordered four. Competition for Concorde was expected from a much bigger and faster American design and from a very similar-looking but much less capable Russian Tupolev Tu-144. Both of these aircraft eventually fell by the wayside, the American design being cancelled in 1971 after having had as much money spent on it as Concorde, and although the Tu-144 achieved very limited operational service, it

was soon withdrawn.

Two Concorde prototypes were built, followed by two pre-production aircraft and two early production models, none of which were ever to enter service. Authorisation to build a total of sixteen production aircraft was received in 1974, but sadly Concorde's market had collapsed. Following Pan-American and TWA's decisions to cancel their options, no other airline placed orders, leaving just British Airways and Air France as customers. Thus the eventual total of Concordes built was twenty and only fourteen of these ever entered airline service.

By 1975, after six years of exhaustive and unprecedented testing, Concorde was declared ready for commercial use. The next obstacle to overcome, however, was one which had not been foreseen in 1962. A carefully orchestrated campaign of protest against the perceived environmental impact of supersonic airliner operations had been underway for

TOP: *Since 1977 Concordes have successfully maintained a twice-daily supersonic link between London and New York as well as operating charters to many hundreds of places around the world. In this photograph G-BOAE taxies from Terminal 4 to operate the morning BA001 service to New York, a routine operation which nonetheless never fails to impress most observers.*

ABOVE: *Jetting-off into an evening sky 'Speedbird Concorde Three' will soon catch up with the setting sun as it cruises westbound at twice the speed of sound high over the North Atlantic. Three hours later as G-BOAB slows down and descends towards New York the sun will once again be seen to set ahead of it.*

some time. In America, after the Boeing 2707 supersonic airliner had been cancelled, attention focused on Concorde and the aircraft was banned from flying there. Whether or not this was entirely motivated by environmental concerns remains open to debate, but removing the ban was essential to the success of the entire Concorde project. As the matter was being debated in the American courts, Concorde was readied for service and on 21 January 1976 finally carried its first fare-paying passengers. British Airways flew G-BOAA from Heathrow to Bahrain whilst Air France flew its first service from Paris to Rio de Janeiro via Dakar. The Bahrain route was not ideal for Concorde as much of it was flown subsonically over Europe, but a saving of 2.5 hours over the usual sector time was still achieved. This was seen as the first leg of a proposed service to Australia, the next one being an extension from Bahrain to Singapore in association with Singapore

Airlines. Services from Heathrow via Bahrain to Singapore commenced in December 1977 and were to be flown three times a week until problems with a supersonic routing through Malaysian airspace forced their suspension after only three flights had been operated. In January 1979 services resumed, usually flown by G-BOAD which had been painted with Singapore Airlines colours on the port side, but were abandoned in November 1980 because of poor loads, never having been extended to Australia.

Meanwhile, the battle to land in America had been won, at least for a sixteen-month trial period, but not initially to the desired destination of New York JFK. Services to Washington-Dulles IAD commenced with a simultaneous arrival by British Airways and Air France Concordes on 24 May 1976 and were finally followed on 22 November 1977 by flights to JFK after a successful noise abatement trial had been performed. At last Concorde was operating on the route for which it had been designed and soon settled into a twice-daily service which has continued ever since. Other scheduled Concorde services in America have been experimented with over the years. An unusual agreement was reached between Braniff International Airways and British Airways/Air France for the operation of Concordes on Braniff services between Washington and Dallas-Fort Worth, beginning on 12 January 1979 with G-N94AE. These were flown subsonically by Braniff crews and in order to satisfy the airworthiness authorities on both sides of the Atlantic, the aircraft were all given hybrid registrations, hence G-BOAE became G-N94AE. The eventual aim was for Braniff to operate Concordes on its South American services but an economic recession forced the airline to stop using the aircraft in June 1980. The Heathrow–Washington service was extended once again from 27 March 1984 when British Airways itself flew the aircraft on to Miami, making full use of an over-water route to operate supersonically. Miami was served by Concorde three times per week until March 1991 when flights once again terminated at Washington, and in November 1994 after more than eighteen years, Washington's supersonic link to London ended.

Operationally, Concorde was remarkably successful and had suffered from very few problems for such a technically advanced machine. Commercially, however, its future remained uncertain and during the early 1980s was threatened by the British Government's decision to terminate support for any Concorde costs incurred by its manufacturers. An earlier agreement, in February 1979, had seen British Airways accepting full responsibility for the operating costs of its Concordes. The government had agreed to write-off the £160m purchase cost of these five aircraft and would continue to support the manufacturers costs in return for receiving 80% of any future Concorde operating profits. The two unsold aircraft at Filton were also handed over to British Airways for operation on similar terms. This was all to change, however, and so the airline entered into a lengthy period of negotiations with the government and British Aerospace to see if a satisfactory formula to ensure the future of Concorde operations could be found. In March 1984, after eighteen months of negotiations, an agreement was announced whereby British Airways took over full responsibility for funding Concorde costs and the requirement to pay 80% of operating profits to the government was dropped. British Airways paid £16.5m for all Concorde spares and test equipment, including the stored first production aircraft G-BBDG at Filton, which has been retained as a valuable source of spare parts. With its Concorde operation on a more secure financial footing, British Airways further developed the use of its aircraft and has set up long-term plans to ensure that their operation well into the future will be properly supported.

The seven-strong Concorde fleet is now fully utilised thanks to the development of some very innovative ideas to market the aircraft's unique abilities. Although three aircraft are fully utilised operating the twice-daily New York schedules and others are grounded for maintenance checks, which are much more frequent and time-consuming than those for subsonic airliners, there is still enough spare Concorde time for other work. Since 1987 regular services have operated for four months during the winter from Heathrow to Barbados either once or twice a week. From February 1999 these have been joined by flights from New York JFK to Barbados. Other occasional scheduled flights operate to Toronto and Washington. The main source of extra work, however, comes from charters which now account for approximately 20% of the fleet's annual utilisation. These began back in the early 1980s with local flights from Heathrow for people who wanted to experience supersonic flight without the expense of a flight to New York. The charter market has since then been extensively developed and agencies now offer many different packages. A trip on Concorde can be linked with excursions to interesting places or events (e.g. day-trips to see the Pyramids, to Lapland at Christmas or to Monaco for the Grand Prix) or combined with other exotic forms of transport such as the QE2 or the Orient Express. Even more ambitious are the occasional round-the-world charters which can take the aircraft away for several weeks. As a result of these activities, Concordes have been seen at hundreds of places around the globe, at airports which otherwise would never have seen the aircraft and which always provide a warm welcome. British Airways is justly proud of its use of Concorde to enable people from all walks of life to experience the thrill of an afterburner take-off and the sight of the earth's curvature from 60,000 feet whilst cruising supersonically and sipping champagne!

For the future, Concorde is expected to remain in service for many more years. The airframes have recently undergone thorough inspections which have confirmed their excellent condition. Although they are now all over twenty years old, each Concorde flies for an average of just three hours per day, a quarter of that achieved by a typical long-haul subsonic airliner. Another factor which uniquely favours Concorde is that the heat generated by supersonic flight dries out any moisture in the airframe and virtually eliminates any possibility of corrosion in unseen areas. Supersonic transport research is once again underway in the USA and somewhat surprisingly this has led to the reactivation of a stored Tupolev Tu-144 for NASA-sponsored trials in Russia during 1997–8. Even if this research eventually leads to the development of a new supersonic airliner, it would take at least fifteen years to actually build one and by then Concorde would have been in British Airways service as the world's only supersonic airliner for almost forty years!

CHAPTER FIVE

AIRCRAFT TYPES
NO LONGER OPERATED

This chapter looks at aircraft types which are no longer part of the British Airways fleet, mainly those inherited with the merger of BEA and BOAC, but also including aircraft such as the TriStar and DC-10 acquired since that time but which have also gone. Background information about the acquisition and operational use of each type is followed by details of its disposal. Many such aircraft have gone on to lead long and productive lives after leaving British Airways and a summary of how they have fared since retirement is given.

Aircraft types: Boeing 707
BAC VC-10
BAC One-Eleven
HS 748 and BAe ATP
HS Trident
Lockheed TriStar
McDonnell Douglas DC-10
Shorts Skyliner
Vickers Viscount
Vickers Vanguard / Merchantman

Note: Details of each individual aircraft's history can be found in Appendix Two.

Boeing 707

Throughout the 1960s, the mainstays of BOAC's long-haul fleet were Boeing's classic workhorse, the 707, and its charismatic British rival the VC-10. With the dawn of the new wide-bodied airliner age in 1970 both types survived to wear the new British Airways colours, the 707 ultimately outliving the VC-10 and flying well into the 1980s.

The 707 was the first long-haul jet to achieve true worldwide airline acceptance, the market leader of a new generation of intercontinental airliners which began a complete transformation of long-haul air travel. Even after Boeing's 747 began to supersede it, the 707 continued to be built for another twenty years, the last examples being produced for such decidedly non-airline roles as in-flight refuelling and as Airborne Early Warning radar platforms. Boeing finally closed the line after the 856th 707 had rolled out in 1991. During October 1998, as the 707 reached 40 years of commercial service, over 130 were still in use and several programmes were underway to hush-kit or re-engine these aircraft to prolong their lives well into the next century.

Two of British Airways' Boeing 707s were photographed soon after the merger. G-APFP, a Rolls-Royce Conway-powered 707-436 was soon to be retired from service and never received the airline's new colour scheme, whereas 707-336C G-AVPB served as a freighter and then a passenger airliner until 1983.

TOP: *Although most 707-436s had been withdrawn from British Airways' scheduled services by March 1975, four were retained to operate charters to North America for another two years. Three of these are seen at Heathrow along with two Standard VC-10s in June 1976.*

ABOVE: *G-AXGW climbs out from Heathrow during January 1977 at the beginning of a flight to Barbados. British Airways operated eleven turbofan-powered 707-330B/Cs, eight of which flew as passenger airliners and three as freighters. Poor economic conditions combined with the availability of longer-range TriStars brought about the retirement of all 707s from scheduled services by 1983.*

BOAC's purchase of 707s in addition to its order for VC-10s resulted from the airline's determination to overcome political opposition and obtain an aircraft type with sufficient range to operate its North Atlantic routes. The initial fleet of fifteen Rolls-Royce Conway-powered 707-436s arrived at Heathrow during 1960 and was eventually increased to twenty. Eighteen from this total survived to join British Airways in 1974. BOAC also acquired eleven of the later and more capable Pratt & Whitney JT-3D turbofan-powered 707-320B/Cs from a variety of sources, to boost capacity during the 1960s and also to take over the freighter routes. All but two of these were built as convertible passenger/freighter 707-320Cs, although in later years with British Airways only three aircraft (G-ASZF, SZG, TWV) regularly flew as freighters, with G-AXGX converted as required. Two 707s, G-AXXY/XXZ, were purchased as pure passenger 707-336Bs with extra range for the demanding Moscow–Tokyo sector.

When the 747 finally took to the air with BOAC during 1971, phasing out of the early-model 707-436s began. Over the following two years seven were converted to a high-density 189-seat configuration and transferred to BEA's charter subsidiary BEA Airtours to replace its Gatwick-based fleet of Comet 4Bs. BEA Airtours, which later became British Airtours, eventually operated thirteen different 707-436s on its extensive medium-range European charter network which imposed a punishing high-cycle utilisation rate on this long-haul airliner. Boeing ultimately took twelve of the eighteen 707-436s as part of purchase deals for new 747s.

By March 1975 British Airways Overseas Division had withdrawn all 707-436s from scheduled services, retaining just four to operate summer season Affinity Group charters to the USA for another two years. British Airtours maintained an operational fleet of up to nine 707-436s throughout the 1970s for its own charter services and also for sub-lease to carriers such as Air Mauritius to operate their scheduled services. By the time they were replaced with new 737s in 1981, the few remaining 707-436s were twenty years old, costly to operate and difficult to maintain. Although a few were sold to small airlines, most were soon grounded and eventually broken up. Today the only place to see a fine example of this once proud fleet of early transatlantic jet-airliners is the RAF Museum, Cosford, near Wolverhampton, where G-APFJ is displayed as part of the British Airways Collection.

As for the turbofan 707 fleet, poor economic conditions prevalent at the beginning of the 1980s forced the airline into a radical review of its entire network and the many diverse aircraft types used to serve it. One of the resultant decisions called for a simplification of the fleet structure, which in turn opened the final chapter for British Airways' operation of the Viscount, VC-10 and Boeing 707-320B/C, all of which had gone by early 1984.

The passenger 707-320B/C fleet was reduced at the rate of two per season from the summer of 1981 when six were flown, decreasing to four for the winter and just two for 1982–3. All three freighters were withdrawn by the end of March 1982. The final 707 services were actually flown by British Airtours during March 1984 using 'XXY, one of two transferred from BA in April 1981 and May 1982 for North Atlantic charter work.

British Airways' fleet of 707-320B/Cs proved to be a much more saleable commodity than the earlier and much less economical 707-436s. All eleven soon found buyers and left for new and varied careers which in some cases proved to be somewhat short-lived. By 1985 two of the 707s had been written-off whilst operating in Africa, but others survived for much longer, mostly operating for small freight carriers in remote parts of the world. One exception,

which has led something of a charmed life and looks set to outlive all other ex-BA 707s, is G-AXGX. During May 1981 'XGX was wet-leased to the Qatar Government which, in July 1984, purchased the aircraft and flew it as A7-AAC, still with BA crews. During 1995 it was sold to Grumman Aerospace as VR-BZA and ferried to the USA to join nineteen other ex-airline 707s awaiting their turn for conversion into E-8C J-Stars radar intelligence aircraft for the USAF. In its new military role 'XGX will probably have another twenty or more years of flying ahead of it!

Vickers VC-10

BOAC brought a total of twenty-seven VC-10s to the marriage with BEA in 1974, just half of the fleet size originally envisaged by supporters of this supremely elegant and majestic airliner, and exactly half of the total number of VC-10s ever built. Whilst much loved by its pilots and the first choice of many passengers, the VC-10 had been fatally damaged by years of arguing about its role and specifications and, sadly, very few were built. Although all VC-10s had left British Airways service within seven years of the merger, ten of them still fly today in a vital military role and are expected to continue operating well into the twenty-first century, some forty years after first entering service.

The VC-10 was conceived in an atmosphere of conflict between Her Majesty's Government and the State-owned airlines over support for British-built airliners. For some time British industry had consistently failed to deliver the suitable modern long-haul types which were desperately needed to replace BOAC's uneconomical and uncompetitive post-war fleet. The Britannia and Comet, both ultimately excellent aircraft, matured much later than required by BOAC and these delays forced the government to approve its purchase of additional and expensive stop-gap airliners from America. For the next generation of long-haul airliners, however, another new British design was emerging which BOAC was expected to support.

During the mid-1950s, as BOAC defined its requirements for the coming decade, two somewhat different requirements emerged which could not be satisfied by one type alone at such an early stage in the development of jet airliners. For its North Atlantic routes BOAC wanted Boeing 707s, and in October 1956 was given permission to buy fifteen Rolls-Royce-powered 707-436s. However, for the more demanding requirement to operate long-haul services from difficult airfields at hot and high African locations such as Nairobi and Johannesburg, or from airfields with poor runways throughout the airline's eastern network, Vickers' VC-10 proposal was tailor-made and the best available candidate.

BOAC placed an order for thirty-five VC-10s and took out options for another twenty in January 1958, many more than it wanted, but a necessary minimum to justify the huge cost of launching the new airliner. This set the scene for many years of haggling, with the government urging BOAC to accept the full order and use the excess aircraft on its Atlantic routes. Ten stretched Super VC-10s, which had sufficient range to operate comfortably from Heathrow to New York JFK, were ordered during June 1960 at a cost of £25m, but BOAC continued to press for additional 707s. During 1961 the number of VC-10s on firm order changed to twelve Standards and thirty Supers, but even when the prototype first flew on 29 June 1962, BOAC could not foresee a use for so many VC-10s.

The Standard VC-10 entered service on 29 April 1964 from Heathrow to Lagos, settling in quickly on BOAC's African routes and receiving praise for its 'swift, silent and serene' characteristics! However, for much of its growing worldwide network the airline still did not want VC-10s and fought hard to cancel the entire Super VC-10 order. It was becoming increasingly obvious that even this improved version would not be able to compete with the latest turbofan-powered 707/DC-8s, which could take full advantage of the newly extended runways at many North American airports. The VC-10's large wing and heavy structure meant that it would always be at a disadvantage on routes where airfield restrictions were not a factor. The final outcome saw BOAC taking delivery of twelve Standards and seventeen Supers, after many years of uncertainty and dispute which seriously damaged future sales.

The Super VC-10's debut was on 1 April 1965, flying from Heathrow to New York JFK and it soon became established on the new 'Monarch' service to JFK and Bermuda, and to San Francisco. All seventeen were flying with BOAC by 1969 and the type reigned supreme for a few short years on the North Atlantic before the 747 began to change long-haul travel forever during the early 1970s. Pilots, who were licensed to fly either the Super or Standard, quickly came to favour the VC-10 with its docile flying characteristics, good airfield performance and spacious flight deck. Passengers also liked it, many choosing to fly on a VC-10 where possible because of its comfortable quiet cabin – a direct benefit from the rear-mounted engines. Residents close to airports frequented by the VC-10 did not, however, quite share this enthusiasm for its *external* noise characteristics!

Following the merger consummation in 1974, British Airways kept its VC-10 fleet intact for a very short time. The Standards soon fell victim to a series of world events which were to upset the long-term fleet plans of most airlines and condemn many relatively youthful jet airliners to an early retirement. An unprecedentedly large rise in fuel costs had been triggered by conflict in the Middle East and the resulting economic downturn led to a reappraisal of fleet requirements. In British Airways' case the Standard VC-10s, then barely ten years old, were deemed to be too costly to operate and were promptly withdrawn.

Airframe durability was not a factor in the relatively short airline career of the VC-10 (corrosion during the ageing process had taken much less of a toll than on the 707), their early retirement being brought about purely on economic grounds. Of the eleven Standards, five went on to fly for Gulf Air and two became ideal prestigious VIP transports for Arab Heads-of-State. Three others were not so fortunate and were cut up at Heathrow after being traded to Boeing as part of 747 purchase deals. The remaining aircraft, G-ARVM, survived for some years as a crew trainer for the Super VC-10 fleet before its eventual retirement to the British Airways collection at the Cosford Aerospace Museum (now known as the RAF Museum, Cosford) in 1979.

The fifteen-strong Super VC-10 fleet (two of the original aircraft had been destroyed by terrorist action in 1970 and 1974) continued in service for a further seven years. During this period, before long-range ETOPS-capable twin-jets became available, replacement of both the VC-10 and 707 on the many long-haul routes which did not need the capacity offered by wide-bodied airliners proved to be very difficult. The Super VC-10 continued to fly intensively on 'thin' routes to Africa, the Middle East, North America and on the airline's longest route of all. This began with the VC-10 flying from Heathrow to Hong Kong and Tokyo. The aircraft then undertook two round-trips from Tokyo to Johannesburg, routing via Hong Kong, Colombo and the Seychelles. Finally

Two of British Airways' Standard VC-10s were adapted for use as prestigious executive transports for Arab Heads of State. One of these was G-ARVF which flew for the United Arab Emirates in this splendid livery from 1974 to 1981. The VC-10 was then donated to a museum in Germany where it can still be viewed today.

Looking considerably more menacing than during its airline days is RAF VC-10 tanker ZA140 which was once British Airways' G-ARVL. 'The Empire Strikes Back' markings and mission symbols were acquired during the 1991 Gulf War when the rugged construction and impressive performance of the VC-10s enabled them to excel in their new role. Unfortunately, the ever increasing maintenance and operating costs of the VC-10s as they approach forty years old means that their retirement will probably be brought forward and the RAF is currently examining replacement candidates.

the VC-10 returned from Tokyo through Hong Kong to London, the whole trip taking six days.

The Super VC-10's replacement on some of British Airways' prestigious services to the Middle East began during 1976, when a small number of highly unsuitable short-range TriStar-1s were converted to a long-haul configuration. Competitor airlines, such as Gulf Air and Saudia, were flying TriStars and BA had little choice but to follow suit or be left behind. This was followed by the delivery of six new long-range TriStar-500s and eight -200s between 1979–81, allowing the VC-10s to be retired, followed soon after by the 707s. The looming recession of the late 70s/early 80s also hastened their retirement, with the result that some routes which could not support TriStars were dropped.

The first Super VC-10 to retire was G-ASGC, following an Amsterdam to Heathrow service on 22 October 1979. Flown to join the Duxford Aviation Society's large collection of British airliners in April 1980, 'SGC is today proudly displayed in BOAC's final regal blue and gold livery. As TriStars progressively took over from the VC-10s, the surplus aircraft were redeployed to boost short-haul capacity (to the delight of many passengers, but at what cost to the airline!) serving routes to Amsterdam, Athens,

Larnaca and Lisbon. Another nine VC-10s were withdrawn by the end of March 1980 and flown to Prestwick for storage, leaving five in service for the final year of operations. Attempts to sell the entire fleet came to nothing, as did a plan to transfer them to British Airtours. The final scheduled VC-10 service at Heathrow was an arrival from Dar es Salaam and Larnaca on 29 March 1981, and after some spirited enthusiasts' charters around the UK, the VC-10's airline career drew to a close.

The VC-10's flying career was, however, far from over as another long-term operator fully appreciated the strong, durable and capable nature of its airframe and wanted more of them. The RAF needed a new in-flight refuelling tanker to begin replacing its old Victor K2s and was not too concerned about the excessive fuel-guzzling, noise-generating habits of the VC-10, thirteen of which were already operated as transports. During March 1978 five of the surviving ex-British Airways Standard VC-10s, plus four ex-East African Airways Supers, were acquired and flown to British Aerospace at Filton for tanker conversion and eventually entered service with 101 Squadron at Brize Norton during 1984–5. Meanwhile, the fourteen redundant Supers were purchased for possible tanker conversion and put into long-term storage at Abingdon and Brize Norton during April and May 1981 to await a decision. In 1990, with the remaining Victors rapidly running out of airframe life, a contract to convert five of the stored Super VC-10s into tankers was finally awarded to British Aerospace. They were withdrawn from storage, ferried to Filton and, after an extensive overhaul and conversion programme, joined 101 Squadron between April 1994 and March 1996. The remaining nine ex-British Airways Super VC-10s have been dismantled for spares, although some sections still survive for training purposes.

The RAF today still operates twenty-seven VC-10s from Brize Norton and Mount Pleasant in the Falklands, an impressive fleet which includes five Standards and five Supers from a British Airways fleet which had also numbered twenty-seven at its peak. Remarkably, over twenty-five years after they first began to leave British Airways' service these fine aircraft continue to serve the RAF in a demanding role which is far removed from that for which it was designed. With no replacement due for some years yet, the 'swift, serene' (but not so silent) VC-10 will continue to be admired over the Oxfordshire countryside well into the twenty-first century. Another three of the ex-British Airways aircraft can also be admired at much closer quarters in museums.

TOP: *Such was the affection within British Airways for the VC-10 that an angry reaction was sparked when three redundant Standards were scrapped in the Heathrow Engineering Base during the autumn of 1976. They were literally torn to pieces in full view of those who had carefully maintained and operated them for many years, provoking letters of protest to the airline's newspaper!*

ABOVE: *G-ASGG crosses the threshold of Heathrow's Runway 28-Left for a typically gentle landing in September 1979. Super VC-10s served primarily on long-haul routes which could not support the much larger 747 such as those to Africa, the Middle East and to some North American destinations. However, increasing wide-bodied competition, the availability of long-range TriStars and an economic recession led to their retirement by March 1981.*

BAC One-Eleven

British Airways' extensive use of the BAC One-Eleven finally came to an end in August 1998 with the retirement of franchise partner Maersk Air's two remaining Series-500s, thereby ending a highly successful career which began thirty years earlier with BEA's acceptance of the first Super One-Elevens. BEA was actually a reluctant customer, preferring the One-Eleven's American competitors, but this flexible, robust and very popular little jet soon proved its worth and went on to give sterling service to British Airways across its domestic, internal German, and European networks. Many more examples joined the fleet, including the surprise late addition of thirteen British Caledonian (BCAL) aircraft in 1988. Following their displacement from the hub airports of Heathrow and Gatwick by larger aircraft, One-Elevens moved on to become the foundation for the development of regional hubs at Birmingham and Manchester.

Development of the One-Eleven originally began with a design by Hunting Aircraft in 1956 for a jet-powered replacement for the highly successful Vickers Viscount. The H.107 would have been a thirty-two-seat twin-jet, but the project had to be put on hold until a suitable engine became available. Further studies by the British Aircraft Corporation (BAC), which had absorbed Hunting in 1960, finally led to the launch of the new BAC One-Eleven with an order from British United Airways (BUA) for ten in May 1961. The new design, which had by that time grown into a much larger airliner, would use two Rolls-Royce Spey turbofans to power it, engines which were already under development for the Hawker Siddeley Trident. For it to operate on the intensive short-haul networks flown by the propeller-driven airliners then in service, the One-Eleven needed to have excellent airfield performance characteristics and be independent of as many ground facilities as possible. The structure was therefore designed to be very strong and features such as front and rear airstairs and a powerful Auxiliary Power Unit (APU) were incorporated. This led to strong interest from US carriers which soon translated into orders from Braniff, Mohawk and American Airlines.

By the time of the first flight on 20 August 1963, orders for sixty One-Elevens had been received from many prestigious airlines, but noticeably the list of

In February 1968 the first production stretched 'Super One-Eleven' took to the air, the first of 18 for BEA. G-AVMH was photographed with British Airways in April 1984, still looking as good as new and without the 'Stage Two' hush-kits which would soon be required. Currently 'VMH is stored at its original birthplace at Hurn to await 'Stage Three' hush-kits, which could further extend its career with owners European Aviation.

British Airways' entire fleet of 18 One-Eleven-510s was retired during 1991/2 and placed in open storage at Hurn whilst a buyer was sought. For a while prospects looked bleak because of their unique cockpit layouts and a sale to Okada Air of Nigeria fell through even after eight had been repainted. Eventually, two went to museums and sixteen were sold to European Aviation.

customers did not include BEA. First to enter service was a Series-200 of BUA which, fitted with sixty-nine seats, flew from Gatwick to Genoa on 9 April 1965. Increased weight -300/400s soon appeared and these were followed in 1967 by the longer fuselage -500, the variant which was eventually bought by BEA.

During 1966, BEA's need for a Viscount replacement on routes which were suffering from jet competition had become urgent, particularly so on the Internal German Services (IGS) where Pan-American was using Boeing 727s. A request to the government for permission to order Boeing 737s was rejected, forcing BEA to look to a suitable version of the One-Eleven to meet its requirement. BAC offered a One-Eleven with a 13 feet 6 inches fuselage stretch which could take another four rows of seats and accommodate a total of ninety-seven passengers. More powerful Spey engines and extended wing tips were fitted to the Series-500 and the structure was strengthened so that a full passenger load could be carried over distances of up to 950 miles. BEA accepted the proposal and ordered eighteen One-Eleven-500s in January 1967, enabling BAC to go ahead with its development and leading to the first flight of a prototype on 30 June 1967, followed by the first of BEA's Series-510s in February 1968. BEA specified several modifications which were only ever incorporated into its eighteen -510s. In later years this decision led to crew rostering restrictions when other One-Elevens joined the fleet because the differences were so great that crews could not operate both types. These changes included a different cockpit instrumentation layout, fitting a Smiths Industries flight director and deletion of the forward airstairs. The first Series-510s entered regular service in November 1968 and seven had been delivered by the end of that year. An intensive operation was soon established from Berlin Tempelhof to the German

cities of Bremen, Cologne, Dusseldorf, Frankfurt, Hamburg, Hanover, Munich and Stuttgart and the new Super One-Elevens were soon achieving up to twelve sectors per day! With the delivery of another ten in 1969 the -510s were also deployed on Manchester's scheduled service network and from London to German destinations.

One-Eleven deliveries peaked at forty-one aircraft during 1969 but fell back to single figures by 1972. Attempts by BAC to rejuvenate the aircraft by offering further stretched and re-engined versions came to nothing and British production finally ended in 1982 after 235 had been built. During that same year the first One-Eleven to be assembled in Romania took to the air, as part of a programme which was ultimately meant to see six built there each year, but only nine were ever completed.

Another seven One-Elevens had joined BEA by the time of its merger with BOAC, resulting in a total of twenty-five being transferred to British Airways in 1974. The extra aircraft were all second-hand Series-400s and consisted of four bought by Cambrian Airways in 1970–71 and three for BEA's regional base at Birmingham, although these were delivered as the merger was being implemented and entered service painted in the new British Airways colours. Other examples used during the 1970s were single aircraft leased from Gulf Air (-400), Cyprus Airways (-500) and BCAL (-500) to operate Regional Division services. The final One-Elevens to be bought were three more Series-500s, this time standard production models without the 'improvements' which had been incorporated into the earlier eighteen -510s. The -539s were delivered to Birmingham in 1980 and replaced two Series-400s which were traded back to the manufacturer.

During the mid-1980s, as British Airways took delivery of its second large batch of Boeing 737-236s

In April 1988 thirteen One-Eleven 500s unexpectedly joined British Airways as part of its amalgamation with British Caledonian. They were soon redeployed from Gatwick to Birmingham and Manchester and served the airline until July 1993, outliving all other One-Elevens in the fleet. G-AXJK waits for its passengers at Birmingham's Eurohub shortly before the type was finally retired.

(BEA's original choice of aircraft from twenty years earlier), One-Elevens began to be displaced from some of their traditional roles. Boeing 737s and BAe 748s had taken over their IGS commitment by March 1986 and some of the surplus Series-510s took on the somewhat less demanding role of Shuttle back-up from the last Tridents. The One-Eleven fleet was, however, to receive one final and unexpected boost when thirteen Series-500s arrived during April 1988 as a result of a merger with British Caledonian (BCAL). They were redeployed from their Gatwick base by October 1988 to Birmingham and Manchester to replace the -400s which were put into storage to await sale.

As the 1990s decade began, the One-Eleven's career with British Airways appeared to be drawing rapidly to a close. It was perceived by many to be too noisy and out of date, but in reality was actually the ideal aircraft for services from regional hubs and one which would prove very difficult to replace. Therefore, even though the airline finished its own operations with the aircraft in 1993, it was to be another five years before the last One-Eleven to serve in British Airways colours would retire.

The three Series-539s were sold during 1991 and the delivery of new 737-436s to Heathrow finally displaced the One-Eleven-510s, allowing several to be withdrawn from service. This left two One-Eleven bases, Birmingham with the ex-BCAL aircraft and Manchester with the remaining -510s. By December 1992 the last of the -510s were retired, to be followed by the airline's final One-Elevens, at Birmingham on 1 July 1993.

As noted above, this was not to be the end of British Airways' association with the One-Eleven. Birmingham European Airways acquired five of the airline's Series-400s in 1990 and used them to operate scheduled services from its Birmingham base to many European cities. A merger with Brymon Airways occurred in October 1992 to form Brymon European Airways, but this was soon superseded by another reorganisation in August 1993 when Maersk Air of Denmark acquired the Birmingham operation and renamed it Maersk Air Ltd. Also at that time, a franchise agreement was reached for the operation of Maersk Air's network of routes under BA service numbers. So, just after British Airways had retired its final One-Elevens, Maersk Air repainted its fleet of four One-Eleven-400s and one -500 back into British Airways colours! A second Series-500 joined Maersk Air in August 1994, followed by a third which was leased from European Aviation in April 1996. They were all reconfigured to offer BA's comfortable two-class Club Europe product and flew schedules to Amsterdam, Belfast, Copenhagen, Cork, Lyons, Milan and Stuttgart. Replacements began arriving in the form of 737-500s from October 1996, leading to the sale of the four Series-400s by April 1997, and in 1998 a fleet of new Canadair Regional Jets entered service. The last One-Elevens in British Airways

service, two Series-500s of Maersk Air, were finally retired after G-AWYS had flown from Copenhagen to Birmingham on 4 August 1998, barely one month short of thirty years since G-AVMJ had operated the first One-Eleven services for BEA, on 1 September 1968.

One-Elevens have fared remarkably well since leaving British Airways service, especially the original Series-510s which are now well over thirty years old! Of the eighteen -510s built, twelve are still in an airworthy condition and are undergoing several modification programmes which should ensure their continued productive use well into the twenty-first century.

After a period of storage during the early 1990s it appeared that the -510 fleet would remain unsold, mainly because of their lack of commonality with any other One-Elevens. Two were donated to museums and flew from storage at their original birthplace of Hurn Airport to Cosford and Duxford. In May 1993, however, the remaining sixteen were bought by European Aviation Ltd who quickly set about returning the One-Elevens to service. Four ex-BCAL Series-500s were also acquired and by August 1998 sixteen ex-British Airways One-Elevens were operational with the company. European set up a charter subsidiary, European Aviation Air Charter (EAC) to operate the fleet on ad hoc and series charters as well as to operate scheduled services on behalf of other airlines. These have included Air France, Air Liberté, Air UK, Jersey European, Ryanair and Sabena. An aircraft was also leased to Maersk Air and operated once again from Birmingham in full British Airways colours until May 1998. To achieve commonality with the more-capable ex-BCAL Series-500s, European has converted the cockpits of some of its -510s to a similar layout and has also installed more powerful Spey engines and forward airstairs. A hush-kit has been developed in association with Quiet Technology Venture of the USA which should ensure that the notoriously noisy One-Eleven can continue to operate in Europe after Stage Three noise restrictions come into effect. All of this investment by European Aviation demonstrates the company's absolute faith in the One-Eleven and should ensure its future use for many more years.

Of the other British Airways One-Elevens, all seven Series-400s eventually flew south to new homes in Africa. Three ended their days having flown with Okada Air of Nigeria, but the ex-Maersk Air aircraft are fit and well, flying scheduled services with Nationwide Air Services from Johannesburg and with EAS from Lagos. Two of the Series-539s also joined Okada Air, whilst the third remained in the UK and has taken up a military identity to undertake radar trials with the Defence Evaluation and Research Agency. The nine ex-BCAL aircraft which did not join European Aviation have all found their way to overseas buyers, with two going to Romania and the others joining the large fleet of One-Elevens in Africa.

Highland Division's HS-748 G-BCOF 'Glen Fiddich' cruising above the typical rugged island terrain of its Scottish homeland. (ADRIAN MEREDITH PHOTOGRAPHY)

Hawker Siddeley HS-748

British Airways began its long association with Hawker Siddeley's tough little airliner in 1975, when two new HS-748s were delivered to operate the airline's difficult Scottish routes. Many more examples served during the 1980s until a replacement fleet of new ATPs took over from 1988. Although the ATP, which British Aerospace built as a successor to the 748, has recently left the fleet, many others fly with franchise partners British Regional Airlines and Sun-Air, thereby maintaining the link back to 1975.

The HS-748 itself dates back considerably earlier than 1975. Avro decided to build a new airliner in the late 1950s in a bid to do what many other manufacturers have also attempted, and that was to replace the immortal Douglas DC-3! With several thousand ageing Dakotas still in use, Avro foresaw a huge market for a modern replacement and designed its new HS-748 accordingly. The basic requirement, therefore, was for a transport which would do everything that a Dakota could do, and more. This meant that, as well as being able to operate from virtually any airfield, be largely self-sufficient and independent of ground equipment and be economical and easily maintained, the new aircraft would also have to offer better performance and much improved comfort levels for its passengers

and crew. Rolls-Royce's proven Dart turboprop was chosen and Hawker Siddeley (of which Avro was a part) gave the go-ahead as a private venture project in January 1959. The first HS-748 flight took place in June 1960 and first deliveries were made to Aerolineas Argentinas in January 1962.

Throughout the 1960s the HS-748 sold well to both civil and military customers from all parts of the world. Specialised military versions were produced and licence production got underway in India. The basic aircraft was regularly updated, with the more powerful Series-2 and -2A offering increased operating weights, and from 1971 customers could specify the installation of a large freight door.

So by the time of British Airways' order for two 46-seat Series-2As in 1974, the HS-748 was a proven, highly reliable and rugged airliner with 300 sold worldwide. Entry into service began in August 1975 on Scottish routes from Aberdeen to Kirkwall in the Orkney Islands, Lerwick in Shetland and Glasgow. Lerwick in particular benefited from the HS-748's ability to uplift a full load compared with the Viscount's restricted payload. Another three HS-748s arrived at Aberdeen on lease from Dan-Air in March 1982 to allow the retirement of the final Viscounts. An autonomous Highlands Division was established which transformed the traditionally loss-making Scottish routes into profitability with the HS-748 fleet. An order for two new Series-2Bs plus a third fitted

Hawker Siddeley 748s of British Airways were familiar sights on the island of Jersey on summer weekends throughout the 1980s, bringing holidaymakers from Scotland. G-AZSU, one of 17 HS-748s flown by the airline, was nearing the end of its three-year lease from Dan-Air when photographed there in October 1984.

with a freight door was placed for delivery by January 1985 to replace the leased HS-748s. The two earlier Series-2As were then modified by the airline at Glasgow to a similar Series-2B standard, a complicated task which included fitting uprated engines and extended wing tips. To further increase capacity, from 1986 additional HS-748s were leased-in from Dan-Air and Euroair, and in 1988 three arrived from the German airline DLT, followed by one from BAe in 1990. In all, British Airways used seventeen different 'Budgies' as the HS-748 became affectionately known.

As well as their domination of the airline's Scottish Highlands and Islands network, HS-748s appeared on lengthy sectors to the Channel Islands from Aberdeen and Edinburgh during summer weekends from 1984 and also operated scheduled cross-border flights to Birmingham and Manchester. From June 1986 until the arrival of ATPs in April 1989, HS-748s operated Internal German Services from Berlin Tegel to Bremen and Munster, replacing BAC One-Elevens. Once ATP deliveries began to grow, the leased HS-748s returned to their owners and others were traded back to BAe. The final HS-748 services were flown by G-HDBD on 15 April 1992.

British Aerospace ATP

The ATP (Advanced Turboprop) was British Aerospace's attempt to extend the life of its HS-748 which by the mid-1980s had become obsolete as a new production aircraft. Although based on a stretched HS-748 airframe with the same fuselage cross-section, the ATP was developed as a completely new aircraft. New Pratt & Whitney Canada PW127 engines driving slow-turning six-bladed propellers were installed, a new nose section with a fully updated electronic cockpit fitted and an eighteen-foot longer fuselage with a new interior and seating for up to seventy-two passengers was developed, all of which made the ATP the largest twin-turboprop regional airliner of its time. The prototype first flew

on 6 August 1986 and deliveries to airlines began in May 1988.

British Airways ordered eight ATPs in 1988 and took out options for the acquisition of eight more. Deliveries began in December of that year and all eight from this initial order, each fitted with sixty-four seats, had entered service at their Glasgow base by July 1989. They operated routes from Aberdeen, Edinburgh and Glasgow to Birmingham and Manchester, plus Manchester to Hanover and Berlin, and IGS services from Berlin to Bremen, Hanover and Munster. Another five were ordered in August 1991 and one final aircraft, which was already in service on lease from BAe, was acquired in July 1994, taking the fleet strength to fourteen. Other ATPs have also been operated on lease. After withdrawing from the IGS routes in 1991 all of the ATPs returned to Highland Division and operated an intensive network of internal Scottish routes as well as services to Birmingham, Manchester and Belfast.

Sadly for BAe, sales were slow and the type was finally dropped after an attempted relaunch as the upgraded Jetstream 61 failed to stimulate sales in 1994. Production ceased after just sixty-eight had been built, not all of which were delivered.

The ATP fleet size began to decrease at the end of 1996 when the airline's Scottish internal routes were transferred to BA Express franchise carriers, allowing the return of four ATPs to BAe. Further departures took place from May 1998 as several Scottish–UK routes transferred to Brymon and by January 1999 the fleet had been completely phased out as BA Regional concentrated on operating nothing smaller than a 737. G-ATPJ flew the final ATP service, BA1865, on 26 January 1999 from Edinburgh to Manchester. The ATP, however, continues to fly in British Airways colours with British Regional operating ten on a wide range of franchise services throughout the UK and Ireland, and Sun-Air which flies three on its network in Scandinavia as well as between Billund and Manchester.

British Airways was one of the main operators of the ATP, which was built by British Aerospace in an unsuccessful attempt to derive a modern commuter airliner from the ageing HS-748. Highland Division began receiving ATPs from December 1988 and eventually built up a fleet of 14 which were used on its extensive network of UK domestic routes and until 1991 on the Internal German Services. G-BTPL was photographed about to touch down at East Midlands on a flight from Jersey in August 1992.

Hawker Siddeley Trident

Despite having left our skies forever during the mid-1980s, many Tridents still linger today at airports around the UK, stirring the memories of those associated with the type and perhaps the curiosity of those who are too young to recall seeing it fly. The Trident was a fine example of the innovative designs and technological advances which British manufacturers were famous for during the 1950s and '60s, and, by delivering tremendous advances in speed and comfort over the previous generation of propeller-driven airliners, enabled BEA to move successfully into the new age of European jet travel during the mid-1960s. Following from this Tridents went on to play a significant role in British Airways' early years with a total of sixty-five assorted models inherited from BEA forming the backbone of the airline's European fleet, as well as being the aircraft used to establish domestic Shuttle operations in 1975. Sadly this pioneering airliner was destined to face a premature retirement when tough new noise legislation and the drive for reduced operating costs caught up with it.

The Trident was designed specifically to operate BEA's medium-range European routes where high speed was seen to be essential, leaving the slower Vanguards to operate shorter and domestic routes. An order for twenty-four plus options for another twelve was placed during 1959 and the new airliner flew for the first time in January 1962. Although de Havilland had originally proposed building a bigger and more powerful airliner with longer-range capability, BEA's requirement for a maximum of 100 seats, 600 mph speed and 1,000-mile range prevailed. Unfortunately this decision to shrink the Trident to satisfy the needs of just one customer dealt a fatal blow to its sales prospects, leading to just 117 being built compared with thousands of the competing American designs.

The Trident One entered service with BEA in April 1964 and twelve had been delivered by the end of that year. BEA was very happy with the performance of its swift new airliner and passengers loved its comfort and quietness (on the inside, that was!). De Havilland, which became part of Hawker Siddeley in 1960, had designed the Trident to incorporate an autoland capability and after many hundreds of trial landings a BEA Trident from Paris made the first ever automatic landing with passengers on board on 10 June 1965. During the years to come Tridents were able to take full advantage of this remarkable technology to land in weather conditions which grounded all other types, saving much money for the airline and giving it a tremendous competitive advantage.

BEA placed its next order for fifteen longer-range Trident Twos during August 1965 for delivery during 1968. Uprated Spey engines and bigger wings enabled the new variant to reach cities such as Athens, Moscow and Tel Aviv. Also at that time evaluations were under way to define the characteristics of the next generation of bigger airliners for the 1970s. Whilst BEA favoured buying Boeing 727-200s or the BAC 2-11, other alternatives examined included a 300-seater 'Airbus' proposal from a consortium of European manufacturers which, whilst supported by influential ministers in HM Government, was much too big for the airline. Politics finally prevailed and in 1968 an order was placed for twenty-six Trident Threes plus options for another ten worth £83m in total, although BEA was promised compensation of £25m as the airline felt that the new Trident would be too small for its needs.

The Trident Three, which entered service in March 1971, featured a seventeen-foot fuselage stretch, allowing it to comfortably accommodate up to 140 passengers, but with no increase in wingspan and a reduced fuel capacity it became payload-limited beyond 1,100 miles, whereas the Trident Two could carry its full load over 1,700 miles. To achieve acceptable take-off performance an RB162 boost engine was fitted for use in difficult conditions, giving the aircraft an untidy-looking cluster of five engines (including the APU) around the tail. Despite this extra 'boost' the Trident's notoriety for its general lack of airfield performance persisted and became almost legendary when the next generation of twin-jets with their excess of power began to arrive. For example, the 'Ground Gripper' apparently only ever became airborne by taking advantage of the Earth's curvature and only managed to return by means of a 'controlled crash'!

The final Trident Three was delivered in April 1973 and one year later British Airways adopted twenty T1s, fifteen T2s, twenty-six T3s plus four hybrid Trident 1Es from Regional Division. This impressive total of sixty-five Tridents dominated the Heathrow-based short- and medium-range network and continued to perform that role, in gradually decreasing numbers, for over ten more years.

TriStars began to take over some of the busier European routes from January 1975 and by the late 1970s an expanding British Airways was in desperate need of many more medium-sized airliners for growth and to begin replacing the Tridents with a more economical and environmentally acceptable type. Noise regulations were also being formulated which would ultimately call time on the first generation of jets which could not realistically be hush-kitted. Many of the original Trident Ones retired to Prestwick during the recession of 1974–5, although others found a new lease of life flying as Shuttle back-ups, an ideal task for such range-restricted aircraft. The low utilisation achieved with this type of operation worked in the Trident One's favour, keeping direct operating costs to a minimum and making good use of a fully written down asset.

During 1977–8 British Airways experienced an acute shortage of aircraft for its European routes which led, amongst other measures, to a search for additional Tridents to provide a temporary capacity

TOP: *The Trident in this photograph in a hybrid colour scheme can easily be identified as a Trident Three by the RB162 booster above the number two engine which was incorporated to improve the take-off performance of the bigger and heavier stretched variant. It was often said that with three Rolls-Royce Speys, a boost engine and an APU the Trident Three was British Airways short-haul's only five-engined airliner! G-AWZJ was one of the last Tridents in service when new noise regulations effectively grounded the type in December 1985.*

MIDDLE: *The last airworthy Trident Two departs from Heathrow on a flight to Glasgow during March 1985, just one month before operating its final service. Although the extended-range Trident Twos were designed to satisfy BEA's requirement for an airliner to operate services to eastern Mediterranean and Eastern European destinations, towards the end of their flying careers much of their time was spent performing the undemanding role of back-up aircraft for the domestic Shuttle operation.*

ABOVE: *The final sunset for Trident operations came on 31 December 1985 as new noise restrictions came into effect which the aircraft stood no chance of meeting.*

increase. Part of the problem resulted from the discovery of severe cracking in the wings of its Trident Three fleet which necessitated each aircraft returning to British Aerospace at Hatfield for approximately two months' worth of strengthening modifications. Two Cyprus Airways Tridents, a 1E and a 2E, were discovered lying abandoned at Nicosia following conflict on the Cypriot island during 1974. After some temporary patching up both were ferried to Heathrow wearing a hybrid Cyprus/BA livery in May 1977 and entered service some months later after major overhauls. One of these aircraft, G-AVFB, survives today with the Duxford Aviation Society airliner collection.

Time was however beginning to run out for the Trident fleet. The first of an order for replacement 737-236s entered service in 1980, followed by the larger 757 which began to take over from Trident Threes on high-density Shuttle routes during February 1983. These new two-pilot, twin-engined types brought a dramatic improvement to the operating economics of the airline's short-haul routes and rapidly displaced the Tridents. The first Trident Three retirement, G-AWZA, occurred in October 1982 and the last Trident One, G-ARPZ, flew its final service from Glasgow to Heathrow on 2 April 1983. By that time half of the Trident Twos had also gone and the process continued inexorably with the last Trident Two services flown in April 1985. Finally the last two Trident Threes, G-AWZO and 'WZU returned to Heathrow on 31 December 1985 to make simultaneous landings on parallel runways, bringing the Trident's passenger carrying days with British Airways to a close. Noise regulations had brought the use of this pioneering British airliner to a final, irrevocable and perhaps premature end in Europe. Without that unyielding deadline, perhaps the Trident Threes would have continued in use for a few more years, after all many were less than fifteen years old and had flown less than 25,000 hours, a fraction of their design life. Having said that, however, the vastly improved operating economics of the replacement Boeings would almost certainly have forced them from the fleet before too much longer.

During the early part of 1986 many Trident Threes were lined up in the Heathrow Engineering Base awaiting their fate. With no prospect of further employment in Europe most of those which were not scrapped were destined to become museum exhibits or emergency service training airframes. Many Trident Ones and Twos had earlier been despatched on their final flights to airfields around the UK for emergency services training, and during the early months of 1986 several Trident Threes followed suit. Two flew to Tees-Side for the CAA Fire Service Training School, where they joined the remains of four Trident Ones and one Trident Two which had arrived there between 1981–3. Other more fortunate examples were despatched to Hatfield and Wroughton for preservation and British Airways retained Trident Two G-AVFG and Trident Three G-AWZK to train ground crews in the arts of de-icing, loading and towing. Both were painted into the new 'Landor' livery and can be seen today at Heathrow, 'WZK preserved in a clipped-wing condition and still used for ground training, and 'VFG serving the fire crews but now in a very poor condition.

Only five ex-British Airways Tridents survived

A scene repeated many times at Heathrow during the early mid-1980s was that of Tridents being scrapped en masse as quieter and more efficient Boeing twin-jets replaced them. Sadly, from the entire fleet of 67 Tridents only five Trident Threes sold to Air Charter Service of Zaire ever saw commercial service after leaving British Airways. Many others found new uses as emergency services training airframes at airfields around the country and four have been preserved.

to fly again commercially, albeit for a limited time, in a country where ICAO Chapter Three noise restrictions had probably never been heard of. G-AWZC left for Ostend in November 1984 as 9Q-CTM on the first leg of its delivery to Air Charter Service of Zaire (now the Democratic Republic of Congo), followed by 'WZF, WZD, WZG and finally WZV during the next eighteen months. How ACS coped with operating such complex and temperamental airliners on cargo services in the demanding environment of central Africa is not known and reports of their use are few, but it is generally assumed that they did not survive for very long and their eventual fate is unknown.

Today a surprising number of Tridents survive across the UK including two publicly displayed in museums, G-ARPH at Cosford and G-AVFB at Duxford, plus G-AWZM held in store by the Science Museum at Wroughton. Another fourteen are believed to survive on various airfields as training airframes plus the remains of some of the seven Tridents at Tees-Side. Although most of these will undoubtedly deteriorate and eventually be broken up, the future of the three museum Tridents plus the Trident Three at Heathrow looks secure.

Lockheed L-1011 TriStar

The Lockheed TriStar formed a significant part of British Airways' fleet for twenty years, beginning in the early days of the airline with the delivery of Series-1s, from an inherited BEA order, to operate European scheduled services and continuing with additional purchases of Series-200s and -500s for long-haul use. Other TriStars were leased-in when necessary and the original Series-1s were progressively upgraded and then converted for charter work and were ultimately the last of the type to leave the fleet. The TriStar, with its beautiful clean lines (especially when compared with the more rugged-looking DC-10!) was regarded with great affection within the airline, but in engineering terms was often thought of as overly complicated and somewhat difficult to maintain.

Although BA pioneered the use of wide-bodied airliners on European scheduled services with the TriStar, it was not an early customer nor was it the first airline to fly the type in Britain. Lockheed launched the TriStar in March 1968 primarily to satisfy the requirement for a new US domestic airliner and received orders from Eastern Airlines, TWA and Air Holdings. The first flight took place on 16 November 1970 and Eastern Airlines flew the first TriStar service during April 1972 from New York to Miami.

Following from the December 1970 cancellation of BEA's preferred choice of airliner, the 250-seat BAC Three-Eleven, the airline was forced to look elsewhere and placed an order for six TriStar-1s plus options for another twelve during August 1972, each to be powered by three of Rolls-Royce's new 42,000 lb

thrust RB-211-22Bs. Although ordered by BEA, the aircraft were bought with the forthcoming merger in mind and the options were taken with a view to replacing BOAC's 707 and VC-10 fleets if and when longer-range TriStars became available. The number on firm order was increased during October 1973 by three, and again in November 1974 by another six, taking the total to fifteen, all Series-1s.

The first British TriStars were two brightly painted examples (one orange, one pink!) operated in a 400-seat configuration by holiday airline Court Line from March 1973 until its sudden bankruptcy in August 1974. The first aircraft for British Airways, less dramatically painted in the new corporate livery, arrived at Heathrow soon afterwards in October 1974. Route proving took place during December and the first TriStar services were flown in January 1975, later than originally planned due to industrial problems, to Brussels, Madrid, Malaga, Palma and Paris CDG. By the summer of 1975 five TriStars were in service and operating additionally to Alicante, Amsterdam, Athens, Faro and Tel Aviv in a 20F/300Y layout. By that time, however, the effects of the Middle East war were being felt in the form of soaring fuel costs and a deepening world economic recession. British Airways was losing money and suffering from an excess of capacity and needed to make cuts in its operations. Very few European routes could profitably support aircraft as big as a TriStar and so a gradual move to long-haul operations began. A 1976 agreement to form a combined pilot force enabled the use of TriStars on Overseas Division services and two basic, range-limited Series-1s in a spacious 38F/202Y configuration began flying to the Gulf and India in April.

The development of higher-powered engines enabled Lockheed to offer extended-range and increased weight TriStars more suited to longer-range services. British Airways placed the launch order for a short-fuselage, extended-range TriStar-500 powered by 50,000 lb thrust RB211-524Bs in August 1976 after an intense competition with versions of the DC-10 and A300. The order was worth £140m and converted the airline's six remaining options into firm orders whilst adding another six options. The TriStar-500s were acquired to replace VC-10s and 707s on routes which needed a long-range capability but could not support the capacity of a 747, routes such as the Gulf, the west coast of the USA, and Caribbean. The first Series-500 G-BFCA flew from Palmdale during October 1978 after being 'baptised' by Princess Margaret (the aircraft was later named 'Princess Margaret Rose' and made an appearance at the Farnborough Airshow as such in September 1980). Entry into service occurred in May 1979 from Heathrow to Abu Dhabi, a route which was later extended to Singapore. The TriStar-500 incorporated many new ideas to maximise range and more modifications were incorporated after delivery, including active ailerons, extended wing tips and engine upgrades. A new route to New Orleans and

Mexico City was flown during 1981, ideal for the size and range of the Series-500.

Additional long-range aircraft were required for the early 1980s to enable the airline to complete the replacement of its Super VC-10 and 707 fleets. Lockheed designed a version of the standard-body TriStar which offered sufficient range to comfortably operate Middle East and east coast USA routes. An initial order for two TriStar-200s to take over from the Series-1s on Gulf routes was placed in January 1979 and this was followed in September 1979 by British Airways' final TriStar order, for six Series-200s. When the last of these aircraft entered service in May 1981 the TriStar fleet had reached its twenty-three aircraft peak, comprising nine Series-1s, six -500s and eight -200s, an impressive but short-lived total.

The six short-fuselage TriStar-500s delivered during 1979–80 became the shortest serving sub-fleet after their surprise sale to the RAF in 1983. Although performing well in service, the TriStar-500s were expensive to operate and the opportunity was taken to sell the entire fleet and raise much needed cash to help the airline weather a recession.

In its post-Falklands war reviews the RAF had identified an urgent requirement for a long-range strategic airlifter which could also perform in-flight refuelling, and saw the TriStar-500 as a suitable candidate. The first to be withdrawn from scheduled services was G-BFCF in December 1982, with the others following by the end of March 1983. However, the airline had not quite finished with the type as British Airtours leased back G-BFCB from the RAF for long-haul charter work from May to October 1983 and leased G-BFCE for similar work between June and September 1985. One important task performed by this fleet after its sale involved G-BFCD, which was leased by British Airways in October 1983 to undertake a Royal tour of Africa and India the following month. Following this the TriStar joined the tanker conversion line with Marshall Aerospace at Cambridge.

The RAF initially operated two of its new TriStar-500 fleet in the passenger-carrying role whilst the tanker conversion programme was established. British Airways undertook to provide initial crew, engineering and operational support and both aircraft (G-BFCA/CE) were regular visitors to Heathrow for maintenance until 1985. Their initial livery consisted of the basic BA scheme modified with the addition of RAF roundels. The badge of 216 ('Two-Sixteen') Squadron appeared on their tails when the unit was reformed in November 1984 to operate the TriStars. The first tanker commenced test flying in July 1985 and deliveries began in March 1986, with the complete modification program taking until the end of 1990 to complete. Four of the TriStars (originally G-BFCA/C/E/F) have also had large freight doors cut into their fuselages and strengthened floors fitted and, designated KC1s, operate in the mixed passenger/freight and refuelling roles. The other two

(ex-G-BFCB/D) are K1s without the freighter modifications and operate as passenger aircraft or tankers. No. 216 Squadron has subsequently acquired another three TriStar-500s and proudly boasts that it flies the largest and heaviest aircraft ever operated by the RAF. In practice the TriStars spend much of their time employed as long-range transports whilst another ex-BA airliner type – the VC-10 – undertakes most of the day-to-day refuelling tasks.

Unfortunately the TriStar-500's departure left British Airways with a gap in its long-haul fleet which became more apparent in 1985 when BCAL's South American licences were acquired as part of a transfer of routes. The solution was found in the form of two Air Lanka TriStar-500s which were leased to operate scheduled services from April 1985 to March 1988. At this point mention should also be made of another TriStar operated on lease – 'The Ghost Ship' as it was often known! The aircraft concerned was an Eastern Airlines TriStar-1 N323EA, leased in full BA livery to operate European scheduled services from October 1978 until February 1980. The rather sinister nickname stemmed from the tragic crash of another Eastern TriStar in the Florida Everglades in December 1972, and the rumoured sighting of apparitions aboard their TriStars ever since!

Changes in the role and capabilities of the TriStar fleet continued throughout the 1980s with the type never quite seeing the measure of stability and air of permanency in any particular area as achieved by, for example, the larger 747 or smaller 757. In fact, it was the appearance of the new Boeing 757 in large numbers from 1983, followed some seven years later by its larger cousin the 767, which finally drove the TriStar from scheduled services. The 757's ability to provide a good balance between capacity and frequency on many European routes released TriStars for long-haul and British Airtours use. Three Series-1s (EAK, EAL, EAM) were originally built with Series-50 capability and in 1985 were quickly converted by fitting heavier duty wheels to allow the carriage of an extra nine tonnes of payload. Five other Series-1s (BAE, BAF, BAH, BAI, BAJ) transferred to British Airtours from 1985, and between 1989 and 1991 four of these underwent conversion to TriStar-100 standard, which involved increasing their operating weights and upgrading the engines. Throughout the late 1980s the disposition of British Airways' seventeen-strong TriStar fleet continued to change from one season to the next as aircraft moved between short-haul, long-haul and charter operations.

By 1990, the final full year of TriStar scheduled flying, only one Series-1 remained on short-haul services from Heathrow. One other was Gatwick-based for Cairo services and the other four were with Caledonian, along with Series-50 G-BEAL. The other two TriStar-50s and eight -200s performed long-haul work from Heathrow and were also used for services from Gatwick to New York-JFK and Accra and regional services from Manchester and Glasgow to JFK.

After receiving an initial nine medium-range TriStar-1s British Airways turned its attention to acquiring longer-range versions. Six short-fuselage TriStar-500s capable of flying from London to the US west coast entered service during 1979/80. The first TriStar-500 to fly was G-BFCA, seen here landing at Farnborough in September 1980.

The summer 1990 fleet breakdown was as follows:

LHR short-haul	1	TriStar-1	(BAF)
LHR/LGW long-haul	8	TriStar-200	
	2	TriStar-50	(EAK, EAM)
	1	TriStar-1	(BAG)
Caledonian A/w	1	TriStar-1	(BAI)
	1	TriStar-50	(EAL)
	3	TriStar-100	(BAE, BAH, BAJ)
	17	**Total operated**	

A rapid rundown of the fleet soon followed, the intention being to withdraw all TriStars by May 1991, with the exception of six Caledonian aircraft and two Series-200s which were retained to operate Manchester/Glasgow–JFK until the end of the summer season.

Withdrawn TriStars were flown to Cambridge and to desert storage at Mojave, California, to await sale. Two of the Series-200s soon returned from Mojave to begin three year leases to Air Lanka and two from Cambridge flew for Kuwait Airways from June to October 1992, replacing aircraft lost during the Gulf War. The first TriStar to be sold was Series-1 G-BBAG which went to Cathay Pacific from Mojave in March 1993 to be operated by its Dragonair subsidiary as VR-HMW. The others languished in storage for some time until yet another new career opportunity arose for this flexible airliner in 1994. American International Airlines purchased three of the TriStar-200s and took out options on another five for conversion into freighters. Marshall Aerospace, using experience gained with the RAF conversions, was contracted to perform this work and the first one (N102CK ex-G-BHBM) flew from Cambridge in August 1995 and was delivered to Detroit in September. All eight TriStar-200s plus two Series-50s

have since been purchased by American International Airways which became Kitty Hawk International in 1999.

With British Airways, commercial use of this technically advanced and undeniably beautiful aircraft came to an end during March 1995 when the remaining five TriStars along with operator Caledonian Airways were sold to package-tour operator Inspirations PLC.

For just over twenty years a total of twenty-three owned TriStars plus three leased examples gave sterling service in many different versions and on a wide variety of routes, but were ultimately displaced by the newer technology and better economics of new twin-jet Boeings. After leaving British Airways the TriStar has fared well, carving out market niches undreamed of at the time of its conception. With all twenty-three aircraft currently flying or stored in a potentially flyable condition, many of these TriStars appear to have a bright future ahead, but the type is unlikely to be seen with BA again.

McDonnell Douglas DC-10

Throughout the 1970s McDonnell Douglas fought many tough battles with arch-rival Lockheed for sales of its wide-bodied airliner products and, although DC-10 sales eventually reached almost double those of the TriStar, the company consistently failed to win any orders from British Airways. However, despite the DC-10's initial lack of success, two separate fleets did find their way onto the airline's long-haul routes. In fact, after the incorporation of BCAL's DC-10 fleet in 1988 the type became a valuable long-haul performer, long outliving its earlier rival in British Airways' service as the TriStar was never able to match the DC-10's excellent long-range capabilities.

TOP: *After the TriStar-500s had entered service Lockheed introduced a series of improvements which turned them into very capable performers on the airline's thin long-haul routes. Despite this the fleet survived for only four years and was sold to the RAF in December 1982 to raise much needed cash. G-BFCD and FCE are seen soon after their withdrawal from service at the end of March 1983.*

ABOVE: *Once G-BFCE of British Airways, ZD952 was photographed at Brize Norton as a fully converted TriStar KC1 with a large main-deck cargo door and in-flight refuelling equipment on the underside of the rear fuselage. Most of the RAF's strategic transport and tanker force now comprises ex-airline TriStars and VC-10s, many of which are ex-British Airways aircraft.*

The DC-10 and TriStar both evolved from a 1966 American Airlines' requirement for a new domestic airliner capable of carrying 250 passengers from Chicago to the west coast. Douglas developed the DC-10-10, powered by three new-technology high-bypass ratio General Electric CF-6 engines, and received launch orders from American Airlines and United Airlines in 1968. The first flight took place from Long Beach in August 1970 and service entry came one year later with both carriers. Douglas also realised that the DC-10 had the potential to complement Boeing's new 747 on 'thin' long-haul routes and wasted no time in launching an intercontinental version, the DC-10-30, which entered service in December 1972.

Lockheed's response to the 1966 US domestic requirement was the similarly-configured TriStar, powered by Rolls-Royce's RB-211 engine. This aircraft eventually won the competition for an order from BEA in September 1972 and TriStars went on to serve British Airways in a variety of short- and longer-range versions, keeping the DC-10 largely at bay for the next fifteen years. Apart from a four-year arrangement for the use of Air New Zealand aircraft during the 1970s, British Airways' operation of the DC-10 came much later in the aircraft's career

following the British Caledonian merger in 1988. None were ever purchased from McDonnell Douglas.

British Airways' first use of DC-10s came about through a leasing arrangement with Air New Zealand (ANZ) which was entered into during the mid-1970s to solve a serious capacity problem on the Heathrow to Los Angeles service. To remain competitive with Pan-Am and TWA on this important route the airline badly needed to replace its 707s with wide-bodies, but 747s were much too big and TriStars just did not have the necessary range. ANZ offered the use of spare DC-10-30 time and agreement was reached for the use of this through an interchange of aircraft at Los Angeles beginning in May 1975. This arrangement, which relied upon good punctuality from both airlines, worked as follows:

Every day ANZ would operate a DC-10 from Auckland to Los Angeles, whereupon the aircraft would be transferred to British Airways for its service to London. Meanwhile, another DC-10 would be operating the reverse of this route, from Heathrow to Los Angeles with BA and then on to Auckland for ANZ. The aircraft remained in ANZ's full Maori-style livery, but between Los Angeles and Heathrow were operated entirely by British Airways' flight and cabin crews.

British Airways' first use of DC-10s came about through the operation of Air New Zealand aircraft on its Los Angeles services from May 1975. This successful arrangement proved the value of the DC-10-30 on such lengthy routes but as the airline had a substantial commitment to the Lockheed TriStar, none were ever ordered. Sadly the aircraft shown here at Heathrow in July 1978 was destroyed during an ANZ sight-seeing flight over Antarctica after the interchange had ended in 1979.

DC-10s proved to be ideally suited to the lengthy Los Angeles route with their comfortable 24 first and 219 economy seat configuration and their ability to uplift substantial cargo loads. Another benefit to both airlines from this arrangement was the opportunity to carry passengers between London and Auckland on the same aircraft. By 1978, with one year of the interchange agreement still to run, British Airways introduced 747s to Los Angeles five days a week and re-deployed the DC-10s onto five Miami and three Montreal services, plus two to Los Angeles in order to feed the aircraft back into ANZ's network. These revised arrangements increased the amount of DC-10 flying so that the equivalent of two aircraft were being used by British Airways, one quarter of ANZ's fleet. The highly successful interchange agreement ended in April 1979, having clearly demonstrated the reliability and commercial capabilities of this excellent long-haul airliner. Sadly, one of the DC-10s which had been seen regularly on these services came to grief not long afterwards when

ZK-NZP crashed into Mount Erebus in Antarctica during a sight-seeing flight on 28 November 1979.

A more permanent involvement with the type came in April 1988 when eight DC-10-30s of varying ancestry joined British Airways as a result of its merger with British Caledonian (BCAL). BCAL had achieved great success with its DC-10 fleet, beginning with an initial delivery of two from McDonnell Douglas in early 1977, building up to six by April 1981 and topped-up with a further two 'pre-owned' examples during 1985. One of these was a battle-scarred Ariana Afghan Airlines aircraft which was rescued from Kabul; the other one came from Air Zaire. The final three BCAL DC-10s acquired 'personalised' registrations: G-DCIO for obvious reasons, G-MULL to highlight the airline's Scottish connections and G-NIUK – 'Nippon International UK' – referring to the aircraft's financing arrangements.

During May 1988 G-BEBL became the first DC-10 to appear in British Airways colours. The fleet

British Airways finally acquired its own fleet of eight DC-10s in April 1988 through a merger with British Caledonian Airways which had built up a substantial long-haul presence with the type. G-MULL had originally been operated by Ariana Afghan Airlines and was rescued from war-torn Kabul in 1985 to fly for BCAL.

TOP: *British Airways' fleet of DC-10s continued to be Gatwick-based for the rest of their time with the airline. G-BEBM, seen taxying from the North Terminal, was the first DC-10 delivered to BCAL in February 1977 and was also the first to be retired from service in October 1998 after serving for more than 21 years at Gatwick.*

ABOVE: *This once familiar sight of a line of DC-10 tails at Gatwick's North Terminal has now gone forever with the retirement of the type in March 1999. Here half of the DC-10 fleet is prepared for the regular late-morning exodus of long-haul flights heading for destinations in southern USA and Africa.*

remained at Gatwick to operate basically the same route network as before, flying mainly to the southern USA (Atlanta, Dallas and Houston) and to West Africa (Accra, Kano and Lagos). Once again the DC-10 came to be greatly admired for its capabilities and rugged reliability, so much so that the acquisition of two additional examples was evaluated in 1988 and again in 1990 when two ex-Eastern Airlines aircraft were seriously considered. In the end none were acquired and an order for nine of the new MD-11s held by

BCAL at the time of the merger for delivery between 1990–93 was transferred to American Airlines.

A reduction in the fleet took place during 1993–4 with the transfer of two DC-10s to charter subsidiary Caledonian Airways. Following the sale of Caledonian in April 1995 both aircraft remained with them on lease although one, G-NIUK, was reconfigured with a two-class 32J/279M layout for Caledonian to operate British Airways' scheduled services to Tampa, San Juan, and Nassau/Grand

Cayman. G-BHDH meanwhile continued to operate worldwide charters for Caledonian in a single-class 356-seat configuration until October 1995. Once again all eight DC-10s were back in British Airways colours, seven flown by the airline itself plus 'IUK operated on its behalf by Caledonian.

From April 1997 the operation of 'IUK on British Airways' leisure routes was taken over by Airline Management Limited (AML) and flown by BA flight crew with Flying Colours Airlines cabin crew. From April 1998 this operation increased with the transfer of two additional aircraft to AML, the expanded fleet serving Montego Bay/Kingston four times a week, Cancun, Puerto Plata and Tobago, as well as the previously listed destinations, in a revised 26J 279M configuration.

Other new routes served by DC-10s in recent years have included Gatwick–Abu Dhabi–Colombo twice a week from November 1995 and Gatwick–Phoenix–San Diego daily from July 1996, a route which stretched the DC-10's performance abilities to the limit because of the extreme summer temperatures experienced at Phoenix. By April 1998, however, the route structure of the DC-10 fleet had changed completely. As noted above, three aircraft had transferred to the AML operation and the remaining five were deployed on services to Abidjan, Accra, Baku, Dar es Salaam/Entebbe and Tel Aviv.

This small fleet of DC-10s came to British Airways unexpectedly and surprised many by surviving for so long, seemingly inseparable from Gatwick where they were such familiar sights for more than twenty years. Basically, their continued operation was because the aircraft's attributes – reliability, ease of maintenance and suitability for many of the long routes flown from Gatwick – made them difficult to replace economically and operationally. Although the DC-10s were expected to remain in service until at least the early part of the twenty-first century, this changed during 1998 when their early retirement was announced as part of a plan to reduce the number of long-haul aircraft types. All eight were sold and withdrawn from service from October 1998, replaced by a similar number of Boeing 767/777s. The last scheduled DC-10 services arrived back at Gatwick early on 28 March 1999 with 'HDJ arriving from Baku just thirty-seven minutes after sister ship 'CIO from New York.

Most of the 386 DC-10s built for commercial use are still flying, many having found a new lease of life as freighters. Federal Express has accumulated over fifty and these are undergoing significant upgrades to become two-crew 'MD-10s'. Others are being used to replace the previous generation of 707/DC-8 freighters with smaller operators throughout the world. Three of the ex-British Airways aircraft have found new careers as part of Gemini Air Cargo's growing fleet of DC-10 freighters, and the remainder are expected to find similar employment and continue flying for many more years.

Shorts Skyliner

BEA took delivery of two new Shorts Skyliners in March/April 1973 to replace its long-serving Herons on Scottish services. The Skyliner, which was basically the STOL transport Skyvan fitted out with a more comfortable interior for up to nineteen passengers, became the smallest fixed-wing aircraft in the new British Airways fleet. Both were Glasgow-based and continued to maintain daily scheduled services to Campbeltown on the Scottish mainland plus Barra, Islay and Tiree in The Hebrides. Aberdeen and Inverness were later added but both Skyliners were withdrawn from service and sold during 1975.

G-AZYW SH1903   Sold as LN-NPG 5/75. To 9Q-CDA.
G-BAIT SH1908   Sold as LN-NPC 3/75. To SE-GEY, OH-SBA, OH-BBA.

Vickers Viscount

The Viscount, a supremely elegant and pioneering airliner from a bygone era, an aircraft which until recently was such a familiar sight and sound, sadly has now disappeared from British skies after a career spanning almost half a century. During that time the Viscount became the best selling British airliner of all time with 444 built (a title now hotly pursued by the BAe/Avro 146/RJ family!).

During the years immediately after World War Two, the willingness of Vickers to expand the horizons of design and technology to produce this revolutionary new airliner led directly to the introduction of new levels of speed and comfort for passengers everywhere and delivered much greater efficiency levels to the airlines. Thus, following from July 1950 when a Viscount became the world's first turbo-prop airliner to carry passengers, the previous generation of short/medium-haul piston-engined transports were rendered virtually obsolete. Passengers loved its smooth, quiet ride and features such as the large oval-shaped windows, and major world airlines queued up to place their orders during the early 1950s. Viscounts enabled BEA to build an extensive European route network second to none and almost half of its fleet eventually went on to fly with British Airways, some remaining in service until 1982, but, even then, finding economically viable replacements was so difficult that many routes were dropped when the Viscounts finally retired.

Why was the Viscount such a success? Although many other airliner designs from the prolific post-war years were eventually successful in technical terms, most were doomed to commercial failure because of their prolonged development programs, examples being the Ambassador, Britannia and Comet. Vickers, however, managed to achieve that rare and sought-after combination of innovative design and widespread commercial acceptance by producing exactly what the airlines needed at the right time, a fast and economical airliner with a large, pressurised

ABOVE: *This 1953-vintage Viscount is the oldest airliner to have served British Airways since the 1974 merger. It was one of a pair of BEA's original Viscount 701s leased-in to fly feeder services for long-haul flights from Prestwick until March 1976. G-AMOG now resides at RAF Cosford, as part of the British Airways collection of airliners, where it has been fully restored to its early BEA colours.*

BELOW: *British Airways inherited a substantial fleet of 33 Viscount 802/806s from BEA. Although 13 were retired during 1975/6, 20 remained in service for the rest of the decade, providing a valuable service on many UK and Ireland routes and defying all attempts to replace them. When G-APEY was photographed at the end of March 1981 the fleet had reduced to just seven, which were retained primarily to operate the airline's Scottish routes. Two months later, however, they had all been replaced by leased HS-748s, bringing the Viscount's illustrious career with British Airways and its predecessors to an end after almost 30 years.*

cabin. Much of this success was to a great extent due to the relatively trouble-free introduction of the Viscount's Rolls-Royce Dart engines, which soon earned their reputation for being smooth, economical and reliable and became so successful that eventually over 7,000 were built.

At the time of the Viscount's first flight in July 1948, however, none had actually been ordered. BEA bought Airspeed Ambassadors and felt that the initial Viscounts would be too small, but once the new turbine-powered airliner had been demonstrated, the airline's management was won over. An order for twenty 47-seat Viscount 700s was placed in August 1950, the first of which began flying scheduled services from Heathrow to Nicosia via Rome and Athens on 17 April 1953. By the end of 1955 over 300 Viscounts had been sold to major world airlines and customers included such influential carriers as Capital Airlines of the USA, Trans Canada Airlines, Air France, Alitalia, Lufthansa, South African, Trans Australian and Ansett. After ordering another six Series-700s, BEA pressed Vickers to build a larger Viscount. Twenty-four Series-802s seating fifty-seven passengers were introduced into service from

February 1957, followed by nineteen Series-806s with uprated Dart engines and improved performance. In later years as the Viscounts were displaced from BEA's trunk routes their configuration was changed to seventy-one single-class seats.

Viscounts dominated BEA's major routes by the end of 1959 when all deliveries had been completed. Including leased aircraft, the airline operated a total of seventy-eight Viscounts of various models. Through the early 1960s the Viscount 700s left the airline, many transferring to Cambrian Airways, and in 1967 fourteen of the Series-806s joined BKS and Cambrian. By the late 1960s most Viscounts had dispersed to BEA's regional routes and in April 1971 the remaining thirty-four became 'owned' by profit centres as the airline's final organisational structure came into being. This gave the Scottish Airways Division eight -802s, Birmingham-based Channel Islands Division twelve -802s, and British Air Services fourteen -806s, further sub-divided into six with Northeast Airlines and eight with Cambrian.

BOAC's contribution of two ageing Viscount 701s must also be added to the substantial Viscount fleet which was soon to join British Airways! To feed BOAC's long-haul flights at Prestwick, Cambrian received a contract to operate its two remaining 701s on daily feeder services from Prestwick to Belfast and Edinburgh/Aberdeen, beginning in 1972. The old Viscounts, G-AMOG and 'MON, affectionately known as 'Golly' and 'Noddy' by their crews, were painted up in full BOAC colours, later replaced by BA's new scheme, and flown on these services until their retirement in March 1976. British Midland then took over the contract and used their own Viscounts until March 1977.

British Airways inherited thirty-three Viscount 802/806s from BEA (plus the two old 701s mentioned above!) and, although the type had been in service for twenty years, there was no sign of a viable replacement which could operate economically on the short routes flown, particularly those in the Scottish Highlands and Islands. Despite this, however, the fleet would not remain intact for long, as a deteriorating world economic climate forced the new airline to take stock of its operations and implement drastic cuts. During the winter of 1975–6 all but six of the Viscount 802s were retired to Cardiff, with two new HS-748s bought as partial replacements for Scottish services. The thirteen retired Viscounts were hastily scrapped or donated to airport fire services at Birmingham, Jersey, Leeds-Bradford, Liverpool and Newcastle. Operations continued with the remaining twenty Viscounts and studies were undertaken into how best to replace them. Finally, as another economic recession loomed, the decision was taken to reduce the operational fleet to just five Viscounts by March 1980 and close many uneconomic routes. Seven -806s were actually retained in service until the type was finally retired in May 1982, by which time Viscounts had served BEA/British Airways continuously for almost thirty years.

Perhaps surprisingly, this last batch of Viscounts fared considerably better than those retired years earlier and found a ready buyer on the second-hand market with British Air Ferries (BAF). After purchasing an initial six in early 1981, BAF continued to acquire British Airways' redundant Viscounts until eighteen had been delivered to its Southend base by 1984, most of which were quickly pressed into service. BAF took full advantage of the capabilities of this

With its extra large 'British' titling Viscount 806 G-AOYN arriving at Newcastle from Jersey could easily be mistaken for a British Airways aircraft. In fact the photograph was taken in 1987, six years after British Air Ferries had bought the aircraft and at a time when they had adopted the oversized style of titling discarded by British Airways in 1984.

flexible and well maintained fleet during the next seventeen years using them on a wide variety of work. Initially several were leased out for work which ranged from oil support contracts in North Africa to flying scheduled services for established airlines including British Caledonian and Virgin Atlantic. Many fledgling airlines, such as Euroair, Guernsey Airlines, London European Airways and Polar Airways also took advantage of BAF's new fleet. BAF used the Viscounts extensively on passenger charters and during the summer months a steady procession would arrive at Jersey filled with holiday makers from UK regional airfields, just as they had done in their BEA/BA days. During the 1990s as the Viscounts reached the end of their working lives they were retired and after lingering for a while at Southend were scrapped. By 1996, after the final Viscount operations on a long-running contract to carry Shell personnel between Aberdeen and Shetland, the only remaining regular work was flying Parcelforce freight from Coventry to Belfast and Edinburgh. Several British World (the new name for BAF) Viscounts received the bright red overall Parcelforce livery but were rarely seen as the

flying was undertaken at night. Sadly, even this contract was soon to end and in early January 1998 Britain's last Viscounts were withdrawn, the final services flown by veteran Series-802s G-AOHM and G-OPFI (originally G-AOHV), both by then over forty years old!

The Viscount's story has not completely drawn to a close as four of the ex-British Airways aircraft have been purchased for operations in Africa. Unfortunately, no Viscounts fly in Britain today and the prospect of seeing this much loved airliner in operation once again or preserved in flying condition is very remote, a sad situation given its tremendous contribution to the development of modern airliners. Two fine examples of the early Viscount 700s flown by BEA are preserved; G-ALWF, the fifth to be built, is at Duxford and G-AMOG, the seventh Viscount, which also saw service with Cambrian, BOAC and British Airways, is at Cosford. G-APIM, a Viscount 806, survives at the Brooklands Museum and hopefully at least one more example of the Series 802/806s will also be saved once their productive days in Africa come to an end.

Five Merchantmen were retained to operate British Airways Cargo's network of European scheduled services from 1975 to December 1979. G-APEP, one of two to receive the new livery, was photographed early one morning in August 1979 after offloading its cargo from a scheduled Stockholm and Gothenburg service. The large main-deck cargo door is clearly visible.

Weighed down by its heavy load of cargo, G-APEG taxies onto its stand at British Airways' Heathrow Cargo Centre at the end of a busy night's work in August 1979. BEA's Merchantman conversions produced extremely capable freighters which could transport large volumes of cargo weighing up to 19 tonnes over long distances, but by the end of the 1970s all had been disposed of.

Vickers Vanguard

Along with many airlines which were also achieving remarkable success with the Viscount during the mid-1950s, BEA undertook studies into its future needs, concentrating in particular on a higher capacity airliner to accommodate growth on routes which were benefiting from the Viscount's ability to generate extra passengers. Initial discussions with Vickers actually began as early as 1952, when the Viscount had barely entered service, and in 1953 both BEA and Trans Canada Airlines, which were ultimately to be the only customers for the new airliner, came up with their initial set of requirements. BEA basically wanted a larger, faster Viscount with the ability to carry up to 100 passengers and more cargo over distances of 1,000 miles at speeds of over 400 miles per hour. Various designs were evaluated and rejected until Vickers offered an even bigger aircraft which it hoped would have a much wider appeal, and BEA duly ordered twenty of the all-new Vanguards in July 1956.

When it emerged in January 1959, the Vanguard was indeed considerably bigger in all respects than its predecessor. The fuselage was thirty-seven feet longer than that of the largest Viscount and was designed in a 'double-bubble' style with a capacious cargo hold beneath the passenger cabin floor. Although thought to be too big for BEA's initial requirements, the Vanguard offered considerable potential for accommodating the anticipated growth in passenger numbers and cargo through the 1960s. Usual configuration was for 18 first- and 109 tourist-class seats, interestingly with the first-class cabin at the rear of the fuselage, and in later years a 135-seat all-tourist layout was adopted.

Trans Canada Airlines ordered twenty-three increased-weight Vanguards for its longer routes and BEA decided to change its order at a late stage to take advantage of this extra capability. As a result the first six were delivered as Vanguard 951s, followed by fourteen of the heavier and longer-range Series-953s. Entry into service was scheduled for July 1960 but compressor failures in the Rolls-Royce Tyne turboprops delayed this until December of that year when some Christmas extras were flown. By March 1961 the Vanguard began to settle in and over the next twelve months the full complement of twenty was delivered.

Unfortunately for Vickers further sales of the Vanguard were not forthcoming and the company's hopes for success comparable to that achieved with the Viscount were dashed. They had produced a superbly fast and efficient airliner with impressive range and payload capabilities and a comfortable, quiet passenger cabin, but the first short- to medium-haul jet airliners were also entering service and offering a more glamorous alternative for passengers. Caravelles, Comets, Boeing 707s and DC-8s were soon to be joined by BAC One-Elevens, DC-9s and Boeing

727s and whilst Vanguards were only slightly slower on many typical European routes and considerably cheaper to operate, passengers preferred jets! So, as the 1960s progressed, BEA's Vanguards became confined to operating high-density and primarily leisure routes such as Heathrow to Malta and Palma, as well as shorter European and domestic services where jets were less of a threat. They also performed particularly well at restricted airfields such as Gibraltar and Jersey. By the end of that decade, however, BEA was seeking to reduce the number of Vanguards in service and decided to convert several into freighters, a move which made full use of the aircraft's impressive load-carrying abilities.

BEA began to convert its fleet in 1968, G-APEM being the first of two to be sent to Aviation Traders (ATEL) at Southend where the extensive engineering work was performed. This involved removing all passenger fittings from the aircraft, installing a strengthened, roller floor and an upward-opening door in the fuselage side measuring 139 by 80 inches. Eleven 108 by 88-inch pallets could be accommodated, just two fewer than a 707 freighter, and with the aircraft capable of carrying a 42,000 lb payload, this gave BEA an excellent medium-range freighter. Following from these initial conversions, BEA's own engineering department undertook a further seven conversions at Heathrow using parts supplied by ATEL. These nine freighters, renamed Merchantmen by BEA (and soon nicknamed the 'Guardsvan'!) entered service from February 1970 as Argosy replacements, and outlived the passenger aircraft by many more years.

By 1973 several Vanguards, the early Series-951s, had been retired from service and the remainder were soon to follow. British Airways took over the operation of just three passenger-carrying Vanguards in April 1974, in addition to the nine Merchantman freighters. These three Vanguards had only just managed to survive because of their low operating costs during the world's first major fuel crisis which was underway at the time. This was only a temporary reprieve, however, and British Airways' final Vanguard service was flown on 16 June 1974 from Jersey to Heathrow by G-APEU, the last one to have been delivered just twelve years earlier.

Whilst the Merchantmen were to soldier on with British Airways for another five-and-a-half years, the remains of the passenger fleet were soon disposed of, with all but one scrapped. The survivor saw further service with Merpati Nusantata Airlines of Indonesia, and occasionally undertook the long ferry flight back to London for maintenance.

The freighter conversion gave the Vanguard a completely new lease of life, a new career which ultimately was to last for twice as long as the airliner's passenger-carrying days and made the few converted survivors very valuable commodities. British Airways used them on scheduled services to Amsterdam, Milan, Stockholm and Gothenburg as

ABOVE AND BELOW: *Air Bridge/Hunting Cargo Airlines prolonged the life of its Merchantman fleet for as long as possible through the 1990s, gradually retiring aircraft as their airframe and engine hours expired. Finally, in October 1996 G-APEP undertook the last ever flight by a Vanguard when it returned to Brooklands for a well earned retirement, landing on what was left of the runway from which it had first flown 35 years earlier. To accept the aircraft into preservation from its crew were Sir Peter Masefield, Chief Executive of BEA at the time of the Vanguard's conception, and 'Jock' Bryce who had been in command of the type's first flight.*

well as for ad hoc charters. Four Merchantmen were retired during 1975–6, three of which were sold. One of these, G-APES went to East Midlands-based Air Bridge Carriers (ABC) in November 1976 where much of its work over the next eighteen years involved the transport of racehorses and other livestock. This aircraft proved to be such an excellent freighter that ABC quickly snapped up the other five Merchantmen following their retirement in 1979. The final British Airways service was flown by 'PEJ from Stockholm to Gothenburg and Heathrow on 2 December 1979.

ABC, later renamed Hunting Cargo Airlines, used its Merchantman fleet for cargo charters and later to operate lucrative, scheduled, overnight services for the expanding courier and small package delivery companies such as DHL, where full use of

the extensive volumetric capacity of the upper and lower holds was made. This became the main source of work during the 1990s as aircraft began to run out of flying hours and were retired one by one to be used as a source of spares at East Midlands. Following the retirement of G-APES in February 1995, just one Merchantman remained in service. G-APEP continued to operate five nights a week over the route Belfast–Coventry–Brussels until all remaining stocks of spare engines had been exhausted. The last flight ever by a Vanguard was the return of 'PEP to its birthplace at Brooklands on 17 October 1996, where it was accepted for preservation by Sir Peter Masefield, Chief Executive of BEA at the time of the Vanguard's creation, and 'Jock' Bryce who had commanded the type's first ever flight over thirty-seven years earlier.

Whilst the long-term future of G-APEP is secure, sadly the other survivors which had been stored at East Midlands for some time were hastily scrapped, despite moves by a local preservation group and other UK museums to restore and display one more. As a result the wonderful collection of British post-war airliners on display at Duxford is not quite as comprehensive as it could have been with a Vanguard proudly displayed alongside the Ambassador, Viscount, Britannia, Comet, Herald, VC-10 and Concorde etc. Only one other Vanguard is believed to survive today. G-APEK retired to the south of France well over ten years ago to be used as a source of spares at Perpignan for the ill-fated and short-lived Inter Cargo Service, a freight airline which managed to write-off its entire fleet of two Vanguards in 1988–89. Since then 'PEK has remained at Perpignan, minus its engines but otherwise complete. If it is still there today perhaps there is just a faint hope of saving another Vanguard?

CHAPTER SIX

COLOUR SCHEMES

During the last twenty-five years British Airways' airliners have displayed three distinctly different liveries, each designed to reflect a different stage in the airline's evolving corporate identity. The initial and very patriotic red, white and blue scheme of 1973 was replaced by a more sober and business-like 'Landor' design in 1985. This in turn has succumbed to the innovative 'World Image' artwork introduced through 'Project Utopia' in 1997 to take a global British Airways into the twenty-first century. There have also been many one-off and hybrid schemes, and in 1980 oversize 'British' titles appeared throughout the fleet. The background to these liveries and details of their implementation now follows.

1973 – A colour scheme for the new British Airways

A new livery for the emerging airline designed by Britain's Dick Negus was announced as early as July 1973 and began to appear in September after the official adoption of the British Airways name. The first aircraft to be rolled-out was BOAC Boeing 707 G-AXXY and others soon followed, with Viscount G-APEY of Northeast and newly delivered 747 G-AWNN appearing in early November and Trident Three G-AWZC in December.

One of the main factors taken into account during the design of the new identity was that the reborn British Airways would be the result of bringing together two long-established and highly respected airlines, each with its own fiercely loyal workforce. It was therefore decided to incorporate recognisable features from both of their liveries in the new identity and so BEA's Union Jack emblem became the basis of the tail design and BOAC's famous Speedbird logo was also retained, albeit in a much smaller form. Three bold and recognisably British colours, red, white and blue, were employed to project a strong national identity. The scheme comprised a dark-blue fuselage beneath the windows and a white top. The tail was basically white with a red top, a dark-blue triangle and a red diagonal stripe to represent a section of the Union Jack. 'British airways' titles appeared on the forward fuselage above the windows with the Speedbird symbol just ahead. All aircraft adopted the same scheme, which was slightly modified by the addition of small Cambrian, Northeast, Channel Islands and Scottish Airways titles on the lower forward fuselages. The new identity was very well received and perceived to be modern, fresh and very suited to the British flag carrier.

Painting the entire fleet was a costly and time-consuming task which could only be accomplished as individual aircraft reached their next scheduled repaint. In the meantime BEA and BOAC titles were soon replaced by 'British airways' and aircraft could

Super VC-10 G-ASGP models the simple but effective colour scheme created for British Airways which first began to appear in September 1973. Patriotic red, white and blue colours were used and the design incorporated an updated version of BEA's flag-based tail and BOAC's famous Speedbird logo.

Newly delivered 747-236 G-BDXC displays British Airways' livery in 1977. (ADRIAN MEREDITH PHOTOGRAPHY)

be seen flying with this slightly modified livery for many more years. Other hybrid liveries appeared with, for example, two Trident Threes and several 747-136s gaining the new tails and titles whilst retaining their original fuselage colours. G-ARVM became one of only two Standard VC-10s to be repainted, initially with the hybrid new tail and titles and then during 1976 into the full new colour scheme for its role as a Super VC-10 training aircraft. Several Merchantmen flew until their withdrawal in December 1979 with basic BEA colours, and Tridents could still be seen that year with similar liveries. The final BOAC tail did not disappear until February 1977 and it actually took a total of seven years for all traces of the old liveries to disappear.

1980 – The airline becomes 'British'

On 23 June 1980 Boeing 747-136 G-AWNC had the dubious distinction of being the first aircraft to be rolled out wearing extra large 'British' titles in place of the previous 'British airways'. Trident Two G-AVFA followed on 29 June and the entire fleet was soon updated. Perhaps the best looking aircraft to carry this amended livery was 747-236F G-KILO which wore large 'British Cargo' titles during its short stay with the airline. However, as mentioned previously, traces of the old colour schemes lingered on for many years and were still in evidence when this first update to British Airways' livery was made. Several 747-136s still retained their original fuselage colours and this change gave them a rather odd appearance with elements of three different liveries visible – BOAC fuselage colours, British Airways tails and 'British' titling. One such 747, G-AWNK, left Heathrow after its sale to TWA on 31 March 1981 still wearing this peculiar and somewhat tatty livery over seven years after the new identity had been introduced!

1984 – The 'Landor' livery

Along with the change to British Airways plc in April 1984 as part of the run-up to privatisation, the management decided to completely revise the airline's image. The previous livery had lasted for ten years, from the early merger and consolidation phases through a major recession and on into a new era of growth, high profits and commercial freedom. But airline liveries are always evolving and British Airways' was judged to have fallen behind some of the newer and more contemporary schemes then being introduced around the world. Landor Associates of California was chosen to design the new identity which, whilst retaining some elements of the previous one, portrayed a completely different image.

The first physical evidence of an impending change came with the delivery of Boeing 737-236 G-BKYA, which arrived at Heathrow on 15 September 1984 wearing an experimental scheme consisting of the basic British Airways livery applied over a silver fuselage top instead of the usual white. Next came 737 G-BKYB with all-blue undersides and One-Eleven G-AVMM, repainted with blue engine nacelles in place of the usual natural metal. After the final design decisions had been taken, another new 737, G-BKYF, arrived from Seattle on 20 November wearing the basic new colour scheme which was then completed in conditions of total secrecy prior to the launch date of 4 December 1984.

The aircraft livery unveiled on that date was based on a deeper midnight blue for the undersides and engines and pearl grey for the upper fuselage and tail. The familiar, quartered Union Jack was retained but the upper part, which extended further down the tail, was blue instead of red and bore a heraldic crest with the motto 'To Fly To Serve'. A red 'Speedwing' stripe was applied along the lower fuselage and the full airline name reappeared on the forward upper fuselage in midnight-blue Roman capitals. The familiar Speedbird logo, however, had disappeared.

Another newly-delivered 737, G-BKYG, became the first aircraft to enter service in the new scheme on 12 December followed by the first long-haul aircraft, 747 G-AWNO. One problem which soon became

The first change to British Airways' livery was introduced in 1980. The word 'airways' was dropped from the fuselage titling, leaving the single word 'British' which was greatly increased in size.

ABOVE: *The extra-large 'British' titling seen to good effect on TriStar 500 ZD953, previously G-BFCF, awaiting delivery to the RAF in July 1983.*

BELOW: *Experimental changes to the basic livery began to appear during 1984 as plans for a new identity were made. For example, 737 G-BKYA was delivered with a silver fuselage top in place of the more usual white.*

A new corporate identity designed by Landor Associates was unveiled in December 1984, an innovative design chosen to reflect the growing success of British Airways as it progressed towards privatisation. As can be seen from this picture of two 747-236s the basic tail design was retained but used new colours and incorporated a Heraldic crest with the airline's 'To Fly To Serve' motto .

earlier, helped by the delivery of many new airliners and improved painting techniques. Much of the work was subcontracted with most of the 747-136/236s painted in Hong Kong and many 737s in Brussels. As a result the proliferation of hybrid schemes did not occur again.

1997 – 'Utopia'

'Utopia' is the enigmatic code-name adopted by British Airways for a project set up in the mid-1990s to change completely the airline's image through the introduction of a revolutionary and colourful new corporate identity. Although conceived over several years, details of 'Project Utopia' were kept successfully hidden under a blanket of strict corporate secrecy despite some well publicised 'leaks' and wild media speculation. All of this served to stimulate interest and resulted in a very successful high-profile launch for the 'new' British Airways in June 1997.

After ten years with its post-privatisation

The initial Heraldic crest applied to the 747s was deemed to be too small and was soon replaced with a much larger version more in proportion with the size of the aircraft. Here two 747-136s undergoing maintenance illustrate the different-sized tail crests.

apparent on the 747s was that the tail crest was too small. After several had been completed a new and larger decal was applied, but 747s with the small crest were still flying many months later and were to be seen on various publicity photographs throughout the life of the Landor scheme.

The new livery was reviewed as being very innovative and, although not universally well-liked at first, soon came to be accepted as presenting a strongly positive brand for the airline, portraying business-like qualities such as professionalism whilst also being easily recognisable as belonging to the national carrier. Similarly-coloured schemes were later chosen by United Airlines and Canadian Airlines.

Repainting the fleet was achieved in a faster and more orderly way than had been seen ten years

Landor Associates-designed identity, management began to feel that a complete and radical change was once again needed. The livery was by that time perceived to be dated and unsuitable for the 'global and caring' airline image which the company wanted to portray for the forthcoming new millennium. With 60% of business originating from outside the UK, an identity with more relevance to the majority of its customers was to be sought, an identity which would also reflect many far-reaching changes planned for the airline's corporate culture. In conditions of the utmost secrecy which were maintained right up to the launch date two years later, British Airways outlined its requirements to design consultants in April 1995, one of which, Newell and Sorrell, was given approval by the Board in August of that year to go ahead with its ideas.

The first visible signs to the outside world came some time later in January 1997 when aircraft began to appear in an 'interim' livery. Boeing 747-436 G-BNLR was the first of forty aircraft to receive this temporary scheme which was then applied to any aircraft due for a repaint or delivered before the June 1997 launch. As it later transpired this was basically the new white and lighter-blue livery as described further on, but with the 'Speedmarque' omitted and the original tail markings with the 'To Fly to Serve' crest retained. Rumours began to circulate about dramatic new tail schemes, especially as this rather plain livery was obviously just an initial base which could easily be changed or added to in the future, but despite some wild media guesswork and an early preview for the airline's staff, the secrets of 'Project Utopia' remained hidden.

The much anticipated launch finally took place on 10 June 1997 with nine aircraft, each freshly painted with a different tail design, rolled-out at locations ranging from Seattle to Johannesburg. A media preview of Concorde G-BOAF and 747-436 G-BNLO at Heathrow preceded a co-ordinated worldwide event for 30,000 invited guests at 126 locations in 63 countries linked together by satellite television for a simultaneous presentation of the new designs. Other aircraft unveiled were a Loganair Islander at Glasgow, British Regional ATP at Belfast, Maersk 737 at Birmingham, Deutsche BA 737 at Munich, Brymon DHC-8 at Gatwick, a Comair 737 displayed at Johannesburg and then flown over the Victoria Falls, and a new 757 rolled-out at Boeing's Seattle factory. As these aircraft re-entered service, another opportunity to show off the new livery came later that same week when Concorde G-BOAF, newly delivered 777 G-RAES and the first of British Regional's brand-new EMB-145s, G-EMBA, made appearances at the Paris Airshow.

The basic design features of the livery are lighter-blue undersides and a pearl-white top in place of the previous navy blue and grey. 'British Airways'

ABOVE: *Newly repainted 747-136 G-AWNC shares a hangar with Concorde G-BOAF which was about to receive its new colours.*

BELOW: *Although Tridents never flew in the 'Landor' livery two examples were repainted at Heathrow for their role as ground training airframes. The first of these was Trident Two G-AVFG which illustrates the full livery of pearl grey fuselage top, midnight blue undersides with a red 'Speedwing' stripe and revised titles. This was followed by Trident Three G-AWZK which remains in excellent condition at Heathrow today under the care of the Trident Preservation Society.*

titles in a softer typeface and repositioned below the window line are topped by a new company symbol, the 'Speedmarque' – a derivation of the 'Speedwing' flash which ran along the side of aircraft in the old livery. Red, white and blue colour shades chosen to reflect those found on the British Union Flag reinforce the British base of the airline, but for the tail-fins designs which would project a global airline image were used. New works of art were commissioned from creative artists in many of the communities served by the airline and translated into suitable tail designs to form the centrepiece of the airline's dynamic new identity. An initial fifteen designs were unveiled on the launch day and others have been introduced since so that by the end of 1998 thirty-four were in use including a series of 'one-off' special event designs.

Some exceptions to the basic livery have been introduced. Deutsche BA uses black undersides instead of blue and has three tail designs which are unique to the German airline. Concorde has a variation which is basically white, essential for heat dispersion at supersonic speeds, to which the new titles and 'Speedmarque' have been applied. Displayed on the tails of the seven Concordes is a 'rippling flag' in red, white and blue, giving this unique fleet a very effective and popular new image. In October 1998 Air Liberté staged a media event at Orly Airport to relaunch the airline and unveiled a Fokker F100 and a MD-83 repainted with different French images. As with British Airways one year earlier, Air Liberté's aircraft had begun to appear some time before the launch with a basic, blue and white 'interim' livery.

A feature of the new livery, with the exception of Deutsche BA's airliners, is the replacement of individual names previously carried on the outside of each aircraft. The original artists' signatures have been applied to the rear fuselage beneath their work and the title of the artwork to either side of the nose, in English on the port side and in the language of the country of origin on the starboard side. The country of origin of the design has subsequently been added to the rear fuselage. Franchise partner airlines have dropped 'Express' from the titles displayed on their aircraft, preferring to standardise on the new 'British Airways' logo carried by the rest of the fleet.

Observers may wonder why the individual artwork images can vary from one aircraft to another. One reason is that tail shapes differ, compare for example a 737's tail fin to that of a Canadair RJ's. Another reason is that only a small section of the original artwork can be adapted to fit onto the narrow area of an airliner's fin, and often a different section of the design will be chosen for individual aircraft.

The new images are being applied throughout the fleet without necessarily referring to the aircraft's capabilities or the routes likely to be flown by particular types. Thus Loganair's Islander G-BLDV which serves local Scottish routes has an appropriate

Benyhone tartan tail but other aircraft in the fleet display images from parts of the world which are unlikely ever to see a Loganair aircraft. The idea is for a varied selection of different images from around the world to appear on each fleet, thereby illustrating the global nature of the airline. So, although 747-436 G-CIVO (which also has a tartan tail) will rarely be seen in Scotland, it will carry this image throughout the world and Comair's 737-200 ZS-NLN will display its Japanese ink painting in Southern Africa.

Interest in the launch event and the new identity was immense and press coverage extensive, thereby achieving one of the airline's aims! However, initial reactions were somewhat mixed. Some felt that the airline was taking a tremendous risk given the success of the previous livery and by going against the proven 1990s theme of establishing and building upon a recognisable and consistent corporate identity. Some criticised the loss of the Union Jack (which in fact was not carried on the aircraft tails with the previous livery) and others compared pictures of the tail designs to a wallpaper catalogue! Some media comments also suggested that this would become the first stage towards eventually dropping 'British' from the airline's name. Conversely, others felt that British Airways had once again taken a bold and radical step forward, one which would set new standards for the rest of the industry and which was likely to stimulate imitations, as the 'Landor' scheme did. Overseas press comment in particular was overwhelmingly positive.

British Airways responded to the UK press criticism by pointing out the degree of acceptance and enthusiasm from its growing overseas customer base. Comments regarding the loss of British identity were countered by emphasising the return to national red, white and blue colours throughout the fleet and in particular on Concorde's Union Flag scheme, as well as the retention of the full British Airways name. An additional response was to arrange a competition with the *Sunday Times* newspaper to find the best of British designs.

As well as the rapid introduction of the commissioned tail-art, several one-off and special series designs soon began to appear. The first of these was seen on 737-236 G-BKYG, repainted at Tees-Side in the new livery but with a large red poppy on its tail and 'Pause To Remember' fuselage titles to commemorate Remembrance Day on 11 November 1997. 'KYG flew services from its Gatwick base until December and then returned to Tees-Side to have the poppy replaced with the British Olympic Association's 'Lion' logo and the title 'Teaming up for Britain' applied to the fuselage. This scheme soon appeared on Airbus G-BUSC and 757 G-BMRC to promote British Airways' sponsorship of the British Team for the year 2000 Olympic Games in Sydney.

British Airways also took the opportunity provided by the new livery to mark its close relationship with Qantas. Two of the Australian airline's 747s have flown for some time with Aboriginal 'Dreamings' paintings covering their entire fuselages and these images soon appeared on the tails of two 747-436s. G-BNLS adopted the *Wunala Dreaming* scheme in November 1997 followed by G-BNLN as *Nalanji Dreaming* in January 1998. These complement a third 'Dreamings' design, *Water Dreaming*, although this one is not related to a Qantas colour scheme.

Competitions for new tail designs were held during the winter 1997–8 season in order to stimulate further interest and also to counter some of the criticisms of the airline losing its 'Britishness' by adopting too many overseas-based designs. A competition held in conjunction with the *Sunday Times* newspaper to find the best, recognisably British designs which also represent the country in a 'modern or contemporary way' generated a large number of entries and yielded three designs from different categories. Winning the children's section was a cartoon-style portrayal of 'Britain in a teacup' which was painted on the tail of Airbus G-BUSI during

December 1997 and named '*British Blend*'. Then during February and March 1998, 757s G-BMRD/MRJ emerged with *Chelsea Rose* and *Grand Union* artwork depicting the winning entries from the art student and adult sections. Boeing 737-436 G-DOCH appeared from a repaint at Stansted with its *Chelsea Rose* barely dry, in time to represent England by transporting the national football team to the World Cup in France during June 1998. *Chelsea Rose* and *Grand Union* have subsequently been adopted as permanent images, appearing on many more aircraft in the fleet. A competition to give the airline's employees a chance to 'design a tail-fin' produced over 400 entries. The winning entry came from a cabin crew member who based it on traditional Romanian hand-embroidered, floral tablecloth techniques. *Images of Romania* flew on 757 G-BIKY from April 1998.

Painting a fleet of well over 300 aircraft with such a complex new livery is at first sight a very daunting task, especially given that only one dedicated paint bay is available at the Heathrow Engineering Base and that aircraft such as the 757

TOP: *To launch British Airways' widely anticipated new identity in June 1997 a carefully co-ordinated world wide event linked by satellite television took place during which nine newly-painted aircraft at locations ranging from Seattle to Johannesburg were presented to an audience of 30,000 guests. At Heathrow Concorde G-BOAF, 747-436 G-BNLO and a selection of airline vehicles were unveiled.*

ABOVE: *Boeing 747-436 G-CIVW illustrates the revised titles and 'Speedmarque' company symbol which were introduced with British Airways' current identity. The Speedmarque was derived from the previous Speedwing which in turn had evolved from the much-loved Speedbird, giving the airline an ongoing link to its British heritage.*

Whilst red, white and blue colours from the British Union Flag form the base of its livery, British Airways' global image is projected by specially commissioned artwork from around the world which has been applied to the aircraft tails. 15 such images were unveiled on launch day and this had risen to 34 by the end of 1998. Boeing 777 G-VIIN displays the bold forms and shapes found in traditional Pacific Northwest Canadian art in a design known as Whale Rider.

need a week for a complete strip and paint, a 747 up to eight days and Concorde slightly longer. Despite this, progress was rapid, so that by the end of September 1997, just over three months from the launch, forty-four aircraft had been completed. Obviously this was not all achieved in the one paint bay! Many short-haul aircraft went to subcontractors at Stansted and Tees-Side and franchise partners arranged to have their aircraft repainted locally. Many new aircraft arrived either in the full or partial livery and those which

The new identity has enabled British Airways to commemorate special events and run competitions to find new designs for its aircraft. The link with Qantas has been highlighted by the adoption of two Aboriginal 'Dreamings' designs which the Australian carrier uses to decorate two of its 747s. Here 757 G-BMRH displaying Nalanji Dreaming *taxies out behind another 757 with a* Chelsea Rose *design which was the winning entry in a newspaper competition.*

already carried the interim livery soon had their tails repainted and the 'Speedmarque' added.

Ninety aircraft from across the fleets carried the new British Airways image by the end of 1997 and another 125 were completed during 1998, bringing the total to 215. This meant that, on average, another aircraft had appeared somewhere in the world with the new livery every three days! Seventy-eight 737s, twenty-eight 757s and twenty-seven 747s had been painted, reflecting the dominance of these types, especially the 737. Five of the seven Concordes had been painted, as befits the aircraft's high profile 'Flagship' role with the airline, and a wide range of partner airlines' smaller types.

Along with many things in today's dynamic airline business British Airways' latest corporate identity has continued to evolve. Almost two years on from its launch, management decided to give more prominence to the airline's British heritage by concentrating on the Union Flag design for all subsequent repaints and deliveries. They were responding to opinion surveys which clearly showed that people like designs which reflect their own culture and whilst this had been successfully achieved with the world images in overseas markets, a much higher profile for the airline's British customer base was needed. So Union Flag or 'Chatham' which had proved to be one of the most popular world images made its first appearance on the subsonic fleet during April 1999 on Boeing 767 G-BNWR which was used for Her Majesty the Queen's state visit to Korea. Other aircraft soon followed, leading towards a revised target of approximately half of the fleet literally 'Flying the Flag' with this design joining those already painted with other global images, a split which approximates to the airline's mix of British and overseas customers.

CHAPTER SEVEN

ASSOCIATED AIRLINES

This important aspect of British Airways has undergone a complete transformation during the last twenty-five years as the airline has updated its strategic aims and the tactics necessary to achieve them. Whilst the early activities of its subsidiary companies contributed little to the airline itself, since 1992 valuable links with other scheduled service airlines have flourished through the advent of franchising, partnerships and alliances, all of which are set to grow further in the future.

colours. Of the 440 airliners serving the British Airways family at the beginning of 1999, 175 were operated by subsidiary companies or franchise partner airlines.

Airlines which feature in this chapter are those which have taken on a full or part British Airways identity or have operated their aircraft on its behalf. Subsidiary companies now include the major European carriers Air Liberté and Deutsche BA as well as Brymon and Cityflyer Express in the UK,

Although these two airliners at Gatwick are wearing full British Airways colours, they are operated by AML and GB Airways, two members of the extensive and growing family of partner airlines.

The airline's links with other sectors of the air transport industry were initially through the involvement of two inherited subsidiary companies in such 'non-core' activities as offshore oil exploration support and the carriage of Inclusive Tour holidaymakers to Mediterranean resorts. British Airways Helicopters and Caledonian Airways have since been sold and the airline now concentrates on feeding traffic into its scheduled service network through a whole series of agreements with other airlines, which range from simple marketing agreements through to full franchise partnerships where other companies' aircraft fly in British Airways

and 'go', a low-cost, no-frills budget travel subsidiary. Franchise partners began to take on the airline's identity in 1993 and there are now many examples including airlines in The Netherlands, Scandinavia and South Africa. Also included are two airlines which became part of British Airways through merger or acquisition, British Caledonian and Dan-Air.

Airlines which are not included in this chapter are the code-share partners and participants in the **one**world alliance, as they have not adopted a British Airways identity and continue to operate their fleets as separate entities.

This chapter is sub-divided as follows:

1) Subsidiary companies: Air Liberté / TAT
British Airtours /
   Caledonian Airways
British Airways Helicopters
Brymon Airways
Cityflyer Express
Deutsche BA
'go'

2) Mergers or take-overs: British Caledonian
Dan-Air

3) Franchise partners: Airline Management Limited
BASE Airlines
British Mediterranean Airways
British Regional Airlines
Comair
GB Airways
Loganair
Maersk Air
Sun-Air

(1) Subsidiary Companies

Air Liberté (including TAT European Airlines)

Air Liberté became the second-largest airline in France following its amalgamation with TAT European Airlines in 1997. Thus British Airways, through its majority ownership of the newly enlarged airline, was able to increase its access to one of mainland Europe's biggest markets.

British Airways' acquisition of a French subsidiary airline began with the two-stage purchase of TAT in 1993 and 1996, followed by the rescue of bankrupt Air Liberté in December 1996. A major programme to rationalise and restructure the two airlines took place with the identity of Air Liberté adopted and that of TAT dropped. The route structure has since been changed to concentrate mainly on the lucrative French domestic market and a long-term fleet renewal plan implemented.

TAT European Airlines
TAT originated as Touraine Air Transport in 1968, an air taxi company which began scheduled services on the Tours to Lyon route in 1969. The company expanded rapidly and took over many small French regional airlines. TAT also began to operate services on behalf of Air France during the 1970s and many of its Fokker F28 aircraft were painted in the national carrier's livery. The airline name was changed to Transport Aérién Transregional (still TAT) in 1983 to more accurately reflect its size and type of operations and by 1988 the fleet comprised sixteen F28s, nineteen Fairchild F27/FH227, four Twin Otters, five Beech 99s and three King Airs. The long-standing links with the French national carrier were strengthened in 1989 when Air France purchased 35% of TAT. This did not last for long, however, as the European Commission insisted that Air France dispose of its TAT

shareholding as a condition of approving the merger between Air France, Air Inter and UTA.

A further name change, to TAT European Airlines, took place in 1992, at a time when the airline began operating its own international routes from Paris CDG to Bergamo, Copenhagen, Gatwick, and Munich and from Lyons to Gatwick. The fleet had further grown and included new Fokker 100s, ATR-42/72s and Boeing 737-200s. British Airways acquired an initial 49.9% shareholding in January 1993, with an option to purchase the remainder by April 1997. Joint BA/TAT services began in March 1993 and soon expanded to include Paris CDG to Stockholm, Stockholm–Nice–Rome, Gatwick–Lyons–Rome, Nice to Brussels and Rome, and Manchester–Nice–Rome using Fokker F28s and Fokker 100s painted in British Airways colours. However, by 1995 many of these routes were dropped as substantial losses had been incurred and a decision was taken that TAT should concentrate on increasing its share of the large French domestic market which for many years had been dominated by Air Inter/Air France.

A change in French ownership law allowed British Airways to complete its purchase of TAT in August 1996, just as the final legislation to liberalise air transport within the European Union came into effect allowing airlines to compete on equal terms outside their own domestic markets. By that time TAT was serving thirty destinations in France and also feeding traffic from Paris Orly to Heathrow and from Lyons and Marseilles to Gatwick using two 737-300s and several Fokker 100s in British Airways colours.

Air Liberté
After commencing operations in March 1988 as a charter carrier with a single leased MD-82, Air Liberté grew rapidly and by 1990 employed two A300-600s, one A310-300 and five MD-83s on services to European resort destinations and from Paris to Montreal and New York. A 747 was also flown in a joint venture with Corse Air International and an associate airline, Air Liberté Tunisie, operated one of the MD-82s.

By 1996, however, the company was in financial difficulties after over-expanding into scheduled services. After filing for bankruptcy in September 1996, Air Liberté became the subject of several rescue bids from airlines interested in acquiring its valuable Paris Orly slots and because of its excellent reputation as a young, innovative airline in the French marketplace. One such bid came from British Airways through its TAT subsidiary in conjunction with a French bank. This was accepted by the administrator in December 1996 and resulted in BA paying £12m to cover debts and injecting another £55m of share capital for restructuring, giving it a 70% holding in its second French subsidiary.

Initial plans were for Air Liberté to dispose of its A300/310 fleets and some 737-200s, retaining thirteen

ABOVE: *TAT European Airlines Fokker F28 F-BUTI departs Manchester on a scheduled service to Nice and Rome during August 1994. After British Airways' initial purchase of TAT shares in January 1993, several new intra-European routes were opened but were soon dropped to allow the airline to concentrate on more profitable French domestic services.*

BELOW: *British Airways acquired a second French subsidiary through its rescue of struggling Air Liberté in December 1996. A full merger with TAT soon followed, creating France's second largest airline which was re-launched in 1998 using the Air Liberté name. The airline's new identity is very similar to British Airways' but features distinctive French images as illustrated by MD-83 F-GRML at Heathrow in February 1999 with 'L'esprit Liberté' markings.*

aircraft – three DC-10s, seven MD-83s and three 737-200s. All domestic routes and those to French overseas territories were retained. Together, Air Liberté and TAT were taking 22% of the French domestic market, a strong enough base from which to compete effectively at last with Air France.

Further developments soon followed as British Airways announced in April 1997 that its two French subsidiaries were to be jointly managed in the run-up to a full merger. Air Liberté would be the surviving name with all references to TAT ceasing by the end of the year. The new Air Liberté became France's second-largest airline with thirty-nine aircraft serving thirty-three destinations and carrying four million passengers per year. A 20% share of the important Orly market was held, including up to seventeen daily flights to Toulouse. The only routes flown under BA service numbers during summer 1997 were from Paris Orly to Heathrow and from Bordeaux and Toulouse to Gatwick.

During March 1998 Air Liberté began the process of rationalising its fleet from nine types to three. Fleet plans showed the remaining 737-200s withdrawn during 1998 and the F28s by 2003, leaving three DC-10s and eight ATRs plus up to thirty new medium-range jets, presumed to be Airbus A319/320s from BA's August 1998 order. Long-haul flights to Africa, Asia and Canada were dropped, but services to the French territories of Fort-de-France in Martinique, Pointe-à-Pitre in Guadeloupe and Réunion in the Indian Ocean were retained. Services on major French domestic routes from Paris Orly to Bordeaux, Montpellier, Nice, Perpignan, Strasbourg and Toulouse were boosted and flights from a total of thirty-two French towns and cities maintained. Air Liberté was relaunched during October 1998 and introduced its own variation of the new British Airways livery featuring French images.

Air Liberté fleet

Aircraft registration	Aircraft type	Constructor's number	Date*	Notes
F-BUTI	Fokker F28	11034	1/93	TAT. BA c/s 4/94. Lse to Sabena and Air Sicilia '95. T/f to Air Liberté 10/97. To Time Air as C-GNCR 3/98.
F-GBBR	Fokker F28	11051	1/93	TAT. BA c/s 5/94. Lse to Sabena, ret 11/96. T/f to Air Liberté 10/97. To Time Air as C- 2/98.
F-GDUS	Fokker F28	11053	1/93	TAT. T/f to Air Liberté 10/97
F-GDUT	Fokker F28	11091	1/93	TAT. T/f to Air Liberté 10/97.
F-GDUU	Fokker F28	11108	1/93	BA c/s 3/93. T/f to Air Liberté 10/97.
F-FDUV	Fokker F28	11109	1/93	BA c/s 3/93. T/f to Air Liberté 10/97.
F-GIOA	Fokker 100	11261	1/93	TAT. BA c/s 11/94. T/f to Air Liberté 10/97.
F-GIOG	Fokker 100	11364	1/93	TAT. T/f to Air Liberté 10/97.
F-GIOH	Fokker 100	11424	1/93	TAT. BA c/s 6/95. T/f to Air Liberté 10/97.
F-GIOI	Fokker 100	11433	3/93	TAT. Ex-DBA. BA c/s 4/94. T/f to Air Liberté 10/97.
F-GIOJ	Fokker 100	11454	1/93	TAT. BA c/s 6/93. T/f to Air Liberté 10/97.
F-GIOK	Fokker 100	11455	1/93	TAT. BA c/s 5/94. T/f to Air Liberté 10/97.
F-GIOV	Fokker 100	11248	1/93	TAT. BA c/s 6/94. To Air UK as G-UKFJ 2/96.
F-GIOX	Fokker 100	11249	1/93	TAT. To Air UK as G-UKFK 1/96.
F-GNLG	Fokker 100	11363	1/93	TAT. Originally op as F-GIOF. Lse to DBA as D-ADFE 10/94. Ret TAT 4/97 as F-GNLG. T/f to Air Liberté 10/97.
F-GNLH	Fokker 100	11311	1/93	TAT. Ret from DBA lse 9/97. T/f to Air Liberté 10/97.
F-GNLI	Fokker 100	11315	1/93	TAT. Originally op as F-GIOD in BA c/s 2/93. Lse to DBA as D-ADFC 4/94. Ret Air Liberté 10/97 as F-GNLI.
F-GNLJ	Fokker 100	11344	1/93	TAT. Ret from DBA lse 9/97. T/f to Air Liberté 10/97.
F-GNLK	Fokker 100	11307	1/93	TAT. Ret Air Liberté from DBA lse 12/97.
F-GLLD	737-3Y0	23926	4/96	TAT. Ex-PT-TEJ. BA c/s. T/f to Air Liberté 11/97. To 'go' as G-IGOH 11/98.
F-GLLE	737-3Y0	23927	3/96	TAT. Ex-PT-TEK. BA c/s. T/f to Air Liberté 11/97. To 'go' as G-IGOG 9/98.
F-GFZB	MD-83	49707	12/96	Air Liberté.
F-GHEB	MD-83	49822	12/96	Air Liberté.
F-GHED	MD-83	49576	12/96	Air Liberté.
F-GHEI	MD-83	49968	12/96	Air Liberté.
F-GHEK	MD-83	49823	12/96	Air Liberté.
F-GHHO	MD-83	49985	12/96	Air Liberté.
F-GHHP	MD-83	49986	12/96	Air Liberté.
F-GJHQ	MD-83	49668	12/96	Air Liberté.
F-GPZA	MD-83	49943	4/98	Air Liberté.
F-GRML	MD-83	49628	12/98	Air Liberté. Ex-AOM French Airlines.
F-GPVA	DC10-30	47956	12/96	Air Liberté.
F-GPVC	DC10-30	48265	12/96	Air Liberté.
F-GPVD	DC10-30	47865	12/96	Air Liberté.

* Date into service

British Airtours / Caledonian Airways

In 1969 BEA formed a charter division called BEA Airtours based at Gatwick and using redundant Comet 4Bs, ten of which were eventually flown. The company was renamed British Airtours in 1973, by which time a fleet of ex-BOAC Boeing 707-436s had taken over from the Comets. The airline thrived, initially by operating package-tour charter flights to Mediterranean resort destinations and later by branching out into long-haul work. By 1978 the fleet consisted of nine 707-436s and flights were operated throughout Europe and to Far Eastern and west coast USA destinations. Fleet updates continued with the old 707-436s replaced with a fleet of brand-new 737-236s from 1980 and two 707-320B/Cs transferred from British Airways for North Atlantic charter flying in 1981–2. Many TriStars from the BA fleet were operated from 1981 onwards with transfers taking place to cover the seasonal peaks of both airlines. Although Series-200 TriStars were operated initially and -500s flown for short periods, it was six of the earlier TriStar-1s which became the mainstay of the Airtours – later the Caledonian – fleet. Several Boeing 747s have also been operated on lease, primarily for North American charter work.

Caledonian Airways was created from British Airtours during March 1988 as a result of the merger between British Airways and British Caledonian. BA decided to capitalise on the strong image of BCAL and re-branded its charter subsidiary with a similar yellow and blue livery with a lion on the tail, and tartan uniforms for the staff. The initial fleet was four TriStars

ABOVE: *British Airtours' early fleet consisted of veteran ex-BOAC/British Airways 707-436s, long-haul airliners which were less than ideally suited to the rigours of package-tour flying to Mediterranean resorts. G-ARRC was photographed on a damp January day in 1977 in between operating Air Mauritius' services from Heathrow.*

BELOW: *British Airtours was re-constituted as Caledonian Airways following the merger of British Airways and British Caledonian in April 1988. Charter services continued, initially with a fleet of four TriStars and five 737-236s. G-BEAL, a TriStar-50, taxies out to Newcastle's wet Runway 07 in August 1988 in the new Caledonian livery which was derived from the well-known BCAL 'Golden Lion' scheme.*

and five 737-236s and the first to appear in the new livery was TriStar G-BBAI, rolled-out at Hong Kong after repaint in February 1988. Also during that month two 757-236s were ordered, the first of an eventual fleet of seven for Caledonian and the first BA-owned 757s to be delivered with improved RB211-535E4 engines. These enabled Caledonian to use its 757s on ETOPS services to satisfy the demand for charters to Asia, North America, Africa and the Caribbean. Two DC-10s were also leased from British Airways from 1993.

British Airways sold Caledonian to package-tour operator Inspirations plc in April 1995, a transaction which included the final five TriStars in the BA fleet and the continued use of two DC-10s and three 757s for the summer 1995 season. Caledonian was also contracted to operate DC-10 G-NIUK from April 1995 in a two-class configuration on British Airways' scheduled leisure services from Gatwick to San Juan, Tampa and Nassau-Grand Cayman. This continued until 'IUK arrived at Gatwick on 30 March 1997, whereupon its operation was transferred to Airline Management Limited. The final links with British Airways were severed in December 1997 with the transfer of TriStar maintenance to FLS.

British Airtours and Caledonian Airways fleets

Aircraft registration	Aircraft type	Constructor's number	Date	Notes
G-APFB	707-436	17703	4/75	British Airtours. To Boeing at Kingman 11/76 stored then b/u.
G-APFD	707-436	17705	2/73	BEA/British Airtours. Lse to Air Mauritius 10/77–4/79. To Boeing 11/79. b/u Fort Lauderdale 8/86.
G-APFF	707-436	17707	5/74	British Airtours. To Boeing at Kingman 5/81, stored then b/u.
G-APFG	707-436	17708	3/73	BEA/British Airtours. wfu Stansted 11/80. To Aviation Traders 3/81 for use as an apprentice trainer. b/u 2/89.
G-APFH	707-436	17709	1/72	BEA/British Airtours. To Boeing 5/75. Stored Marana b/u '77.
G-APFI	707-436	17710	2/75	British Airtours. To Boeing at Kingman 11/76 stored then b/u.
G-APFJ	707-436	17711	2/77	British Airtours. To Cosford Museum 6/81. Preserved.
G-APFK	707-436	17712	12/71	BEA/British Airtours. w/o training at Prestwick 17/3/77.
G-APFL	707-436	17713	12/72	BEA/British Airtours. To Cargo Charter Co as 9Q-CRW 4/80. To Coastal A/w as 5X-CAU 1/81. wfu Entebbe 1/83.
G-APFO	707-436	17716	11/72	BEA/British Airtours. To Boeing at Kingman 3/81,stored, b/u.
G-ARRA	707-436	18411	11/76	British Airtours. wfu Stansted 11/80. To Europe Air Serv 3/81. To Coastal A/w as N4465D 8/83. w/o by fire Perpignan 10/83.
G-ARRC	707-436	18413	12/76	British Airtours. wfu Stansted 11/80. To Europe Air Service 3/81. To Coastal A/w as N4465C 8/83. b/u at Kinshasa 4/95.
G-ARWD	707-465	18372	1/73	BEA/British Airtours. Lse to Air Mauritius 4/79–4/81. To Boeing at Kingman 5/81, stored then b/u.
G-AVPB	707-336C	19843	4/81	British Airtours, lse from BA, ret 10/83.
G-AXXY	707-336B	20456	4/82	British Airtours, lse from BA, ret 3/84.
G-AYSL	707-321	17599	5/79	British Airtours, lse from Dan-Air, ret 10/79. Stored Lasham. To International Air Leases as N80703 11/79. To Kivu Air Cargo for spares 1/83, b/u at Lasham 2/83.
G-BGDP	737-236	21804	4/82	British Airtours, lse from BA. Ret '83.
G-BGDR	737-236	21805	4/82	British Airtours, lse from BA. Ret '83.
G-BGJE	737-236	22026	3/80	British Airtours, del new. Op by BA 10/82–3/84. Ret BA 3/88.
G-BGJF	737-236	22027	4/80	British Airtours, del new. Op by BA 1/82–4/85. T/f Caledonian 3/88. Ret to BA 11/88.
G-BGJG	737-236	22028	4/80	British Airtours, del new. Op by BA 1/82–4/85. T/f Caledonian 3/88. Ret to BA 11/88.
G-BGJH	737-236	22029	5/80	British Airtours, del new. Op by BA 9/83–5/86. T/f Caledonian 3/88. Ret to BA 11/88.
G-BGJI	737-236	22030	10/80	British Airtours, del new. Op by BA 5/83–4/85. Ret BA 11/87. To Caledonian 4/88. Ret BA.
G-BGJJ	737-236	22031	12/80	British Airtours, del new. Op by BA 82–3/84. Ret to BA 11/87.
G-BGJK	737-236	22032	3/81	British Airtours, del new. Ret to BA 9/83.
G-BGJL	737-236	22033	4/81	British Airtours, del new. Op by BA 9/83–'84. w/o Manchester 22/8/85.
G-BGJM	737-236	22034	4/81	British Airtours, del new. Ret to BA 9/83.
G-BHWE	737-204	22364	4/85	British Airtours. Lse fm Britannia A/w. Ret 3/87.
G-BKBT	737-2K2	20943	5/84	British Airtours. Lse fm Transavia. Ret 4/85.
G-BLEA	737-2K2	21397	5/84	British Airtours. Lse fm Transavia. Ret 3/85.
G-BMEC	737-2S3	21776	5/83	British Airtours. Lse fm Air Europe. Ret 4/84.
G-BMHG	737-2S3	21774	11/84	British Airtours. Lse fm Air Europe. Ret 4/85.
G-BMOR	737-2S3	21775	5/83	British Airtours. Lse fm Air Europe. Ret 4/84.
G-BMSM	737-2S3	22279	11/84	British Airtours. Lse fm Air Europe. Ret 4/85.
G-BRJP	737-2S3	22660	11/83	British Airtours. Lse fm Air Europe. Ret 4/85. Lse again from Air Europe 11/85–4/86.
G-DDDV	737-2S3	22633	11/84	British Airtours. Lse fm Air Europe. Ret 4/85. Lse again 11/85–4/86, 11/86–4/87 and from 10/87. T/f Caledonian 3/88, sub-lse to GB A/w but op by Caledonian. Ret to lessor 11/89.
G-IBTW	737-2Q8	21960	4/89	Caledonian. Lse fm BA/GPA. Ret to BA 11/89.
G-IBTZ	737-2U4	22576	4/89	Caledonian. Lse fm BA. To GB A/w 2/90.
G-BDXL	747-236	22305	3/84	British Airtours. Lse from BA, delivered ex-storage in USA. Ret to BA 11/84.
G-BLVE	747-2B4	21097	10/87	British Airtours. Lse from BA/MEA. Ret To MEA 5/90.
G-BMGS	747-283	20121	3/86	Ex-LN-AEO of SAS. Lse by British Airtours. To BA 10/87. Lse by Caledonian 6/89. Ret to BA 11/89.

(Continued)

British Airtours and Caledonian Airways fleets (continued)

Aircraft registration	Aircraft type	Constructor's number	Date	Notes
G-BMRJ	B757-236	24268	3/89	Caledonian, del. new. Op by BA 11/89–3/90. Ret to BA 11/90.
G-BPEA	B757-236	24370	3/89	Caledonian, delivered new. Lse to North American A/l 1/90–3/90. Lse to El Al 3/90–4/90. Lse Nationair 12/90–3/91. Op by BA 11/91–3/92. Lse to Nationair 12/92–3/93. Lse to LAPA 12/93–3/94 and 12/94–3/95. Ret to BA 11/95.
G-BPEB	B757-236	24371	4/89	Caledonian, delivered new. Lse to Nationair 12/90–4/91 and 12/91–4/92. Ret to BA 11/95.
G-BPEC	B757-236	24882	11/90	Caledonian, delivered new. Lse to Nationair 11/91–4/92 and 10/92–2/93. Ret BA 10/95.
G-BPEE	B757-236	25060	5/91	Caledonian, delivered new. Ret to BA 11/94.
G-BPEF	B757-236	24120	5/92	Ex-Air Europe G-BOHC. Op BA 10/93–4/94. Ret BA 10/95.
G-BPEH	B757-236	24121	5/92	Ex-Air Europe G-BNSE. Ret to lessor 4/95.
G-BHDH	DC10-30	47816	5/93	Lse from BA. Ret 10/95.
G-NIUK	DC10-30	46932	10/94	Lse from BA. Op by Caledonian for BA from 4/95. Returned to BA 3/97.
G-BBAE	TriStar-1	1083	4/85	British Airtours. T/f Caledonian 3/88. Lsd Worldways as C-FCXB 11/88–4/89 & 12/89–4/90. Conv to Series-100 6/90.
G-BBAF	TriStar-100	1093	4/91	Caledonian. Lse to Aer Lingus 6/96–9/96 & 5/97–10/97.
G-BBAH	TriStar-1	1101	5/90	Caledonian. Conv to Series-100 5/91.
G-BBAI	TriStar-1	1102	4/85	British Airtours. Ret BA 11/87. To Caledonian 3/88. Lse to Worldways as C-FCXJ 12/88–4/89 & 12/89–4/90.
G-BBAJ	TriStar-1	1106	4/82	British Airtours. Ret BA 11/86. To British Airtours 5/87. T/f Caledonian 3/88. Conv to Series-100 12/89.
G-BEAK	TriStar-50	1132	4/87	British Airtours. Ret BA 11/87.
G-BEAL	TriStar-1	1145	4/83	British Airtours. Ret BA 3/84. Conv to Series-50 1985. To British Airtours 5/87. T/f Caledonian 3/88, ret BA 4/89. Lse Caledonian 11/89–1/90, 3/90–10/92, 7/93, ret BA 10/93. Lse to Air Ops as SE-DPM. Lse Caledonian 5/96 as G-CEAP. To Classic Airways 11/97. wfu Stansted.
G-BEAM	TriStar-1	1146	4/82	British Airtours. Ret BA 11/84. Conv to Series-50 1985. To British Airtours 4/85–10/86 & 4/87, ret BA 3/88.
G-BFCB	TriStar-500	1159	5/83	Lse from RAF/BA. Ret to RAF as ZD949 11/83.
G-BFCE	TriStar-500	1168	6/85	Lse from RAF/BA. Ret to RAF as ZD952 9/85.
G-BHBP	TriStar-200	1211	5/81	British Airtours. Ret BA 3/82. To British Airtours 5/85, ret BA 10/85.
G-BHBR	TriStar-200	1212	5/81	British Airtours. Ret BA 12/81. To British Airtours 5/85,

British Airways Helicopters

British Airways Helicopters (BAH) was sold in 1986, ending almost forty years of ownership by BEA and British Airways of a subsidiary which was one of the leading pioneers of commercial helicopter operations anywhere in the world. Established by BEA as a small trials unit in the early post-war era, it was not until 1964 that a viable use was found for its passenger helicopters through the operation of flights between Penzance and the Isles of Scilly, now the longest running scheduled helicopter service anywhere. It was, however, the discovery of vast oil and gas reserves under the North Sea during the early 1960s which was the catalyst for transforming this small, loss-making unit into a thriving subsidiary, enabling it finally to reach profitability. The civilian helicopter had at last found a useful role in what is a very challenging environment, and a period of explosive growth soon followed which led to a fleet of almost forty helicopters in service by the early 1980s.

BEA formed its Helicopter Experimental Unit in July 1947 based at Yeovil in Somerset with a fleet of three Sikorsky S-51 and two Bell 47B-3 helicopters imported from America. Its role was to find out whether the helicopter had any practical commercial uses and if so to develop them. The initial helicopters were obviously too small and expensive to carry passengers at a profit in competition with fixed-wing airliners, but experimental scheduled services were flown to assess their operational viability. Trial mail-carrying services were also operated in Scotland and southern England and, although demonstrating great reliability, were soon abandoned as being uneconomical. Also, by 1956, after trying five different routes, attempts to operate scheduled passenger services were given up to await the development of larger and faster helicopters in the future. Various large types were developed and flown during the late 1950s such as the twin-rotor Bristol 173 and the Fairey Rotodyne, but none of them were

BEA's Helicopter Experimental Unit was established in 1947 and for many years flew a variety of early designs as it attempted to establish whether the helicopter could be developed for commercial use. This Bristol 171 was one of the earliest types flown but proved to be too small and costly to operate. (British Airways Archive)

A Sikorsky S-61N at Penzance Heliport. This civil version of the US Navy's Sea King enabled BEA Helicopters to establish viable commercial helicopter operations on scheduled services from Penzance to the Isles of Scilly and to support oil exploration work in the North Sea. Some of the original S-61Ns are still in service today with the now independent British International Helicopters. (BRITISH AIRWAYS ARCHIVE)

LEFT: Six 44-seat BV-234 Chinooks entered service with British Airways Helicopters during 1981/2 at a time when oil exploration support work was at its peak. Unfortunately, despite their impressive range and payload capabilities the Chinooks proved to be too big and expensive to operate and were sold off from 1985. (MAP)

commercially viable. So BEA's Helicopter Experimental Unit was left to find whatever work it could by operating passenger charters and lifting various cargoes whilst it waited for helicopter technology to mature. This began to happen in 1964 when the Unit, which was renamed BEA Helicopters (BEAH), took delivery of two Sikorsky S-61Ns, the helicopter which would dramatically change its fortunes.

The S-61Ns were acquired to operate what has proved to be the ideal helicopter route, from Penzance in Cornwall to the Isles of Scilly, which are twenty-eight miles west of Land's End in the Atlantic Ocean. BEA wanted to withdraw the three ancient Dragon Rapides from its Land's End–Isles of Scilly service, but the lack of a suitable airfield on the islands for other aircraft types led to a bold decision to employ helicopters on scheduled services from a purpose-built heliport at Penzance. The first S-61N entered service in May 1964, initially from St Just Airfield at Land's End until the heliport opened in September. The service was immediately popular and passenger numbers soared. Even though traffic is very seasonal with a huge increase in summer passenger numbers, it has continued to be operated year-round and has been flown by the S-61Ns ever since, with the exception of a few short periods when other types have substituted.

The Sikorsky S-61N which made this route such a success was developed from the US Navy's SH-3 Sea King anti-submarine warfare helicopter of the late 1950s. The features which enabled it to become the first really practical large commercial helicopter are its 26–30 passenger seating, 400-mile range, twin-turbine powerplants, and an amphibious capability which made it particularly suited to its next and most important role, that of oil rig support.

Soon after introducing the Isles of Scilly service BEAH began to deploy its new S-61Ns in support of the flourishing search for oil and gas under the North Sea. This initially meant supplying rigs with personnel and equipment from a base at Beccles near Lowestoft on the East Coast from 1964, but as the search moved further north, additional bases were established at Aberdeen in 1967 and at Sumburgh in the Shetland Islands in 1971. This work, which is still carried out today by some of the same helicopters, involves difficult and dangerous flying in a frequently hostile environment, with some of the worst weather conditions experienced by aviators anywhere on a daily basis. As a result many new procedures have been developed over the years to ensure that operations to and from the tiny, isolated rigs 150 miles out to sea are as safe and reliable as possible.

British Airways therefore inherited a thriving and also a profitable helicopter operation in 1974. Seven S-61Ns were being flown on oil support contracts and the Isles of Scilly service. A twelve-passenger Bell 212 was also in use and a single four-

seater Augusta-Bell Jet Ranger was based at the Gatwick headquarters for charter work. British Airways Helicopters (BAH) was at the beginning of a period of rapid growth, as the search for oil under the North Sea had taken on a new urgency following conflict in the Middle East which had led to a worldwide shortage of oil. By 1978 the S-61N fleet had grown to twenty-three, mostly based at Aberdeen and Sumburgh, and two 18-seat Sikorsky S-58Ts were also in service. However, this was not yet the peak as a much larger long-range helicopter was soon to arrive to serve the Brent oilfield from Aberdeen. Six Boeing-Vertol BV-234 Chinooks capable of carrying forty-four passengers were ordered at a cost of £6m each and began entering service in July 1981. They could fly the 250–300 miles from Aberdeen to the Brent rigs in less than three hours, thereby avoiding a much longer two-sector trip via Sumburgh. This in turn reduced the number of S-61Ns required at Sumburgh. Several other helicopter types were also introduced to take advantage of their particular size and range characteristics to service different oil company contracts.

By early 1982 BAH was operating a fleet of thirty-six helicopters:

British Airways Helicopters fleet – 1982		
Boeing-Vertol BV234 Chinook	44 seats	5 (plus 1 on order)
Sikorsky S-61N	24 seats	23
Westland WG-30	17 seats	1 (plus 1 on order)
Bell 212	12 seats	2
Sikorsky SDHC-76A	12 seats	4
Augusta-Bell Jet Ranger	4 seats	1
Total		**36**

By 1982, Aberdeen had become one of the busiest airports in Europe with helicopters of BAH and other operators plus many fixed-wing support aircraft constantly arriving and departing. From then on, however, business began a slow decline as the level of exploration for new sources of oil and gas was falling. Production work from existing platforms continued, but as this is much less labour intensive a smaller level of helicopter support was required. The Chinooks became too big and expensive to operate on such work and began to be sold off in 1985, replaced by three new long-range Super Pumas fitted with twenty-one seats. Overseas contracts were also sought as a way of utilising some of the excess capacity.

Mention should also be made of other vitally important work which BAH has undertaken. From 1971 to 1979, BEAH/BAH held a contract to provide a S-61N and crew on twenty-four-hour standby at Aberdeen Airport for Air-Sea Rescue flights over the North Sea and northern Scotland. This was followed by another similar contract at Sumburgh from 1979 to 1983. Many difficult and courageous rescues were performed and many lives were saved as a result.

In September 1986, British Airways sold its Helicopter subsidiary to the Mirror Group of

Newspapers which subsequently renamed it British International Helicopters. The company has continued to serve in the same markets as its predecessor and today still operates many of the original Sikorsky S-61Ns of BEA Helicopters which date back to 1965!

British Airways Helicopters fleet

Aircraft registration	Aircraft type	Constructor's number	Date	Notes
G-AWGU	J.Ranger	8044	4/68	Sold 9/84.
G-ASNL	S-61N	61220	1/64	Ditched in North Sea 11/3/83. To USA for possible rebuild.
G-ATBJ	S-61N	61269	4/65	To BIH 9/86.
G-ATFM	S-61N	61270	5/65	To BIH 9/86.
G-AWFX	S-61N	61216	6/68	To BIH 9/86.
G-AYOM	S-61N	61143	1/71	To BIH 9/86.
G-AYOY	S-61N	61476	3/71	To BIH 9/86.
G-AZCF	S-61N	61488	8/71	To Shell Brunei 3/82.
G-BBUD	S-61N	61711	12/73	To BIH 9/86.
G-BCEA	S-61N	61721	6/74	To BIH 9/86.
G-BCEB	S-61N	61454	10/74	To BIH 9/86.
G-BDDA	S-61N	61746	7/75	To Aérospatiale 7/84.
G-BDES	S-61N	61747	8/75	To BIH 9/86.
G-BDKI	S-61N	61755	2/76	To Aérospatiale 7/84.
G-BEDI	S-61N	61754	10/76	To Aérospatiale 7/84.
G-BEIC	S-61N	61222	12/76	To BIH 9/86.
G-BEID	S-61N	61223	2/78	To BIH 9/86.
G-BEJL	S-61N	61224	6/77	To BIH 9/86.
G-BEON	S-61N	61770	6/77	W/o in sea near St Mary's, Isles of Scilly 16/7/83.
G-BEOO	S-61N	61771	8/77	To BIH 9/86.
G-BEWL	S-61N	61769	7/77	To BIH 9/86.
G-BEWM	S-61N	61772	9/77	To BIH 9/86.
G-BFFJ	S-61N	61777	2/78	To BIH 9/86.
G-BFFK	S-61N	61778	3/78	To BIH 9/86.
G-BFPF	S-61N	61490	6/78	Leased from Court Helicopters until 1981.
G-BCLN	S-58T	585139	1/74	Sold 1981.
G-BCLO	S-58T	581658	1/74	Sold 1981.
G-BAFN	Bell 212	30550	11/78	Sold 9/83.
G-BFJB	Bell 212	30881	10/78	Sold 9/83.
G-BFJG	Bell 212	30878	9/78	To Irish Helicopters as EI-BFH 9/78.
G-BHYB	S-76A	760079	3/81	To BIH 9/86.
G-BIAV	S-76A	760110	10/81	To BIH 9/86.
G-BIAW	S-76A	760111	6/81	To BIH 9/86.
G-BZAC	S-76A	760018	5/80	To BIH 9/86.
G-BISN	BV234	MJ005	6/81	To BIH 9/86.
G-BISO	BV234	MJ002	9/81	Ditched North Sea 2/5/84. To Columbia Helicopters 1985.
G-BISP	BV234	MJ006	11/81	To BIH 9/86.
G-BISR	BV234	MJ003	6/82	To BIH 9/86.
G-BJAC	BV234	MJ001	2/81	To Columbia Helicopters 1/85.
G-BWFC	BV234	MJ004	6/81	To BIH 9/86.
G-BIWY	WG-30	001	1/82	To BIH 9/86.
G-BKGD	WG-30	002	10/82	To BIH 9/86.
G-OGAS	WG-30	008	6/83	To BIH 9/86.
G-BKZE	AS332L	2102	11/83	To BIH 9/86.
G-BKZG	AS332L	2106	12/83	To BIH 9/86.
G-BKZH	AS332L	2107	1/84	To BIH 9/86.

Brymon Airways

Brymon Airways is a wholly-owned subsidiary of British Airways, but operates with complete independence under agreements which are similar to those of the franchise partner airlines.

Brymon was founded in 1972 by sports journalist Bill Bryce and racing driver Chris Amon (hence the name Brymon) to provide services from its Plymouth base. A network soon built up from both Plymouth and Newquay to many UK destinations including Gatwick, Heathrow, the Channel Islands and the Isles of Scilly. The Brittany region of north-western France was also served. Aircraft in the fleet included the Twin Otter and a Herald, later replaced by de Havilland Canada Dash-7s, an ideal aircraft for operations from Plymouth's short runway. Brymon also deployed Dash-7s to Aberdeen for oil exploration support charters, where two are still operated today by a subsidiary, Brymon Offshore Air Charter (BOAC!).

Although British Airways acquired a shareholding during the 1980s, full ownership came about in 1993 when Brymon European Airways, the short-lived product of an October 1992 merger between Brymon Airways and Birmingham European Airways, was split up. British Airways acquired Brymon along with Plymouth Airport while the

British Airways bought Brymon Airways in 1993 and quickly set about expanding its network of UK domestic and cross-Channel services. Four de Havilland Canada Dash-7s served in British Airways Express colours until 1996 and although ideal for operations from Plymouth's short runway, they were too slow and uncompetitive for most of the airline's routes and were replaced with additional Dash-8s in 1996. Two Dash-7s have however been retained to operate oil support charters from Aberdeen with a Brymon subsidiary called BOAC!

Brymon Airways has standardised on operating the fast and modern turboprop Dash-8. By 1999 fifteen stretched Series-300 were in service the first of which, G-BRYI, was photographed in British Airways Express markings at Jersey in May 1995.

G-BRYW seen shortly after delivery wearing Polish Cockerel of Lowicz artwork was one of eight new DHC-8-300Qs acquired by Brymon during 1998. This latest version of the Dash-8 is fitted with a cabin Noise and Vibration Suppression System and new interiors to improve passenger comfort levels. (JOHN M. DIBBS)

Birmingham-based network went to Maersk Air. Brymon's services began operating as British Airways Express flights in August 1993 and its fleet of DHC Dash-7s and -8s were repainted into BA livery. Brymon at that time was operating two DHC Dash-8-100s and two stretched Dash-8-300s on its expanding scheduled service network, and based one aircraft at Newcastle from October 1993 to operate twice-daily Paris CDG services. The growth in passenger numbers on Brymon's schedules under its BA Express banner was such that an order for five additional Dash-8-300s was placed in January 1996 to replace three Dash-7s and two Dash-8-100s.

Summer 1996 saw a big increase in services through Brymon's newly established hub at Bristol, from where its enlarged fleet served Edinburgh and

Brymon Airways fleet

Aircraft registration	Aircraft type	Constructor's number	Date	Notes
G-BRYA	DHC-7	62	8/93	Transferred to 'BOAC' 4/96.
G-BRYB	DHC-7	66	8/93	To DHC 8/96 as C-FYXT. Stored Calgary.
G-BRYC	DHC-7	54	8/93	To DHC 8/96 as C-FYXV. Stored Calgary.
G-BRYD	DHC-7	109	8/93	Transferred to 'BOAC' 4/96.
G-BRYE	DHC-7	50	8/93	To Arkia as 4X-AHJ 5/94.
G-BOAY	DHC-7	112		White, Brymon t/t. To 9M-TAL 11/95.
G-BRYG	DHC-8-102	237	8/93	wfu Plymouth 4/96. To TransTravel as PH-TTA 10/96.
G-BRYH	DHC-8-102	241	8/93	wfu Plymouth 4/96. To TransTravel as PH-TTB 2/98.
G-BRYI	DHC-8-311	256	8/93	
G-BRYJ	DHC-8-311	319	8/93	
G-BRYK	DHC-8-311	284	96	Returned to Bombardier Inc. 2/99.
G-BRYM	DHC-8-311	305	3/96	wfu 2/99 at Plymouth.
G-BRYO	DHC-8-311	311	4/96	
G-BRYP	DHC-8-311	315	4/96	
G-BRYR	DHC-8-311	336	5/96	
G-BRYS	DHC-8-311	296	5/97	
G-BRYT	DHC-8-311	334	3/97	
G-BRYU	DHC-8-311	458	4/98	
G-BRYV	DHC-8-311	462	4/98	
G-BRYW	DHC-8-311	474	6/98	
G-BRYX	DHC-8-311	508	10/98	
G-BRYY	DHC-8-311	519	12/98	
G-BRYZ	DHC-8-311	464	10/98	
G-NVSA	DHC-8-311	451	11/98	
G-NVSB	DHC-8-311	517	1/99	
G-BXPZ	DHC-8-311	422	3/98	ex-OE-LTE Tyrolean A/w. Leased as back-up aircraft, white with BA markings. Ret 6/99.

Glasgow five times per day, Newcastle–Aberdeen twice, Paris CDG three times as well as Guernsey, Jersey, Plymouth and Cork. Five of the seven Dash-8s were based at Bristol for this work, plus one at Newcastle and one at Plymouth for the four-per-day Heathrow services. Another two Dash-8s arrived for summer 1997 and frequencies on the Bristol–Edinburgh and Glasgow services increased to six a day. After many years of operating to Heathrow, the Plymouth/Newquay services transferred to Gatwick at the end of March 1997, where extra slots were available for a frequency increase to five a day.

Figures for the 1997–8 financial year illustrate just how quickly Brymon was growing. Passenger numbers increased by 30% over the previous year and the airline's profit was £3.6m from a £38m turnover. Growth continued during 1998, helped by British Airways Regional's decision to phase out its fleet of ATPs and concentrate on operating routes which could sustain 737/A319-sized aircraft. Brymon benefited from this move by taking over the Aberdeen to Birmingham and Manchester routes from May 1998 followed by some Manchester to Edinburgh and Glasgow services later in the year. Additional aircraft were required for this expansion, so in March 1998 Brymon placed a £60m order for eight DHC Dash-8Q-300s. These latest Dash-8s came equipped with new interiors and a Noise Suppression System (Dash-8Q = quiet!) to reduce interior noise levels and took the fleet total to fifteen by early 1999.

New routes from the spring of 1999 were Newcastle to Belfast served three times per day plus Newcastle to Copenhagen and Aberdeen to Oslo, both once a day.

To accommodate such continuing growth Brymon will introduce a fleet of new regional jets from 2000. Seven 50-seat Embraer EMB-145s are on order and options for another fourteen held, which can be delivered as 35-seat ERJ-135s or 70-seat ERJ-170s as required. They will initially be used to upgrade services from the Bristol hub and to introduce flights from Birmingham under contract to British Airways.

Cityflyer Express

Cityflyer Express pioneered British Airways' franchise partner concept, becoming the first airline to implement such an agreement, in August 1993.

The origins of Cityflyer date back to 1984 when Connectair began operations from Gatwick with a fleet of Shorts 330 and SD-360s. Scheduled services to Antwerp, Dusseldorf, Rotterdam and from Manchester to Rotterdam commenced, along with night mail services. During October 1988 Connectair took on the identity of Air Europe Express, becoming part of the rapidly expanding International Leisure Group to act as a feeder to the extensive scheduled service network of Air Europe at Gatwick. Troubled times lay ahead, however, as the entire International Leisure Group collapsed in March 1991 taking Air Europe Express with it into liquidation. Fortunately all was not lost, as a management buy-out resurrected the commuter airline as Euroworld, which restarted services with four Shorts SD-360s operating from Gatwick to Antwerp, Guernsey and Rotterdam, the first being a Gatwick to Guernsey flight on 1 July 1991. A name change to Cityflyer Express took place in February 1992 and services on the ex-Dan-Air route from Gatwick to Newcastle commenced with new Franco/Italian-built ATR-42s in November of that year, the first time this type of aircraft had been operated by a UK airline.

From 1 August 1993, Cityflyer's aircraft began to appear in British Airways Express colours, operating under BA service numbers and with crews wearing BA uniforms as the new five-year franchise agreement was implemented. The fleet comprised three 48-seat ATR-42s, with another two on order, and four 36-seat Shorts SD-360s. As the Gatwick-based route network expanded and passenger numbers increased, orders were placed for an initial two 66-seat ATR-72s for delivery by January 1995 and during October of that year the last Shorts SD-360s finally left the fleet. In addition to the scheduled services, an extensive programme of summer weekend charters to Jersey is flown, summer 1995 for example seeing Cityflyer

Cityflyer was the pioneer of British Airways' highly successful franchise partner concept. Since signing up in August 1993 the Gatwick-based carrier's fleet of Shorts 3-60s and ATR-42s has grown rapidly and now comprises twelve ATR-42/72 turboprops and seven 110-seat RJ-100 regional jets. The ATR-42s are gradually being phased out as they are now too small for the airline's busy routes.

During July 1999 Cityflyer inaugurated its thirteenth route from Gatwick for British Airways, a twice-daily service to Nice using 100-seat RJ-100s. One of these, G-BZAU with Irish 'Colum' tail-art, was photographed approaching Gatwick during April 1999.

services operating from East Midlands, Luton, Manchester, Manston and Shannon.

By the time Cityflyer introduced its fourth ATR-72 and seventh ATR-42 in March 1996 the route network radiating from Gatwick had developed considerably, expanding to such an extent that British Airways was by then the only airline holding more Gatwick slots. Cities served were Amsterdam, Antwerp, Cologne, Cork, Dublin, Dusseldorf, Guernsey, Jersey, Leeds, Newcastle and Rotterdam. Passenger numbers continued to increase steadily, so

Cityflyer placed an order for two British Aerospace/Avro RJ-100s for delivery by April 1997, plus options for another two. Initially used for Amsterdam and Dublin services, the options were soon confirmed and a fifth RJ was ordered for June 1998 delivery, by which time six ATR-42s and five ATR-72s were also flown.

Recent route changes have seen Cityflyer ATRs serving Gatwick–Bremen from March 1997 in place of Deutsche BA, Luxembourg introduced with three daily ATRs in May 1997 and Zürich with three

Cityflyer Express fleet

Aircraft registration	Aircraft type	Constructor's number	Date	Notes
G-BUEA	ATR-42	268	5/92	
G-BUEB	ATR-42	304	6/92	
G-BVEC	ATR-42	356	4/93	
G-BVED	ATR-42	315	11/93	
G-BVEF	ATR-42	331	4/94	
G-BXEG	ATR-42	329	4/95	
G-BXEH	ATR-42	306	3/96	Ex-Lao Aviation, leased. Ret to lessor 1/98.
G-BVTJ	ATR-72	342	1/95	
G-BVTK	ATR-72	357	10/94	
G-BWTL	ATR-72	441	12/95	
G-BWTM	ATR-72	470	3/96	
G-BXTN	ATR-72	483	10/97	
G-BYTP	ATR-72	473	4/99	Leased from British World.
G-BXAR	Avro RJ-100	E3298	3/97	
G-BXAS	Avro RJ-100	E3301	5/97	
G-BZAT	Avro RJ-100	E3320	1/98	
G-BZAU	Avro RJ-100	E3328	6/98	
G-BZAV	Avro RJ-100	E3331	7/98	
G-BZAW	Avro RJ-100	E3354	7/99	
G-BZAX	Avro RJ-100	E3356	8/99	
G-	Avro RJ-100	E	(2000)	
G-BVMX	Shorts 360	SH3751	8/93	To Gill A/w 11/95.
G-BVMY	Shorts 360	SH3755	8/93	To Loganair 11/95.
G-BWMW	Shorts 360	SH3750	3/94	To Air Kenya as 5Y-BKP 5/95.
G-BWMZ	Shorts 360	SH3717	3/94	ex-G-BNFA. To Air Kenya 11/95.
OY-SVW	Jetstream 41	41047		Lse fm Sun Air 1-3/98 for Leeds–Gatwick service.
OY-SVS	Jetstream 41	41014		As above 3/98. Operated last Leeds service 27/3.
TF-ELJ	ATR-42	118		Lse from Islandsflug 4/98-6/98.

RJ-100s daily in place of EuroGatwick 737s from March 1998. Leeds, however was dropped from the network at the end of March 1998 because of poor yields and the need to free up slots for other services. The final Leeds to Gatwick service was actually flown by a Sun-Air Jetstream 41 which had been wet-leased to operate the route on behalf of Cityflyer from January 1998 due to a shortage of capacity. An ATR-42 was leased from Icelandic airline Islandsflug from April to June 1998 when the delivery of RJ-100 G-BZAV took the fleet to five 102-seat RJ-100s, six 48-seat ATR-42s and five 66-seat ATR-72s. An order for two more RJ-100s was confirmed during July 1998 followed by another in April 1999 taking the total to eight.

Towards the end of 1998 an agreement for British Airways to acquire Cityflyer for £75m was announced. If approved and implemented, Cityflyer will continue to operate as before, independently managed like Brymon.

In July 1999 Cityflyer began operating its thirteenth route on behalf of British Airways, a twice-daily RJ-100 service from Gatwick to Nice. Cityflyer then had seven RJ-100s in service and had replaced one of its smaller ATR-42s with a leased ATR-72. However, with passenger numbers growing continually and extra slots virtually unobtainable at Gatwick, the airline is expected to outgrow its current fleet once again and the acquisition of larger aircraft in the near future will be the only way to accommodate the extra demand.

Deutsche BA

Ownership of what is now Germany's second-largest scheduled service airline began in March 1992 with the acquisition by British Airways and a consortium of German banks of a small German regional airline. Delta Air Regionalflugverkehr had been established back in April 1978, initially flying a Twin Otter on commuter services from its Friedrichshafen base to Stuttgart and Zürich. By 1992 Delta Air was 40% owned by Swiss regional Crossair and operated a fleet of nine Saab 340s and one Dornier 228 on a scheduled service network of twenty-one German domestic and five international routes.

British Airways' interest stemmed from an evaluation of the likely effects of European Union deregulation and a desire to retain and expand its foothold in the German domestic market, the largest in Europe and with some of the highest yielding routes anywhere. Following from the reunification of East and West Germany in 1990, British Airways was about to lose its rights to operate the Berlin-based domestic routes known as the Internal German Services (IGS) which had been flown since the end of World War Two. The acquisition of an established German carrier provided an ideal base to build upon to achieve these aims and Delta Air was renamed Deutsche BA (DBA) in May 1992. During October of that year British Airways stopped operating its remaining Internal German Services and transferred the routes to DBA. Initially the aim was to transform the reborn airline from a small regional carrier into a viable low-cost competitor for Lufthansa, offering a good two-class service on domestic and international routes with a fleet of new and leased 737-300s, seven of which had arrived on lease from Maersk Air by October 1992. A new colour scheme based on British Airways' but incorporating Germany's national colours was also introduced.

From its Munich base the new DBA expanded rapidly, adding five Fokker F100s on wet-lease from TAT in March 1994 and the first of five new Saab 2000s in March 1995. Routes flown during the summer 1995 season included Berlin Tegel (TXL) to Madrid and Munich, Munich to Gatwick and Paris CDG, Munich–Berlin–Stockholm, Stuttgart–Berlin–Oslo, and Stuttgart to Lyons, Nice and Venice. Gatwick–Bremen was introduced with Saab 2000s during winter 1995, replacing British Airways'

Deutsche BA disposed of its Fokker F100 and Saab 2000 fleets in 1997 to standardise on the Boeing 737-300, 18 of which were operating by early 1999. D-ADBC was photographed at Dusseldorf in September 1997 in the airline's 'interim' colour scheme.

British Airways began its purchase of a German subsidiary in 1992 and by April 1998 had acquired the entire shareholding. During that time Deutsche BA has grown to become Germany's second-largest airline with a large share of the important domestic market and a growing international presence.

Heathrow–Bremen service. Another Gatwick route, to Berlin TXL was introduced with F100s during January 1996, and soon DBA was flying to twenty-seven cities in twelve European countries.

Although DBA had by 1996 become the second-largest scheduled service airline in Germany, with over two million passengers and 35% of the domestic market, it was showing few signs of becoming profitable with its diverse fleet of nine 737-300s, five Fokker 100s, five Saab 2000s and two Saab 340s. Major restructuring was required and began with an agreement in October 1996 for Regional Airlines of France to acquire DBA's Saab 2000 fleet and ten routes flown by the turboprops from Bremen, Friedrichshafen and Stuttgart. The remaining Saab 340s were sold and DBA decided to return its five Fokker 100s by the end of 1997 and standardise on the operation of a single type of aircraft, the 737-300, with the fleet to double in size from nine to eighteen. DBA's new strategy was to concentrate on achieving profitability through the restructuring of its remaining operations with the expansion of German domestic scheduled services given overall priority. The unprofitable international network would be eliminated, with the exception of flights to Gatwick which feed valuable traffic to and from the British Airways network. However, the Gatwick–Bremen

route was transferred to Cityflyer Express in March 1997 after the final Saab 2000 had left the fleet and Berlin to Gatwick was dropped during October 1997, leaving services from Hamburg and Munich to Gatwick as the only remaining international routes. Some night postal and weekend charter flights were also retained.

The last Fokker 100 left DBA in January 1998 and by March, eighteen 737-300s were in service, all of which were fitted with a single-class interior with 136 leather seats, replacing the previous and more expensive two-class configuration. With the arrival of the new 737-300s during 1997–8, German domestic scheduled services increased substantially. Eight per day Munich to Cologne and Hamburg services commenced in January 1997 and frequencies were increased from Berlin to Cologne, Dusseldorf, Munich and Stuttgart, but DBA's most difficult challenge was to enter the Lufthansa-dominated Frankfurt market. An attempt began in November 1997 with the introduction of eight daily services to Munich, but as the result of poor loads and low yields, all were withdrawn by summer 1998.

DBA took part in the 'Utopia' new corporate-identity launch event on 14 June 1997 with 737 D-ADBE displaying its *Bauhaus* tail at Munich, one of four designs from different regions of Germany so far unveiled. Once again DBA has adopted a variation of the British Airways corporate identity, replacing the blue undersides with black and including three tail images which are unique to the German airline.

During July 1997 British Airways purchased another 16% of DBA from a Munich bank, taking its holding to a controlling 65% and by April 1998 had acquired the entire shareholding. Further integration into the British Airways network took place during summer 1998 with DBA contracted to operate services from Gatwick to Frankfurt and Rome. Also during 1998, DBA's growth continued through the introduction of additional frequencies between Munich and Cologne, and on other German domestic routes.

Having achieved an impressive 40% market share on its seven German domestic routes by 1999, DBA began to look internationally once again. Code-sharing services linking the networks of **one**world partners have been introduced: from March 1999 Munich–Hamburg–Helsinki with Finnair and Munich to Madrid with Iberia from June 1999. A similar code-share with LOT may also be introduced.

Deutsche BA fleet

Aircraft registration	Aircraft type	Constructor's number	Date	Notes
D-CDIA	Saab 340	071	3/92	To Air Ostrava 12/95 OK-REK.
D-CDIB	Saab 340	075	3/92	To Andesmar, Argentina as LV-WON 2/96.
D-CDIC	Saab 340	116	3/92	To Air Nelson 11/96 ZK-NLT.
D-CDID	Saab 340	124	3/92	To Air Nelson 11/96 ZK-NLQ.
D-CDIE	Saab 340	026	3/92	To Crossair HB-AHF 4/97. To Hazleton A/l 10/97.
D-CDIF	Saab 340	038	3/92	To Crossair HB-AHG 4/97. To Hazleton A/l 11/97.
D-CDIG	Saab 340	040	3/92	To Chautauqua as N40CQ 7/95. (Continued)

Deutsche BA fleet (continued)

Aircraft registration	Aircraft type	Constructor's number	Date	Notes
D-CDIH	Saab 340	043	3/92	To Chautauqua as N43CQ 6/95.
D-CDIJ	Saab 340	121	3/92	To Chautauqua as N121CQ 8/95.
D-ADSA	Saab2000	013	3/95	To Regional A/l 5/97 F-GTSA.
D-ADSB	Saab2000	014	4/95	To Regional A/l 5/97 F-GTSB.
D-ADSC	Saab2000	016	5/95	To Regional A/l 5/97 F-GTSC.
D-ADSD	Saab2000	023	10/95	To Regional A/l 5/97 F-GTSD.
D-ADSE	Saab2000	025	10/95	To Regional A/l 5/97 F-GTSE.
D-ADFA	Fokker 100	11307	3/94	Lse fm TAT ex-F-GIOB. Ret to Air Liberté 1/98 F-GNLK.
D-ADFB	Fokker 100	11311	3/94	Lse fm TAT ex-F-GIOC. Ret to Air Liberté 9/97 F-GNLH.
D-ADFC	Fokker 100	11315	3/94	Lse fm TAT ex-F-GIOD. Ret to Air Liberté 10/97 F-GNLI.
D-ADFD	Fokker 100	11344	3/94	Lse fm TAT ex-F-GIOE. Ret to Air Liberté 12/97 F-GNLJ.
D-ADFE	Fokker 100	11363	4/94	Lse fm TAT ex-F-GIOF. Ret to Air Liberté 4/97 F-GNLG.
D-ADBA	B737-3L9	26441	6/92	Lse fm Maersk as OY-MAL. Regd D-ADBA.
D-ADBB	B737-3L9	26440	6/92	Lse fm Maersk as OY-MAK. Regd D-ADBB 12/92.To Frontier A/L as N310FL 4/99.
D-ADBC	B737-3L9	26442	6/92	Lse fm Maersk as OY-MAM. Regd D-ADBC 12/92. To Cronus A/L as SX-BGI 3/99.
D-ADBD	B737-3L9	27061	9/92	Lse fm Maersk as OY-MAN. Regd D-ADBD 10/92.
D-ADBE	B737-3L9	24569	10/92	Lse fm Maersk. Ret Maersk 10/98 as OY-MMD.
D-ADBF	B737-3L9	24571	10/92	Lse fm Maersk, ex-OY-MMF. Ret Maersk 10/98, lse to Istanbul A/l as TC-IAE 11/98.
D-ADBG	B737-3L9	25125	10/92	Lse fm Maersk, ex-OY-MMW.
D-ADBH	B737-3L9	27336	1/96	Lse fm Maersk, ex-OY-MAO.
D-ADBI	B737-3L9	27337	4/96	Lse fm Maersk, ex-OY-MAP.
D-ADBJ	B737-3L9	27833	12/96	Lse fm Maersk. Ret 1/98. To GB A/w 3/98 as G-OGBD.
D-ADBK	B737-31S	29055	8/97	
D-ADBL	B737-31S	29056	9/97	
D-ADBM	B737-31S	29057	10/97	
D-ADBN	B737-31S	29058	11/97	
D-ADBO	B737-31S	29059	12/97	
D-ADBP	B737-31S	29060	12/97	
D-ADBQ	B737-31S	29099	1/98	
D-ADBR	B737-31S	21900	1/98	
D-ADBS	B737-31S	29116	3/98	
D-ADBT	B737-31S	29264	9/98	
D-ADBU	B737-31S	29265	9/98	
D-ADBV	B737-31S	29266	2/99	
D-ADBW	B737-31S	29267	2/99	
D-ADBX	B737-36Q	28659	5/97	To BA Regional as G-ODUS 3/98.

Go

British Airways established a new subsidiary airline during 1998 to operate low-cost, no-frills services from Stansted Airport to European destinations. The airline, known as 'go', is run as a separate stand-alone business and was set up to capitalise on a developing market for low-cost flights offering little more than basic transportation, often using secondary airports. The first service was from Stansted to Rome Ciampino Airport on 22 May 1998 using the first of seven leased Boeing 737-300s. Flights to Milan Malpensa, Copenhagen and Lisbon followed by July as more 737s were delivered and a domestic service from Stansted to Edinburgh began with three flights

British Airways' autonomous subsidiary 'go' began low-cost scheduled services from Stansted in May 1998, initially to Rome with the first of seven leased 737-300s. By the end of the year seven European cities were served, including Munich where G-IGOI was photographed.

'go' fleet				
Aircraft registration	Aircraft type	Constructor's number	Date	Notes
G-IGOA	737-3Y0	24678	8/98	Ex-EI-BZK.
G-IGOC	737-3Y0	24546	5/98	Ex-EI-BZH.
G-IGOE	737-3Y0	24547	5/98	Ex-EI-BZI.
G-IGOF	737-3Q8	24698	6/98	Ex-PK-GWF.
G-IGOG	737-3Y0	23927	9/98	Ex-F-GLLE Air Liberté.
G-IGOH	737-3Y0	23926	11/98	Ex-F-GLLD Air Liberté.
G-IGOI	737-33A	24092	11/98	Ex-G-OBMD BMA.
G-IGOJ	737-36N	28872	11/98	Delivered new.
G-IGOK	737-36N	28594	4/99	
G-IGOL	737-36N	28596	6/99	
G-IGOM	737-36N	28599	99	
G-IGOP	737-36N	28602	99	
G-IGOR	737-36N	28606	99	

per day on 12 August. By the end of 1998, 'go' was also serving Bologna, Munich and Venice. Following from its initial success, 'go' announced in October 1998 that it would lease another eight 737-300s to take its fleet to thirteen by 2000 as more routes were added. During the early summer of 1999 'go' introduced services from Stansted to Malaga, Faro, Bilbao and Madrid.

(2) Mergers or take-overs

British Caledonian Airways (BCAL)

The disappearance of an airline is always a sad and emotional event, especially to the people most directly affected, those who worked for it. BCAL's absorption into British Airways during 1987–8 was a prime example of this all-too-frequent occurrence in the history of British airlines, a period when the employees exhibited a fierce loyalty and dedication to the airline which they had built up over many years, but which was about to become just a part of their long-time arch rival. BCAL's disappearance was also controversial because it represented the end of several governments' policies of positive encouragement for a strong and independent British 'second force' airline. Perhaps the time had not yet come for such an airline and BCAL faltered, leaving other thriving independents such as British Midland and Virgin Atlantic to pick up the mantle of providing serious competition for British Airways. One very positive development since 1988, however, has been British Airways' heavy investment to turn Gatwick Airport into a major, scheduled service hub, building on the foundations originally laid by BCAL.

BCAL had existed for almost eighteen years prior to the merger, but could trace its roots back much further through the two airlines, BUA and Caledonian, which came together to create it.

BUA – British United Airlines

By 1970 BUA had grown to become the largest privately-owned airline in Europe, achieved in the ten years since its formation in 1960 from an amalgamation of Airwork and Hunting Clan, and their many subsidiaries, mostly post-war companies but including some which could trace their ancestry back to the early 1930s. BUA was a pioneering airline; for example it was first to order One-Elevens, buying ten in 1961, and later purchased VC-10s for its South American routes. During 1970 a modern fleet of four VC-10s, eight One-Eleven-200s and five One-Eleven-500s operated an extensive Gatwick-based network of UK domestic and European routes, long-haul services to South America and Africa, Inclusive Tour (IT) charters and scheduled cargo services. Unfortunately, BUA was also struggling to reach the size necessary to compete effectively with the State-owned carriers.

Caledonian Airways

Caledonian commenced operating worldwide charters in 1961 with an ex-Sabena DC-7C. By 1964 four DC-7Cs and three Britannias served transatlantic, Far East and Australasian charters and European IT charters. The airline continued to grow and introduced its first Boeing 707s in January 1968 followed by the first of three new One-Eleven-500s in March 1969. By 1970 Caledonian was seeking licences to operate North Atlantic scheduled services and was operating seven 707s and four One-Elevens.

British Caledonian Airways

The formation of BCAL from the two airlines described came about through the same government-sponsored study which eventually led to the merger of BEA and BOAC. The 1969 Edwards Committee Report recommended the setting up of a 'second-force' independent airline through the joining up of Britain's two largest independents, BUA and Caledonian, thereby establishing a larger and viable competitor for the soon-to-emerge British Airways. Caledonian duly bought struggling BUA in November 1970, initially operating as Caledonian//BUA and then BCAL from November 1971.

The initial fleet of this formidable new airline was

made up of thirty-one inherited aircraft – four VC-10s, seven 707s, eight One-Eleven-200s and twelve One-Eleven-500s. In order to strengthen its route network the government transferred licences for BOAC's South American and some African routes to BCAL.

BCAL set about expanding its route network, introducing Gatwick to New York JFK and Los Angeles services during 1973. Unfortunately, the timing was wrong and both routes were dropped the following year because of massive fuel price rises and a recession which forced all airlines into a period of cost savings and retrenchment. Another and more successful attempt at introducing transatlantic schedules came a few years later with the introduction of services to the southern USA cities of Houston, Atlanta and Dallas-Fort Worth. A fleet of DC-10s was bought for these routes and continued to serve them successfully until the mid-1990s, long after the BCAL name had disappeared. A route to Hong Kong via Dubai was opened in 1980.

During the mid-1980s, as the privatisation of British Airways neared, HM Government once again attempted a redistribution of routes to assist the still struggling BCAL. After a hard fought battle BA's Saudi Arabian routes were given to BCAL in exchange for the independent airline's South American network in January 1985, but this did little to improve BCAL's results as it attempted to expand with a selection of second-hand 747s. By 1986 BCAL's scheduled services from Gatwick served North, West and Central Africa, Dhahran, Jeddah and Riyadh in Saudi Arabia, Dubai–Hong Kong, Atlanta, Dallas, Houston, Los Angeles and New York JFK, plus many European and UK destinations. Tokyo came on

line in May 1987 following the arrival of the fourth 747 and further expansion into the Middle and Far East was planned.

Once again, however, the world's airlines were suffering the effects of a recession and BCAL was rapidly running out of cash. British Airways wanted to establish a second hub at Gatwick to relieve congested Heathrow and made an initial bid for BCAL in July 1987. Other bids were received including one from SAS, but after a Monopolies and Mergers Commission enquiry had cleared the way, with a few conditions attached, ministerial approval was granted for a BA and BCAL merger to take effect from April 1988.

The first aircraft to be repainted into British Airways colours was One-Eleven-500 G-BJRT from a fleet of five 747-200s, thirteen One-Eleven-500s and eight DC-10-30s. Orders were held for ten Airbus A320s which were delivered to BA, and nine McDonnell Douglas MD-11s, later cancelled. Many of BCAL's employees transferred to BA and the company's image, which had been so carefully cultivated and promoted over the years, was retained by reforming British Airtours as Caledonian Airways and adopting a variation of BCAL's 'Golden Lion' livery and tartan uniforms.

After the merger British Airways quickly set about developing Gatwick into a major hub using the new North Terminal and, apart from the visible reminder of Caledonian Airways, most traces of the old BCAL quickly disappeared. The DC-10s remained Gatwick-based for many more years but the One-Elevens were soon replaced at Gatwick with 737-236s and the BCAL 747-200s were sold within three years.

One of five 747-200s which joined British Airways in April 1988 with the British Caledonian merger was Combi G-HUGE. BCAL had established a substantial long-haul network to the USA, Africa, and the Middle and Far East with its fleet of DC-10s and 747s.

Ex-British Caledonian aircraft operated by BA

Aircraft registration	Aircraft type	Constructor's number	Date	Notes
G-BEBL	DC10-30	46949	4/88	Delivered new to BCAL 3/77.
G-BEBM	DC10-30	46921	4/88	Delivered new to BCAL 2/77.
G-BHDH	DC10-30	47816	4/88	Delivered new to BCAL 4/80.
G-BHDI	DC10-30	47831	4/88	Delivered new to BCAL 7/80.
G-BHDJ	DC10-30	47840	4/88	Delivered new to BCAL 10/80.
G-DCIO	DC10-30	48277	4/88	Delivered new to BCAL 4/81.
G-MULL	DC10-30	47888	4/88	Ex-YA-LAS, del Ariana Afghan A/l 9/79. Bought BCAL 3/85.
G-NIUK	DC10-30	46932	4/88	Ex-9Q-CLT, del Air Zaire 6/74. Bought by BCAL 6/85.
G-BJXN	747-230	20527	4/88	Ex-Lufthansa D-ABYG, Braniff N611BN. Bought BCAL 4/82.
G-CITB	747-2D3	22579	4/88	Ex-Alia JY-AFS. Bought by BCAL 9/87.
G-GLYN	747-211	21516	4/88	Ex-Wardair C-GXRA. Bought by BCAL 10/86.
G-HUGE	747-2D3	21252	4/88	Combi. Ex-Alia JY-AFB. Bought by BCAL 3/85.
G-NIGB	747-211	21517	4/88	Ex-Wardair C-GXRD. Bought by BCAL 3/87.
G-AWYR	BAC 1-11-501	174	4/88	Delivered new to BUA 4/69.
G-AWYS	BAC 1-11-501	175	4/88	Delivered new to BUA 4/69.
G-AWYT	BAC 1-11-501	176	4/88	Delivered new to BUA 5/69.
G-AWYU	BAC 1-11-501	177	4/88	Delivered new to BUA 6/69.
G-AWYV	BAC 1-11-501	178	4/88	Delivered new to BUA 6/69.
G-AXJK	BAC 1-11-501	191	4/88	Delivered new to BUA 3/70.
G-AXJM	BAC 1-11-501	214	4/88	Delivered new to BUA 3/70.
G-AXLL	BAC 1-11-523	193	4/88	Delivered to BCAL 1/84 ex-Faucett.
G-AYOP	BAC 1-11-530	233	4/88	Delivered to BCAL 3/73 ex-Court Line.
G-AZMF	BAC 1-11-530	240	4/88	Delivered new to BCAL 3/72.
G-AZPZ	BAC 1-11-515	229	4/88	Delivered to BCAL 3/82 ex-Dan-Air.
G-BJRT	BAC 1-11-528	234	4/88	Delivered to BCAL 10/81 ex-Hapag-Lloyd.
G-BJRU	BAC 1-11-528	238	4/88	Delivered to BCAL 10/81 ex-Hapag-Lloyd.

Dan-Air

Dan-Air was, at the time of its demise, Britain's second-largest airline. It was also one of the best known and longest surviving of all British airlines, having begun operating charters back in 1953 with a single DC-3. Sadly in 1992, its name was added to the long list of independent airlines which have disappeared during recent years, joining other familiar names such as Court Line, Laker, BCAL and Air Europe. Dan-Air was only just able to avoid collapsing in the spectacular fashion of Court Line and Air Europe through a last minute offer from British Airways after several other rescue bids had failed. As with BCAL some six years earlier, British Airways mounted a rescue bid to obtain valuable Gatwick slot and route assets, but unfortunately, much less of Dan-Air survived this process. British Airways retained the extensive scheduled service network which Dan-Air had built to connect Gatwick with over twenty European destinations and added this to its own to create a new low-cost European hub operation.

Dan-Air Services Limited began flying as the air charter subsidiary of Davies & Newman shipping brokers in May 1953 with DC-3 G-AMSU. The company soon learned to take advantage of any opportunities to grow during the regulated 1950s and 1960s by, for example, becoming an early operator in the new IT market and operating scheduled freight services on behalf of BEA. After settling at Gatwick in 1960, Dan-Air began flying year-round scheduled passenger services, initially using two Doves from Bristol and Cardiff to Liverpool and Newcastle, followed by other routes and larger aircraft.

As it grew, Dan-Air became well known for prolonging the lives of large numbers of ageing British airliners! After acquiring a total of ten Airspeed Ambassadors the company went on to build the biggest fleet of de Havilland Comets ever operated by one airline. Beginning with two ex-BOAC Comet 4s in 1966, a total of fifty Comet 4/4B/4Cs were bought, thirty-three of which entered service and gave the company many years of valuable service, mainly on IT charter work but also on scheduled services. Twenty-one HS-748s also flew with the airline, with North Sea oil exploration support providing much work for this rugged and adaptable aircraft, as well as the scheduled service network and finally Post Office mail contracts. Twenty-six assorted One-Elevens, all second-hand, also served Dan-Air between 1969 and 1992.

Dan-Air became a public limited company in 1971, the year it acquired the first of an eventual six 707s, which were used initially for transatlantic charters and later for worldwide passenger and cargo charters. Other Boeing jets were soon to follow and became the mainstay of Dan-Air's fleet after the supply of Comets had dried up. Ten 727-100s were bought beginning in 1973, followed by ten 727-200s, six of which were still with the airline at its close.

Boeing 737s came next and true to form, Dan-Air acquired a varied fleet, initially second-hand 737-200s, but from 1985 new 737-300/400s were acquired, primarily to operate the increasing network of scheduled services from Gatwick. A Heathrow to Inverness service began in 1983 by which time one-fifth of all passengers were being carried on scheduled services.

In an unusual move for Dan-Air two new BAe 146 airliners were ordered in 1982, once again providing a British airliner type with support. This support was actually very timely for British Aerospace as it gave them the first 146 order, for two plus two options. The 146 was an ideal aircraft for the Gatwick to Berne route as it is the only jet capable of operating into the Swiss city. Two of Dan-Air's three early Series-100s were exchanged with BAe for updated -300s during 1992 and others were ordered but never delivered.

When British Airways and British Caledonian merged in March 1988, Dan-Air took the opportunity to increase its scheduled service network at Gatwick by adding Brussels, Dublin, Lisbon, Madrid, Nice and Paris CDG. By 1989, however, a loss was made despite carrying over six million passengers. Two Airbus A300s acquired from 1986 for charter flying were disposed of and Dan-Air Engineering was sold to FLS. The situation continued to deteriorate further with a general economic recession followed by the Gulf conflict of 1990–91 which badly hit the charter market. Some operators, in particular Air Europe, took their business away from Dan-Air.

To have any chance of survival Dan-Air was forced to further reduce its dependence on charter work. Scheduled services, in particular those from Gatwick to Europe but also from Berlin, Manchester and Newcastle, were to be developed and the fleet rationalised to just two types, the 146 and 737-300/400s, more of which were ordered. A share issue in the autumn of 1991 raised £53.75m to help achieve these aims and by summer 1992 nine UK and twenty-one European destinations were being served. Unfortunately the charter market remained in the doldrums, leaving Dan-Air with a fleet of expensive under-utilised aircraft (especially the 727s) and knowing that it could not survive the coming winter season, management began talking to Virgin, American and United about possible alliances. These talks achieved nothing and with time rapidly running out a last minute deal with British Airways was agreed.

British Airways paid a nominal £1.00 for the assets and substantial liabilities of Davies & Newman Holdings plc, just hours before the receiver would have been called in. Nine 737-400s and three 737-300s were taken over to continue operating services from Gatwick to Aberdeen, Athens, Brussels, Madrid, Manchester, Montpellier, Nice, Paris CDG, Perpignan, Rome, Toulouse, Vienna and Zürich as well as from Heathrow to Inverness and Manchester to Aberdeen. Regrettably, the rest of Dan-Air could not be saved and all charter flying ceased at the beginning of November 1992. Large numbers of Dan-Air employees no longer had jobs and the rest of the fleet, six 727-200s, eleven One-Eleven-500s, four 737-200s and four BAe 146s was parked at various UK airfields to await disposal.

ex-Dan-Air B737s taken over by British Airways			
Aircraft registration	Aircraft type	Constructor's number	Date
G-BNNJ	737-3Q8	24068	11/92
G-BOWR	737-3Q8	23401	11/92
G-SCUH	737-3Q8	23254	11/92
G-BNNK	737-4Q8	24069	11/92
G-BNNL	737-4Q8	24070	11/92
G-BPNZ	737-4Q8	24332	11/92
G-BSNV	737-4Q8	25168	11/92
G-BSNW	737-4Q8	25169	11/92
G-BVNM	737-4S3	24163	11/92
G-BVNN	737-4S3	24164	11/92
G-BVNO	737-4S3	24167	11/92
G-TREN	737-4S3	24796	11/92

When British Airways bought Dan-Air in 1992 many more European routes were added to its rapidly growing Gatwick scheduled service hub. Nine 737-400s and three 737-300s came with the purchase but the Series-300s were soon disposed of. G-SCUH, photographed pushing-back at Gatwick in December 1992, was sold to the American airline Morris Air six months later.

(3) Franchise Partners

The first airline to become a franchise partner was Cityflyer Express in August 1993. Since then another nine airlines have signed up for what has proved to be an excellent arrangement for both British Airways and the franchisees.

Franchising works as follows: partner airlines continue to operate independently but adopt British Airways' corporate identity on their aircraft, uniforms, tickets etc. and pay fees for the use of the brand and any services provided. Flights operate with BA service numbers and customers are assured of the high standards expected through strict adherence to procedures which are regularly audited. By taking advantage of their lower cost structures the partner airlines are able to operate at a profit many routes which British Airways could not, whilst at the same time obtaining considerable benefits from using BA's brand and support services. British Airways gains by maintaining or establishing a presence in many more markets than it could otherwise have afforded to and through increased passenger feed onto its own network.

Some figures for the year 1997/8 illustrate just how important franchising has now become:
* 5.9 million passengers were flown by the franchise carriers for total net revenues of £542m.
* 3,500 people were employed by franchise airlines.
* BA itself serves nine UK airports but has a presence at forty-five more through franchising.
* BA serves 165 cities in 82 countries. Franchisees add another 74 destinations and 9 more countries.

Further proof of the success of the franchising concept can be found in the impressive growth rates experienced by all of the partners since joining up. Some examples from the first quarter of 1998 are British Mediterranean with an increase of 47% in its passenger totals, Maersk Air which experienced growth of 20% or more on many routes and British Regional which carried 1,118,000 passengers, an increase of 11.7%.

Partner airlines now operate throughout the UK, The Netherlands, Scandinavia and southern Africa. Airliners flown range in size from the 9-seater Islanders of Loganair to the 150-seat Boeing 727-200s of Comair, types which would otherwise never have worn British Airways colours. Route lengths also vary dramatically from the world's shortest scheduled flight flown in the Orkneys by Loganair to the long A320 services of British Mediterranean to the remote cities of central Asia. With so many obvious benefits to both parties, more airlines are expected to become franchise partners in due course.

Note: Cityflyer Express has now joined Brymon Airways as a fully-owned British Airways subsidiary company, (subject to Government approval at the time of writing) but as both airlines are independently managed and operate to agreements which are very similar to those of the franchisees, they are often referred to as part of the family of franchise partners.

Airline Management Limited

Airline Management Limited (AML), a joint venture company established by British Airways and the Flying Colours Group, took over the operation of DC-10 G-NIUK from Caledonian Airways at the end of March 1997. This single DC-10, wearing full British Airways colours, continued to operate a regular pattern of services to Tampa, Nassau, Grand Cayman and San Juan in a two-class 32J/279M layout, flown by BA flight crew and AML-supplied cabin crew. The fleet increased to three in March 1998 with the addition of two DC-10s to operate scheduled services to Montego Bay and Kingston plus new routes to Cancun in Mexico, Puerto Plata in the Dominican Republic and Tobago. Another new destination, San José in Costa Rica was added in November 1998 followed by Havana, Cuba in 1999, all on behalf of British Airways.

The entire British Airways DC-10 fleet, including the three operated by AML, was withdrawn from service between October 1998 and March 1999.

AML began to operate a single DC-10 on some of British Airways' leisure services from Gatwick during March 1997. One year later the fleet increased to three but the DC-10s have since been replaced by new Boeing 777s. One of these, G-VIIO, displaying British Airways' full identity complete with Chelsea Rose *artwork, taxies out at Gatwick for a flight to Cancun in Mexico during April 1999.*

AML Fleet

Aircraft registration	Aircraft type	Constructor's number	Date	Notes
G-BHDH	DC-10-30	47816	3/98	Transferred to AML 3/98. Returned to BA 3/99.
G-BHDI	DC-10-30	47831	3/98	Transferred to AML 3/98. Returned to BA 3/99.
G-NIUK	DC-10-30	46932	3/97	Transferred to AML 3/97. Returned to BA 3/99.
G-VIIO	777-236	29320	1/99	Delivered new.
G-VIIP	777-236	29321	2/99	Delivered new.
G-VIIR	777-236	29322	3/99	Delivered new.

AML introduced three new Boeing 777-236IGWs in a two-class 28J/355M, 383-seat configuration to operate its network of scheduled leisure services. The first service was from Gatwick to Tampa with G-VIIO on 1 February 1999 and by the end of March all three DC-10s had been replaced.

BASE Airlines

BASE Regional Airlines became the tenth British Airways franchise partner in March 1999 and inaugurated a new twice-daily service from Heathrow to the company's home city of Eindhoven (BASE = Business Aviation Services Eindhoven, BV). This introduced yet another new type of airliner to British Airways' network, the 28-seat Embraer EMB-120 Brasilia turboprop, two of which were in service alongside two Jetstream 31s.

BASE was established in 1985 and built up services from the Dutch cities of Groningen, Maastricht, Rotterdam and Eindhoven to several European destinations including Birmingham and Manchester. Small Cessna and Piper twins were supplemented by three Jetstreams from 1991 and the two Brasilias in 1997.

Under the franchise agreement BASE also links Eindhoven and Rotterdam to Birmingham, Gatwick and Manchester and Eindhoven to Zürich.

BASE Airlines fleet			
Aircraft registration	Aircraft type	Constructor's number	Date
PH-KJB	Jetstream 31	648	1/91
PH-KJG	Jetstream 31	690	9/93
PH-BRI	EMB-120ER Brasilia	120235	8/97
PH-BRK	EMB-120ER Brasilia	120253	9/97

British Mediterranean Airways

A franchise agreement with youthful British Mediterranean (B-Med) was initially planned to take effect from October 1996, with its lone A320 operating from Heathrow to Amman, Beirut and Damascus. British Airways had only recently restarted services to these Middle Eastern destinations but was losing money and felt that a smaller carrier such as B-Med would be a more viable option. An agreement could not be reached at that time, however, and it was not until 30 March 1997 that the franchise was implemented.

B-Med originally began operations with a single A320 in October 1994 and served several Middle Eastern destinations from Heathrow via

British Airways' tenth franchise partner, BASE Airlines of The Netherlands, began operating Eindhoven to Heathrow services in March 1999.

TOP: *Landing at Heathrow at the end of a five-hour sector from Beirut in September 1995 is British Mediterranean's first Airbus A320, G-MEDA. A franchise agreement was implemented with British Airways in March 1997.*

ABOVE: *Two additional A320s were delivered in 1997 to serve British Mediterranean's expanding Middle Eastern network. All three are now painted in British Airways' new colours and achieve some of the highest rates of utilisation of any A320s.*

Beirut. When the franchise agreement was implemented another two A320s were leased-in and all three were painted in British Airways colours. Operations also transferred to Terminal Four and Beirut frequencies were increased from five to seven per week, Amman from three to five, and Damascus from two to four to compensate for BA dropping its own services. New destinations of Tbilisi, the Georgian capital city, and Alexandria in Egypt came on line in April 1997, followed later in the year by Bishkek, capital city of Kyrgyzstan. Services to Yerevan in the Republic of Armenia also began and in October 1998 were extended to Ashkhabad, the capital of Turkmenistan. Flights to these remote and distant cities have demonstrated the excellent reliability of this small fleet of A320s which sustains a very high rate of utilisation. Passenger numbers increased during the first quarter of 1998 by 47% over the previous year, with Beirut increasing by 59% and Tbilisi 69%, figures which suggest that larger aircraft will be needed in the not too distant future.

British Mediterranean fleet			
Aircraft registration	Aircraft type	Constructor's number	Date
G-MEDA	A320-231	0480	4/97
G-MEDB	A320-231	0376	4/97
G-MEDD	A320-231	0386	4/97

British Regional Airlines

British Regional Airlines, formerly known as Manx Airlines (Europe), was perhaps the most unlikely airline to join British Airways as a franchise partner because of its ownership by Airlines of Britain Holdings and consequently its ties to rival British Midland (BMA). This has not proved to be an obstacle as the partnership has thrived without conflict and to the benefit of both parties. British Regional has subsequently separated completely from BMA and floated as an independent company.

Manx Airlines in its most recent incarnation dates back to a 1982 agreement between BMA and Air UK to merge and develop their Isle of Man services, with the resulting company becoming a wholly-owned subsidiary of BMA's parent Airlines of Britain Holdings in 1988. The airline known today as British Regional later emerged because Manx Airlines, based in non-EC Isle of Man, needed to establish a UK-based company in order to be allowed to operate scheduled services into mainland Europe. Manx Airlines (Europe) was duly created and began operations in March 1991 flying from a new Cardiff hub with two Jetstream 31s, an ATP and a Shorts SD-360. A large fleet of Jetstream 41s began to arrive in April 1993 and the network quickly expanded to include Belfast City, East Midlands, Glasgow, Liverpool, Manchester and Stansted. Loganair, also a part of the Airlines of Britain Group, had its non-Scottish routes transferred to Manx Airlines (Europe) during 1994 along with its ATPs and Jetstream 41s.

To further increase passenger numbers and profit potential, Manx Airlines (Europe) entered into a franchise agreement with British Airways during January 1995 and its fleet of six ATPs and ten Jetstream 41s soon appeared in BA Express colours. All Isle of Man routes continued to be operated separately by Manx Airlines, with aircraft in its colours. During the first year of its franchise Manx Airlines (Europe) carried 1.2 million passengers, increasing British Airways' presence at many more UK and Ireland destinations such as Belfast City, Cardiff, Kerry, Liverpool, Stansted, Shannon and Waterford, some of which had not seen a BA aircraft since the Viscounts' retirement fifteen years earlier. Further growth came with the acquisition in March 1996 of Leeds-Bradford-based Knight Air's routes to Aberdeen and Southampton, along with its two Jetstream 31s.

Further, more complex, organisational changes were soon to follow. The Airlines of Britain Group decided to establish British Regional Airlines to operate the BA Express services of Manx Airlines (Europe) and Loganair. The new name was felt to be more representative of the carriers' operations as well

as being more marketable, and from its introduction in October 1996 British Regional became Europe's largest regional carrier. British Airways' six Scottish Highlands and Islands routes were transferred to British Regional, but Loganair soon regained its independence through a management buy-out in March 1997, taking with it many local Scottish routes. Following these changes, in April 1997, Airlines of Britain completely divorced its regional airline interests from British Midland, thereby allowing British Regional to further develop its links with British Airways whilst British Midland continued to compete with it! The final and probably the most significant of this series of organisational changes was British Regional's floatation on the London Stock Exchange in June 1998.

Meanwhile, as these corporate changes were taking place, British Regional as an airline was going from strength to strength. The ex-Knight Air Leeds routes were soon upgraded to larger Jetstream 41s and to operate BA's Scottish routes the ATP fleet increased to ten and a Saab 340 was leased from Business Air. Summer 1997 saw the ten ATPs, twelve Jetstream 41s, seven Shorts SD-360s, one Saab 340 and another leased Shorts SD-360 serving an extensive scheduled network of thirty-one domestic and ten international routes from the main hubs at Cardiff, Manchester, Southampton, Belfast Harbour and Glasgow. Traffic was growing at such a rate that larger and faster

British Regional pioneered the use of small regional jets in the UK with the introduction of a fleet of Brazilian-built Embraer EMB-145s from June 1997. Ten of these fast and comfortable 49-seater airliners had entered service by June 1999 with another ten still to be delivered. They have enabled the airline to greatly improve its services from regional airports such as Southampton where these examples were photographed.

One of the many diverse types of airliners now operating in British Airways colours is the Saab 340 which was introduced by British Regional Airlines on the Aberdeen to Kirkwall route during November 1996. G-GNTE displays an appropriate 'Benyhone' tartan livery. (JOHN M. DIBBS)

aircraft were urgently required and British Regional selected the Embraer EMB-145 regional jet, becoming the UK launch customer for the Brazilian-built 49-seater with an order for three in February 1997.

The first Embraer entered service from Manchester to Berlin and Hanover in August 1997. The next two replaced Jetstreams on routes from Southampton to Edinburgh and Glasgow where they provided a tremendous increase in productivity, reducing sector times by twenty-five minutes and increasing the number of seats from twenty-nine to forty-nine. With passengers reacting favourably to the new jets, British Regional wasted no time and placed orders for another ten plus five options in October of that year. Another contract, announced during May 1999, took the total EMB-145 order to twenty plus another five options, all for delivery by 2002. Southampton's growth as a hub has continued and Manchester to Geneva transferred from BA Regional to British Regional in March 1998, also using the Embraer. Elsewhere in the fleet Jetstream 41s displaced by the new jets have replaced Shorts SD-360s, a type which was phased out by the end of 1998. During January 1999 the expanding Embraer fleet began to operate some Birmingham to Edinburgh and Glasgow services, replacing the retired ATPs of

BA Regional, and a new international route was opened from Edinburgh to Paris in February 1999.

Another important development for British Regional came with the transfer from British Airways of its Inverness to Heathrow route in November 1997. Previously flown by EuroGatwick with 737s (the only EuroGatwick flights into Heathrow), the service was initially flown three times a day from Inverness to Gatwick by a BAe 146-200 wearing an appropriate *Benyhone* tartan fin. This was the second 146 flown by British Regional on BA services and in December 1998 a third BAe146, Series-300 G-JEAM, was leased-in to increase capacity on the Inverness–Gatwick route.

With its increasing fleet of Embraers, British Regional continued to grow rapidly during 1999. The regional jets were used to serve six international routes from Manchester and began to be introduced on services from Cardiff to Aberdeen, Belfast, Brussels and Paris from October. In an unexpected move Jetstream 41s displaced by the jets were redeployed to inaugurate six routes from Sheffield City beginning with Belfast and Dublin in June 1999, to be followed by London City, Paris, Edinburgh and Glasgow. This made British Regional the new South Yorkshire airport's largest operator.

British Regional / Manx Airlines (Europe) fleet

Aircraft registration	Aircraft type	Constructor's number	Date	Notes	
G-MANE	ATP	2045	1/95	Manx Airlines (Europe). T/f to B.Regional 9/96.	
G-MANF	ATP	2040	1/95	Manx Airlines (Europe). T/f to B.Regional 9/96.	
G-MANG	ATP	2018	1/95	Manx Airlines (Europe). T/f to B.Regional 9/96.	
G-MANH	ATP	2017	1/95	Manx Airlines (Europe). T/f to B.Regional 9/96.	
G-MANJ	ATP	2004	1/95	Manx Airlines (Europe). T/f to B.Regional 9/96.	(Continued)

British Regional / Manx Airlines (Europe) fleet (continued)

Aircraft registration	Aircraft type	Constructor's number	Date	Notes
G-MANL	ATP	2003	1/95	Manx Airlines (Europe). T/f to B.Regional 9/96.
G-MANM	ATP	2005	1/95	Manx Airlines (Europe). T/f to B.Regional 9/96.
G-MANO	ATP	2006	1/95	Manx Airlines (Europe). T/f to B.Regional 9/96.
G-MANP	ATP	2023	1/95	Manx Airlines (Europe). T/f to B.Regional 9/96.
G-MANU	ATP	2008	12/97	B.Regional. ex-G-BUUP, white, BA titles.
G-MAUD	ATP	2002	3/97	B.Regional.
G-BRLY	ATP	2025	1/95	Manx Airlines (Europe). op on lease fm BAe in blue c/s. Used by Manx/B.Regional as required. Ret to BAe 1/99.
G-BTTO	ATP	2033	4/95	Manx Airlines (Europe). op on lease fm BAe, white with BA titles. Damaged Belfast Harbour 12/11/95. Ret to BAe, to Canarias as EC-CJU 10/96.
G-BUUP	ATP	2008	1/95	Manx Airlines (Europe)/B.Regional. Used as needed on BA services. Damaged in wheel-up landing Manchester 4/8/97. Regd G-MANU 8/97.
G-OEDJ	ATP	2024	8/97	Leased 8-11/97, white, BA t/t.
G-MAJB	Jetstream 41	41018	1/95	Manx Airlines (Europe). T/f to B.Regional 9/96.
G-MAJC	Jetstream 41	41005	1/95	Manx Airlines (Europe). T/f to B.Regional 9/96.
G-MAJD	Jetstream 41	41006	1/95	Manx Airlines (Europe). T/f to B.Regional 9/96.
G-MAJE	Jetstream 41	41007	1/95	Manx Airlines (Europe). T/f to B.Regional 9/96.
G-MAJF	Jetstream 41	41008	1/95	Manx Airlines (Europe). T/f to B.Regional 9/96.
G-MAJG	Jetstream 41	41009	1/95	Manx Airlines (Europe). T/f to B.Regional 9/96.
G-MAJH	Jetstream 41	41010	1/95	Manx Airlines (Europe). T/f to B.Regional 9/96.
G-MAJI	Jetstream 41	41011	1/95	Manx Airlines (Europe). T/f to B.Regional 9/96.
G-MAJJ	Jetstream 41	41024	1/95	Manx Airlines (Europe). T/f to B.Regional 9/96.
G-MAJK	Jetstream 41	41070	9/95	Manx Airlines (Europe). T/f to B.Regional 9/96.
G-MAJL	Jetstream 41	41087	5/96	Manx Airlines (Europe). T/f to B.Regional 9/96.
G-MAJM	Jetstream 41	41096	10/96	B.Regional.
G-GLAM	Jetstream 31	839	3/96	Ex-Knight Air. To Origin Pacific as ZK-JSA 8/97.
G-LOGV	Jetstream 31	761	3/96	Ex-Knight Air. To Origin Pacific as ZK-JSI 7/97.
G-EMBA	EMB-145	145016	6/97	
G-EMBB	EMB-145	145021	9/97	
G-EMBC	EMB-145	145023	10/97	
G-EMBD	EMB-145	145039	1/98	
G-EMBE	EMB-145	145042	2/98	
G-EMBF	EMB-145	145088	11/98	
G-EMBG	EMB-145	145094	11/98	
G-EMBH	EMB-145	145107	1/99	
G-EMBI	EMB-145	145126	4/99	
G-EMBJ	EMB-145	145134	5/99	
G-EMBK	EMB-145	145167	(8/99)	
G-EMBL	EMB-145	145177	(9/99)	
G-EMBM	EMB-145	145196	(11/99)	
G-EMBN	EMB-145	145216	(1/00)	
G-EMBO	EMB-145	145240	(3/00)	
G-GNTZ	BAe146-200	E2036	10/97	Ex-Business Air.
G-JEAM	BAe146-300	E3128	9/98	Lse fm JEA to 10/98. Lse fm BAe from 12/98.
G-MANS	BAe146-200	E2088	4/96	Manx Airlines (Europe). T/f to B.Regional 9/96.
G-BKMX	Shorts 360	SH3608	10/96	Ex-Loganair. To Jersey European 10/98.
G-BLGB	Shorts 360	SH3641	10/96	Ex-Loganair. Wheels-up landing Stornoway 9/2/98. wfu.
G-BMAR	Shorts 360	SH3633	10/96	Ex-Loganair. To BAC Express 12/98.
G-BVMY	Shorts 360	SH3755	10/96	Ex-Loganair. To Flying Enterprise 11/97 as SE-LHY.
G-ISLE	Shorts 360	SH3638	10/96	Ex-Loganair. To ATA Aerocondor as CS-TMN 12/98.
G-LEGS	Shorts 360	SH3637	10/96	Ex-Loganair. To Loganair 11/98.
G-WACK	Shorts 360	SH3611	10/96	Ex-Loganair. To Loganair 2/98. To Pacific Coastal a/l 3/99 as C-GPCE.
G-GNTE	Saab SF340A	133	10/96	Lsd fm Business Air.

Comair

1996 was a very important year for Comair because, in addition to celebrating fifty years of operating in southern Africa, it also became British Airways' eighth franchise partner and the first outside Europe.

From humble beginnings as Commercial Air Services (Pty) Ltd in 1946, Comair evolved into a diverse scheduled service, charter and aircraft

TOP: *Comair's fleet is unique in that it contains the only Boeing 727s ever to have carried a British Airways livery. Five of these elegant airliners are employed to operate the busy and intensely competitive Johannesburg to Cape Town route. ZS-NZV complete with Irish Colum tail-art was photographed at Johannesburg in October 1998.*

ABOVE : *Another of Comair's 727s climbing away from Johannesburg, resplendent in British Airways' world-image livery.*

LEFT: *The Global nature of British Airways today is clearly illustrated in this shot of three Comair airliners at Johannesburg. Boeing 727-200 ZS-OBO, complete with Scottish tartan, taxys onto its stand between another 727 displaying an Irish design and a 737-200 with a geometric pattern from Germany.*

maintenance company. In 1967 the name Commercial Airways or Comair was adopted for the operation of scheduled services from Johannesburg with a fleet of Cessna-twins and DC-3 Dakotas. F-27 Friendships began arriving in 1976 and ten years later the fleet of four F-27s and two DC-3s flew Comair's own routes as well as scheduled services for South African Airways to Richards Bay and Gaborone, and charters which included tourist safari trips to the Kruger National Park. This gradual expansion continued until the government of South Africa introduced airline deregulation in 1991 thereby allowing Comair to operate major domestic routes, beginning with a twice-daily Johannesburg–Cape Town service with a newly acquired fleet of 737s.

By the mid-1990s British Airways was looking

for a partner airline to provide connections throughout southern Africa to feed traffic onto its long-haul services. Comair's expanding route network and long experience of the region satisfied this requirement and a franchise agreement took effect from October 1996. The jet fleet, comprising six 737-200s (two of which had recently been purchased from BA) and two 727-200s, flew schedules from Johannesburg to Cape Town (six per day), Durban (three per day), Port Elizabeth (three per day), one Johannesburg – Cape Town – Port Elizabeth – Durban – Johannesburg and daily international services to Windhoek in Namibia and Harare in Zimbabwe. These airliners were soon repainted into British Airways colours and in June 1997 one of the 737s took part in the 'Utopia' worldwide launch event, flying from Johannesburg over the Victoria Falls. Two ATR-42s and four F-27s operated regional services to Richards Bay, Skukuza, Hoedspruit, Manzizi and Gaborone but in 1997 an agreement was reached to transfer the operation of all of Comair's turboprop routes to SA Express, leaving Comair to concentrate on the major routes with its jet fleet.

Comair has continued to experience a rapid rate of growth in passenger numbers across its network since 1996. Another three 142-seat 727-200s have been added for the very busy and competitive Johannesburg to Cape Town route. Comair's five 727s are the only examples of this classic Boeing airliner to be found in the fleets of British Airways and its partners, and they look particularly elegant with their 'World Image' liveries. By early 1999 Comair was operating over 270 flights each week, including ten daily round-trips from Johannesburg to Cape Town, six to Durban and four to Port Elizabeth.

Comair fleet			
Aircraft registration	Aircraft type	Constructor's number	Date
ZS-NOU	727-230	21113	10/96
ZS-NOV	727-230	21114	10/96
ZS-NZV	727-230	20792	11/97
ZS-OBO	727-230	21623	5/98
ZS-NVR	727-230	20673	5/99
ZS-NNG	737-236	21793	10/96
ZS-NNH	737-236	21797	10/96
ZS-NLN	737-2L9	21686	10/96
ZS-SBN	737-244	20229	10/96
ZS-SBO	737-244	20329	10/96
ZS-SBR	737-244	20331	10/96
ZS-OLA	737-236	23163	5/99
ZS-OLB	737-236	23167	6/99

GB Airways

Originally formed in 1931 by shipping company MH Bland & Co. Ltd to operate between Gibraltar and Tangier, Gibair soon fell dormant and remained that way until BEA took a 51% interest in 1947 and reactivated the route, flown by a DC-3 and then for many years by a Viscount. Services to London, initially to Heathrow with leased BEA aircraft, transferred to Gatwick in April 1979 to be operated by leased Britannia Airways Boeing 737-200s. A name change to GB Airways took place during 1981 and the airline became UK-based in 1989. By 1990 the fleet of three leased 737-200s operated from Gatwick to Casablanca, Funchal, Gibraltar, Marrakech, Tangier and Tunis, as well as from Manchester to Gibraltar and from Gibraltar to Casablanca, Marrakech and Tangier.

British Airways sold its remaining 49% shareholding to the Bland Group in 1995 but maintained the connection as GB Airways became a franchise partner in February 1995. During that year GB introduced two 150-seat ex-BA 737-400s to operate alongside its five 737-200s, and opened new routes to Murcia and Valencia. Passenger numbers during that first year as a franchise partner increased by 22% and as more aircraft and routes were added in subsequent years, equally impressive rates of growth were experienced. During 1997 for example,

By 1989 GB Airways had transferred its base from Gibraltar to London and was building up a substantial network of routes to Iberian and North African destinations. G-DDDV, seen departing from Gatwick's North Terminal, was operated by Caledonian Airways on behalf of GB Airways until November 1989.

when British Airways transferred its South American routes to Gatwick, GB Airways further increased its services to feed passengers through the growing Gatwick hub. Services to Faro, Malaga and Oporto were transferred from British Airways and Malta became a daily service. As a result passenger numbers carried on the fleet of five 737-400s and three 737-200s during the year to March 1998 almost doubled to 815,000.

GB Airways ordered its first ever new aircraft, two 737-300s, for delivery in early 1998 and by the summer of that year operated a modern fleet of five 737-400s and three 737-300s on an intensive schedule to Iberian and North African destinations plus Malta, mainly from the Gatwick hub but also serving Faro and Malaga from Heathrow. Gibraltar was served from Gatwick fourteen times a week, Malaga and Oporto thirteen times and varying frequencies were flown to Faro, Funchal, Jerez, Lisbon, Malta, Marrakech, Murcia, Palma, Tangier, Tunis and Valencia, a total of ninety-two flights per week from Gatwick and twelve from Heathrow. More destinations continue to be added with Seville coming on-line in November 1998 and Alicante in March 1999.

To further update its fleet and in parallel with British Airways, GB Airways placed an order with Airbus during November 1998 for nine airliners from the A320 family and took out options for another five. The first Airbus to be delivered will be an A320 powered by IAE V2500 engines and fitted with 159 seats. Subsequent deliveries, which are all due between 2000 and 2003, will be A320s or A321s, dependent upon the level of demand nearer the time.

oldest carriers in the group, having been formed when the W. Logan construction company took over a Glasgow-based air taxi operator in February 1962. An extensive network of scheduled services was established from 1967, initially inter-island Orkney services and later to the Scottish mainland and other islands, earning it the title 'Scotland's Airline'. The rugged capabilities of aircraft such as the Britten-Norman Islander, Trislander, de Havilland Canada Twin Otter and Shorts 330/360 were put to good use and the Scottish Air Ambulance Service has been maintained using Islanders since 1973. Loganair became part of BMA's Airlines of Great Britain Group in 1983 and expanded its network south of the border with larger aircraft such as the F-27, ATP, BAe 146 and Jetstream 41. During 1994 Loganair was reduced in size to concentrate once again on its Scottish routes using Shorts SD-360s and Islanders.

In July 1994 Loganair became a British Airways franchise partner. The Islanders and Shorts, later supplemented by a Twin Otter, were repainted into BA Express colours and began to operate their traditional Scottish services under BA flight numbers. A further reorganisation in October 1996 created British Regional Airlines from the merged operations of Loganair and Manx Airlines (Europe). For Loganair, however, this proved to be a very short-lived arrangement as a management buy-out in March 1997 took the airline out of the Airlines of Great Britain Group. Since then the Scottish carrier has continued to operate as a British Airways franchise partner and has begun to expand in its homeland once again. As well as opening new routes during 1998, Loganair took over several Scottish schedules from British Regional, which had decided to dispose of its Shorts 360 fleet and associated routes. To operate these Loganair acquired three uprated Shorts SD-360-300s in October 1998 and began flying from Glasgow to Inverness, Kirkwall and Sumburgh and from Edinburgh to Wick and Sumburgh. Two Saab 340Bs entered service during 1999 to further improve services from Edinburgh, Glasgow and Inverness to the Shetland Islands.

As a result of operating in a very remote and difficult environment, Loganair's schedules include some of the most interesting and unusual flying to be found in the British Airways' family of airlines network. One such route has for many years held the world record for being the shortest scheduled commercial air service anywhere, and attracts many passengers as a result. The Westray to Papa Westray sector of a multi-stop route in the Orkney Islands takes an eight-seater Islander just two minutes and provides a vital year-round link to local communities. To the west of Scotland's mainland in the Outer Hebrides another fascinating Loganair operation can be found, one which uses the only Twin Otter to wear British Airways colours. This tough 'STOL' aircraft has proved itself to be the most suitable type for operations from the island of Barra where the only available landing strip is a beach!

GB Airways 737 fleet

Aircraft registration	Aircraft type	Constructor's number	Date	Notes
G-BGDS	737-236	21806	3/92	Lse from BA. Returned 3/98.
G-BGDU	737-236	21808	3/92	Lse from BA. Returned 2/98.
G-BGJF	737-236	22027	1/96	Lse from BA. Returned 3/96.
G-BNNK	737-4Q8	24069	4/95	Ex-BA, lse.
G-BNNL	737-4Q8	24070	3/95	Ex-BA, lse.
G-BUHL	737-4S3	25134	3/96	Ex-BA, lse.
G-TREN	737-4S3	24796	3/97	Ex-BA, lse.
G-OGBA	737-4S3	25596	4/97	Ex-BMA, lse.
G-OGBB	737-34S	29108	1/98	Delivered new.
G-OGBC	737-34S	29109	2/98	Delivered new.
G-OGBD	737-3L9	27833	3/98	Ex-DBA D-ADBJ.
G-OGBE	737-3L9	27834	12/98	Ex-Maersk OY MAS.

Loganair

Loganair, which entered into a British Airways franchise agreement in 1994, is actually one of the

The smallest airliners to be found in British Airways colours are the eight-seater Islanders of Loganair which are used to operate inter-island services off the Scottish coast. These include the world's shortest scheduled flight, a two-minute sector between Westray and Papa Westray in the Orkney Islands. Loganair has flown examples of this rugged type for over 25 years as they have proved to be irreplaceable for such work. (JOHN M. DIBBS)

Loganair became a franchise partner in July 1994 and after several management and ownership changes now concentrates on operating in its Scottish homeland. ATP G-LOGB illustrates an earlier time when the airline had expanded south of the border with a variety of larger airliners. This aircraft now flies for British Regional Airlines as G-MANE.

Loganair fleet

Aircraft registration	Aircraft type	Constructor's number	Date	Notes
G-BEDZ	Islander	544	7/94	W/o Tingwall, Shetlands 20/5/96.
G-BJOP	Islander	2132	7/94	
G-BLDV	Islander	2179	8/96	Replaced G-BEDZ. 'Utopia' launch Glasgow 10/6/97.
G-BLNJ	Islander	2189	7/94	
G-BLNW	Islander	2197	7/94	Scott. Air Ambulance, occasional BA use.
G-BPCA	Islander	2198	7/94	Scott. Air Ambulance, occasional BA use.
G-BVVK	Twin Otter	666	1/95	
G-BKMX	Shorts 360	SH3608	7/94	T/f to Brit.Regional 10/96. To JEA 10/98.
G-BLGB	Shorts 360	SH3641	7/94	T/f to Brit.Regional 10/96. Wheels-up lndg Stornoway 9/2/98.
G-BMAR	Shorts 360	SH3633	7/94	T/f to Brit.Regional 10/96. To JEA 12/98.
G-BMLC	Shorts 360	SH3688	7/94	To Flying Enterprise as SE-LDA 4/96.
G-BVMY	Shorts 360	SH3755	11/95	T/f to Br.Regional 10/96. To Flying Enterprise SE-LHY 11/97.
G-BWMZ	Shorts 360	SH3717	7/94	To Air Kenya as 5Y-BKW 11/95.
G-ISLE	Shorts 360	SH3638	7/94	T/f to B.Regional 10/96. To ATA Aerocondor CS-TMN 12/98.
G-LEGS	Shorts 360	SH3637	7/94	T/f to Brit.Regional 10/96. Returned to Loganair 11/98.
G-WACK	Shorts 360	SH3611	7/94	T/f to B.Regional 10/96. Ret Loganair 2/98. Wfu Exeter 2/99.
G-BNMT	Shorts 360	SH3723	10/98	
G-BNMU	Shorts 360	SH3724	11/98	
G-BPFN	Shorts 360	SH3747	9/98	
G-BNMW	Shorts 360	SH3726	7/99	
G-LGNA	Saab 340B	199	6/99	
G-LGNB	Saab 340B	216	7/99	

Maersk Air

The history of this Birmingham-based airline dates back to the formation of Birmingham Executive Airways in 1983 to operate business-class services from Birmingham to major European and UK destinations, some of which were operated on behalf of British Airways. A Saab 340 and later Gulfstream Ones and Jetstream 31s were operated, followed by the purchase of five ex-BA One-Eleven-400s from January 1990. During October 1992 a merger with Brymon Airways took place to form Brymon European Airways, but this was a short-lived and

TOP: *Maersk Air Limited was established from the break-up of short-lived Brymon European Airways at Birmingham in August 1993. The airline immediately began to operate as a British Airways franchise partner using a fleet of five One-Elevens and a Jetstream 31.*

ABOVE: *Maersk Air's single 29-seat Jetstream 41 entered service during September 1996 on the four-times-daily Birmingham to Newcastle route replacing a 15-seat Jetstream 31 which could no longer accommodate the growing number of passengers. Photographed at Birmingham in June 1998, G-MSKJ taxys past one of the last One-Elevens in British Airways colours which was also operated by Maersk Air.*

Britain's first Canadair Regional Jet, G-MSKK, waits patiently for an Air 2000 757 to pass at Birmingham. Since 1996 Maersk Air has completely updated and expanded its fleet with Boeing 737-500s and Canadair RJs. As deliveries of the new RJs build up Maersk has been able to introduce new routes, such as Birmingham to Geneva and Vienna which were added in early 1999.

Maersk Air Ltd fleet

Aircraft registration	Aircraft type	Constructor's number	Date	Notes
G-WMCC	Jetstream 31	601	8/94	Wfu Birmingham 8/96. To Airport Fire Service 12/97.
G-MSKJ	Jetstream 41	41034	9/96	
OY-MBM	Fokker 50	20103	8/95	Lse from Maersk. Returned 10/95.
G-AVGP	BAC111-408	114	8/93	To Nationwide Air as ZS-OAF 12/96.
G-AWBL	BAC111-416	132	8/93	To Nationwide Air as ZS-NYZ 7/96.
G-BBME	BAC111-401	066	8/93	To Nationwide Air as ZS-OAG 2/97.
G-BBMG	BAC111-408	115	8/93	To Nationwide Air as ZS-OAH 4/97.
G-AWYR	BAC111-501	174	8/94	Lse fm BA. Bought 9/95. To EAS as 5N-ESA 1/99.
G-AWYS	BAC111-501	175	8/93	Lse fm BA. Bought 9/95. To EAS as 5N-ESB 10/98.
G-AWYV	BAC111-501	178	3/96	Lse fm European Avn. Returned 4/98.
G-MSKA	737-5L9	24859	10/96	Lse fm Maersk.
G-MSKB	737-5L9	24928	11/96	Lse fm Maersk.
G-MSKC	737-5L9	25066	12/96	Lse fm Maersk. Utopia launch BHX 10/6/97.
G-MSKD	737-5L9	24778	1/98	Lse fm Maersk.
G-MSKE	737-5L9	28084	1/99	Lse fm Maersk.
G-MSKK	CL600(RJ)	7226	5/98	
G-MSKL	CL600(RJ)	7247	7/98	
G-MSKM	CL600(RJ)	7248	7/98	
G-MSKN	CL600(RJ)	7283	1/99	
G-MSKO	CL600(RJ)	7299	3/99	
G-MSKP	CL600(RJ)	7329	8/99	

unprofitable venture which was reversed in August 1993 when British Airways and Maersk Air of Denmark jointly purchased the airline. BA acquired what had previously been Brymon Aviation at Plymouth and Maersk established Maersk Air Limited to operate the Birmingham-based scheduled service network.

The initial fleet of Maersk Air Ltd comprised four One-Eleven-400s, one Series-500 and a Jetstream 31, all of which were soon painted in British Airways colours as the new airline had entered into a franchise agreement to operate its services with BA flight numbers etc. from August 1993. A second One-Eleven-500 was leased in August 1994 and by the following year the fleet was operating in British Airways' Club Europe configuration from Birmingham to Amsterdam, Belfast, Cork, Copenhagen, Lyons, Milan, Newcastle and Stuttgart. A third One-Eleven-500 joined the fleet on lease from European Aviation in April 1996 and the Jetstream 31 was replaced with a larger Jetstream 41 for the Newcastle services in September.

Traffic levels grew rapidly on most routes and, although Cork was dropped, an eighth route to Berlin started up in January 1997. Fleet renewal had also begun with the introduction of the first of three 737-500s in November 1996, the first time this variant had served in British Airways colours, and the One-Eleven-400s were withdrawn and sold in South Africa. To complete the One-Eleven's replacement, three 50-seater Canadair Regional Jets were ordered for delivery during 1998 and options were placed for another twelve, three of which were confirmed during 1998 for 1999 delivery. A fourth 737-500 also entered service in February 1998 and the final One-Eleven service was operated by G-AWYS from Copenhagen to Birmingham on 4 August 1998. As the RJ fleet built up, new routes from Birmingham to Geneva and Vienna were inaugurated during February 1999 and orders for a further two Canadairs for spring 2000 delivery were announced, taking the total order to eight.

Sun-Air

Danish commuter airline Sun-Air became British Airways' seventh franchise partner in 1996 and, significantly, was the first airline from outside the UK to sign such an agreement. With its extensive network of Danish domestic routes and services to several

British Airways' strong Scandinavian connections are illustrated by this Jetstream 31 of Danish partner Sun-Air, decorated with Swedish 'Flower Field' artwork. Sun-Air was the first airline from outside the UK to become a franchise partner and now provides valuable links to British Airways' Scandinavian services and to its Manchester hub. (JOHN M. DIBBS)

major Scandinavian cities, all of which carry a high proportion of business traffic, Sun-Air provides an ideal feed for BA's scheduled services at Copenhagen, Oslo and Stockholm. A new route from Billund to Manchester was opened in January 1997 and soon proved to be so successful that larger aircraft were bought to serve it.

Sun-Air was established in 1978 by entrepreneur Niels Sundberg, who still runs the airline today, initially as a charter operator and aircraft maintenance company based at Billund in Denmark. Early attempts to begin scheduled services were frustrated by Danish regulations designed to protect SAS, but finally Sun-Air was awarded six routes during 1987 and began flying between Billund and Cologne. However, this lasted only until 1990 and it was not until the opportunity arose to build a hub at Aarhus in conjunction with SAS that Sun-Air's scheduled services became properly established. With Aarhus being just forty miles from Copenhagen, SAS had been unable to operate regional services profitably with its large MD-80s so Sun-Air acquired five 18-seat Jetstream 31s in 1991 and started flights to Oslo and Stockholm. A thirty-seat Jetstream 41 was bought in 1993 and other routes from Aarhus, Billund and Copenhagen were added.

By the mid-1990s, however, profitability was low and the airline felt that it was stagnating without a larger partner to feed traffic and code-share with.

After talking to several major European airlines, British Airways was identified as the most suitable potential partner as it operated frequent flights to the main Scandinavian cities and was also felt to have similar go-ahead attitudes and innovative ideas. A franchise agreement was reached and on 1 August 1996, Sun-Air's ten Jetstream 31s and two Jetstream 41s took to the air with BA Express service numbers and quickly lost their smart red and white colours in favour of the British Airways identity.

To expand the new links Sun-Air introduced its first UK service in January 1997. Jetstream 41s inaugurated twice-daily services from Billund to Manchester, feeding passengers to and from the extensive network of European and long-haul flights at British Airways' third-largest hub operation. Very soon traffic levels had grown to such an extent that larger aircraft became necessary and after evaluating several types an order was placed for two 64-seat British Aerospace ATPs in September 1997. These ex-Seoul Air aircraft had both entered service by January 1998, additionally serving the routes from Oslo to Aarhus and Billund as well as being used for charters. Several Jetstream 31s have since left the fleet and a third ATP has been bought.

Further route expansion is expected in the not too distant future and the purchase of jets by the year 2000 to accommodate the continued growth in passenger numbers is also very likely.

Sun-Air fleet

Aircraft registration	Aircraft type	Constructor's number	Date	Notes
OY-EDA	Jetstream 31	603	8/96	Sold 9/97.
OY-SVF	Jetstream 31	686	8/96	
OY-SVJ	Jetstream 31	711	8/96	
OY-SVK	Jetstream 31	772	8/96	To Airborne of Sweden as SE-LDH 6/97.
OY-SVO	Jetstream 31	773	8/96	To Svea Flyg AB as SE-LGH 8/98.
OY-SVP	Jetstream 31	626	8/96	Damaged on ground at Copenhagen 26/1/98, wfu 3/98.
OY-SVR	Jetstream 31	701	8/96	
OY-SVY	Jetstream 31	781	8/96	To Flying Enterprise as SE-LGM 1/97.
OY-SVZ	Jetstream 31	641	8/96	
OY-SVS	Jetstream 41	41014	8/96	
OY-SVW	Jetstream 41	41047	8/96	Lse to Cityflyer 1-3/98.
OY-SVI	ATP	2061	1/98	
OY-SVT	ATP	2062	12/98	
OY-SVU	ATP	2063	11/97	

CHAPTER EIGHT

LEASED AIRCRAFT

All airlines whether large or small inevitably find themselves short of aircraft from time to time. This may be a temporary problem caused by unexpected commercial demand, or it can result from the long lead-times involved with acquiring new aircraft. One way of overcoming such shortages is to lease-in extra capacity. Large airlines have also learned that some types of flying can be performed much more efficiently by specialist operators, hence for example the expansion of carriers which now operate their freighters on behalf of major airlines.

British Airways has used a large number of leased aircraft, ranging from those employed for short-notice ad hoc charters to the long-term 'dry-lease' of airliners which are incorporated into its existing fleets. Whilst ad hoc charters do not come within the scope of this book and the long-term lease of aircraft such as the Middle East Airlines 747s has been covered elsewhere, there have been many other leases, some of which have introduced new types to the airline's network. These are described here.

Passenger aircraft charters and leases

One of the first examples of leasing-in occurred during November 1977 when Finnair DC-9-41s operated a daily British Airways service between Heathrow and Helsinki for a short period. Finnair provided the flight crew and BA the cabin crew in what was part of the airline's process of evaluating candidate aircraft for its Trident replacement programme. Transavia 737-200s were also evaluated, but over a longer period and flown by British Airways crews.

During the late-1980s the idea of contracting smaller regional carriers to operate some of British Airways' marginal services began to take hold. For example, several cross-border services from Scotland to Birmingham and Manchester were flown by the Gulfstream Ones of Birmingham Executive Airways and Peregrine Air Services. Birmingham Executive took over several other schedules from Birmingham and inaugurated a route from Newcastle to Frankfurt. Some Scottish internal services were also flown by Peregrine, such as Aberdeen to Wick, usually with Cessna 404 Titans. This idea was gradually developed and expanded until the first franchising agreements were signed in 1993.

Also during the late 1980s two other types

which were new to the airline were leased to overcome temporary capacity shortages. An American Trans Air Boeing 727-100 flew domestic scheduled services from Gatwick for three months in 1988 soon after the merger with BCAL. Although British Airways had considered the lease of five 727-200s in 1980 for Shuttle services, this was the first time that Boeing's world-beating tri-jet had operated for the airline. Since then of course, Comair's 727-200 fleet has been repainted into BA colours, but considering that 1,832 727s were built, five is a very small number to have seen service with such a traditionally big Boeing customer! Another popular airliner rarely used by British Airways until the recent acquisition of Air Liberté is the McDonnell Douglas MD-80. In fact, the only previous occasion was when Paramount Airways, a small Bristol-based inclusive-tour charter carrier, flew Shuttle services from Heathrow with its two MD-83s at peak demand periods during 1987–88.

Airliners which have proved to be very useful for providing extra capacity on a number of occasions have been the British Aerospace 146/Avro RJ, aircraft which are now well established with franchise partner carriers. A summary of these and other leased passenger airliners is given below:

Boeing 727
*   American Trans Air 727-22 N284AT operated domestic schedules from Gatwick to Edinburgh, Glasgow and Jersey between May and July 1988. The 727 retained ATA colours but British Airways titles were added.
*   Five 727-200s are currently flown in British Airways colours by Franchise partner Comair in South Africa.

British Aerospace 146 and Avro RJ
*   Two BAe 146-200s, N407XV/N408XV, were leased from the manufacturer to operate Highland Division services due to the late delivery of ATPs. The aircraft came from the American company Presidential Airlines which also provided the flight crew. BA cabin crew were used throughout the lease which lasted from February to August 1989. Following from the success of this lease two 146-100s were provisionally ordered by Highlands with the first aircraft actually painted in full BA colours at the manufacturer's Woodford factory during February 1990. However, the order was never confirmed and

the two 146s G-BRLM/LN were not delivered.

* Other BAe 146 leases involved Loganair's Series-200 G-OLCA from May to July 1990 and BAe's Series-300 G-BTTP from June to August 1992, both for operations from Manchester.

* The first use of an Avro RJ (an improved version of the BAe 146) came with the lease of RJ-70 G-OLXX from Alpine Flightline for two months during the summer of 1995. The RJ was leased to operate scheduled Heathrow to Stuttgart services during a period of runway work at the German airport which prevented the use of BA's own airliners.

* Flightline aircraft were leased once again during 1997, this time to provide extra capacity from Gatwick. From January to March of that year G-TBIC operated services to Bordeaux. The lease was then extended until March 1998 with one of Flightline's 146s (G-OZRH or G-TBIC) operating from Gatwick to Aberdeen/Edinburgh and Glasgow.

* BAe 146s and Avro RJ-100s have become familiar sights in British Airways colours since 1996 through their acquisition by franchise partners British Regional Airlines and Cityflyer Express.

British Aerospace Jetstream 31

* Although Jetstream 31 and 41s are familiar sights today with several franchise partner airlines, the type first appeared as long ago as the mid-1980s on British Airways' domestic services. Birmingham Executive Airways operated from Birmingham to Edinburgh/ Aberdeen from November 1984 and to Southampton from May 1989 with one of its three Jetstream 31s. Aberdeen-based Peregrine Air Services also used its two Jetstream 31s on BA services from Aberdeen to Birmingham and Manchester during 1985.

Grumman G-159 Gulfstream One

* The twin-Dart-powered Gulfstream One was built as a fast executive transport but for a period during the 1980s also operated as a commuter airliner with some small UK airlines. Several examples soon found their way onto BA services.

* Birmingham Executive Airways, forerunner of today's Maersk Air Limited, flew three Gulfstreams (G-BMOW/BNKN/BNKO) on some of BA's Birmingham schedules from 1988 to 1990. A new route was opened from Newcastle to Frankfurt in October 1989 with the Gulfstream.

* Peregrine Air Services, which became Aberdeen Airways in 1990, operated a range of Scottish internal and cross-border Scotland to England services for BA with its Gulfstream One fleet between 1986 and 1989. Services from Birmingham were also flown. Four Gulfstreams were used: G-BMPA/BMSR/ BNCE/ BRWN.

McDonnell Douglas DC-9/MD-83

* Finnair DC-9-41s operated flights BA772/773 Heathrow–Helsinki–Heathrow during November and December of 1977. No specific DC-9s were used and

ABOVE: *Perhaps surprisingly given that 1,831 727s were built, the type did not appear on British Airways' routes until 1988 when a 20-year-old 727-100 of American Trans Air N284AT was leased for three months to operate domestic schedules from Gatwick.*

BELOW: *The excellent airfield performance of British Aerospace's 146 and RJ family was put to good use in 1995 when runway work at Stuttgart meant that they were the only jet airliners capable of landing there. British Airways leased RJ-70 G-OLXX from Flightline to operate its twice-daily services from Heathrow.*

they remained in full Finnair colours but BA cabin crew were used to operate the services.

* A single Paramount Airways MD-83, either G-PATA or G-PATB, was wet-leased to operate Shuttle services during the peak demand periods of December 1987–January 1988 and March–April 1988. Many Air Liberté MD-83s now fly in a French version of British Airways colours.

Freighter aircraft charters and leases

After British Airways had withdrawn its freighter fleet from service in early 1982 all air cargo was transported in the underfloor holds of its passenger aircraft. This left several routes short of cargo capacity so 747 Combis were introduced from 1985. Unfortunately, the mixture of passengers and freight on the main deck did not prove to be a particularly satisfactory arrangement and the operation of Combis was abandoned in 1991. The airline's capacity problem was made worse following the introduction of very-long-range 747-400 flights, many of which were only able to uplift small quantities of freight. Dedicated freighter services were the answer, but as the airline was unwilling to commit to the investment

necessary to re-establish its own operations in this specialised area it began to contract other carriers to operate on its behalf.

Since 1988 many operators have flown services for British Airways World Cargo with a variety of aircraft and on many different routes. Some contracts have been for a few weeks whereas others, particularly for flights to Hong Kong and Africa, have lasted for much longer. Contract carriers are generally responsible for the provision of an aircraft and its crew and operate flights as scheduled BA services. Examples of such cargo charters are summarised below.

Medium- to long-term contracts

Anglo Cargo
From October 1988 an Anglo Boeing 707F operated between Gatwick and Chicago, Hong Kong, and Johannesburg. Throughout the 1990 summer season and continuing until December, one of Anglo's two 707Fs flew the following lengthy itinerary each week:

Gatwick–Chicago–Gander–Heathrow,
Heathrow–Athens–Nairobi–Johannesburg–Nairobi–Cairo–
    Gatwick,
Gatwick–Dhahran–Dubai–Hong Kong–Athens–Gatwick.

TOP: *Another widely-used type which was absent from British Airways' fleet for a long time is the McDonnell Douglas MD-80 family of twin-jets. Until the recent acquisition of Air Liberté none had ever carried the airline's livery but two examples flown by charter airline Paramount Airways were leased to operate Shuttle services at peak periods during 1987/88.*

ABOVE: *A surprising number of light aircraft and even balloons have carried a British Airways identity over the last 25 years, ranging from the light training and touring aircraft of the airline's own flying club to privately owned aircraft. Although details of such aircraft are outside the scope of this publication, a shot of Dragon Rapide G-AKOE at Heathrow in November 1979 has been included here as an example.*

LEASED AIRCRAFT

Atlas Air

Since 1996 Atlas Air has served Hong Kong three times a week with one of its large fleet of 747-200 freighters, initially from Gatwick routing outbound via Dubai and returning via Delhi and Bahrain. During 1997, operations transferred to Stansted and from August 1998 new 747-400 freighters took over and began flying direct to and from Hong Kong.

Cargo Lion

A once-per-week service operated by a DC-8-62F began during 1996 on the following route:

Gatwick–Cairo–Nairobi–Johannesburg–Nairobi–Cairo–Gatwick.

Operations transferred to Stansted in 1997 and have since ended.

Short-term contracts

Anglo Cargo	11–12/91	757F	Gatwick–Athens–Nairobi–Johannesburg 1pw.
DAS Air Cargo	10/93–3/94	707F	Gatwick–Hong Kong 1pw.
Martinair	1–3/94	DC-10F	Gatwick–Hong Kong. Several flights.
Southern Air Tpt.	Summer 94	DC-8F	Gatwick–Hong Kong 2pw.
Southern Air Tpt.	Winter 94	DC-8F	Gatwick–Cairo–Nairobi–Johannesburg.
Heavylift Cargo	12/94	707F	Gothenburg–Glasgow–Columbus
Arrow Air	1–3/95	DC-8F	Gothenburg–Glasgow–Columbus
Cargolux	9–11/95	747F	Gatwick–Hong Kong
Canarias Cargo	1–2/96	DC-8F	Gatwick–Johannesburg
Gemini Air Cargo	Summer 96	DC-10F	Bogota–Miami–Stansted–Ilha Do Sal–Sao Paulo
European Air Tpt.	Summer 96	727F	Gatwick–Gothenburg–Helsinki 2pw
MK Airlines or	Summer 96	DC8	
DAS Air Cargo		707F	Nairobi–Gatwick 3pw.

BELOW: *British Airways World Cargo contracted a number of airlines to operate scheduled cargo services on its behalf after disposing of its own freighters. Anglo Cargo used Boeing 707s for flights to the USA, Africa and Hong Kong from 1988 and a 757 freighter was flown shortly before Anglo ceased trading in early 1992.*

BOTTOM: *N495MC one of Atlas Air's fleet of Boeing 747-400 freighters, received full British Airways World Cargo colours in April 1999 for the operation of three services per week between Stansted and Hong Kong. This is the only 747 freighter since the sale of G-KILO in 1982 to have flown in the airline's colours. (*JOHN M. DIBBS*)*

APPENDIX ONE

INDIVIDUAL AIRCRAFT HISTORIES – CURRENT TYPES

Chapter four gives a brief history of each aircraft type currently in service with British Airways. This appendix details each individual aircraft within those fleets, giving first flight and delivery dates plus information about their use by the airline and subsequent disposal where relevant.

Current British Airways aircraft types:
- Boeing 737
- Boeing 747
- Boeing 757
- Boeing 767
- Boeing 777
- Airbus A319/320
- Concorde

Format of tables: (example)

(1)	(2)	(3)	(4)	(5)	(6)
G-BGDD	236	21793	2/80	2/80	To Comair as ZS-NNG 9/95.

(1) Aircraft registration
(2) Aircraft model number – i.e. Boeing 737-236
(3) Constructor's number
(4) First flight – month/year
(5) Delivery to British Airways – month/year
(6) Notes regarding any significant change in the aircraft's use or disposal details

Boeing 737
737-200s from BA orders

G-BGDA	236	21790	9/79	12/81	To BAR 9/92, to EuroGatwick 3/97.
G-BGDB	236	21791	1/80	2/80	Lse GB A/w 4/92–3/95, to EuroGatwick 5/95, lse GB A/w 3/97–1/98. Disp 2/98. To Winair as N920WA 4/98.
G-BGDC	236	21792	1/80	2/80	Stored 12/94–5/95. Sold 5/95. To LAN Chile as CC-CHR.
G-BGDD	236	21793	2/80	2/80	Stored 11/94–3/95. Lse Transavia as PH-TSE 4/95–9/95. To Comair as ZS-NNG 9/95, repainted BA c/s '97.
G-BGDE	236	21794	2/80	3/80	To BAR 5/93, to EuroGatwick 10/94.
G-BGDF	236	21795	3/80	3/80	To BAR 8/92, BA LHR 3/94–12/94, to EuroGatwick 12/94.
G-BGDG	236	21796	3/80	4/80	To BAR 11/92. To Pegasus Aviation Inc. as N921PG 4/98. To Aerolineas Argentinas as LV-ZEC 6/98.
G-BGDH	236	21797	4/80	4/80	Lse Transavia as PH-TSD 4/95–10/95. To Comair as ZS-NNH 10/95, repainted BA c/s '97. To LAN Chile 4/99.
G-BGDI	236	21798	4/80	4/80	To BAR 1/93. To Pegasus Aviation Inc. as N922PG 7/98. To Aerolineas Argentinas as LV-ZIE 11/98.
G-BGDJ	236	21799	4/80	5/80	To BAR 8/92.
G-BGDK	236	21800	4/80	5/80	To BAR 10/92. Disp 4/98.To First Security Bank as N4361R 8/98. To Winair as N932WA 4/99
G-BGDL	236	21801	5/80	6/80	To BAR 9/92, to EuroGatwick 10/94.
G-BGDN	236	21802	5/80	6/80	To EuroGatwick '94. Sold 6/95. To LAN Chile as CC-CHS.
G-BGDO	236	21803	6/80	7/80	Lse GB Aws 4/92–3/95, to EuroGatwick 4/95, to LHR 9/95, to BAR 3/97.
G-BGDP	236	21804	8/80	8/80	To British Airtours 4/82–83, to EuroGatwick '94. Disp 11/97. To LAN Chile as CC-CZK 1/98, op by LADECO.
G-BGDR	236	21805	9/80	9/80	To British Airtours 4/82–83, to EuroGatwick '94.
G-BGDS	236	21806	9/80	9/80	Lse GB Aws 3/92, repainted into BA c/s 2/95. Ret to BA 3/98.
G-BGDT	236	21807	10/80	11/80	To BAR 10/92.
G-BGDU	236	21808	11/80	11/80	Lse GB Aws 3/92, repainted into BA c/s 2/95. Ret BA 2/98. Disp 4/98. To LAN Chile as CC-CZL 4/98.
G-BGJE	236	22026	3/80	3/80	British Airtours. Op by BA 10/82-3/84. To BA 3/88, to EuroGatwick 5/93.
G-BGJF	236	22027	4/80	4/80	British Airtours. Op by BA 1/82–4/85. To Caledonian 3/88. To BA 11/88, to EuroGatwick 5/93. Lse GB Leisure and sub-lse Sterling European 4/95–10/95. Lse GB Aws 1/96. Ret EuroGatwick 3/96. Disp. 5/99.
G-BGJG	236	22028	4/80	4/80	British Airtours. Op by BA 1/82–4/85. To Caledonian 3/88. To BA 11/88, to EuroGatwick 5/93. Sold 2/94. To Transaero as YL-BAA 4/94.
G-BGJH	236	22029	5/80	5/80	British Airtours. Op by BA 9/83–5/86. To Caledonian 4/88. To BA 11/88, to EuroGatwick '94. To LADECO as CC-CZN 4/99.
G-BGJI	236	22030	8/80	10/80	British Airtours. Op by BA 5/83–4/85. To BA 11/87. To Caledonian 4/88, to EuroGatwick '94. Disp 11/97. To LAN Chile as CC-CZO 12/97, op by LADECO.
G-BGJJ	236	22031	12/80	12/80	British Airtours. Op by BA '82–3/84. To BA 11/87, to EuroGatwick '94. Disp 6/98. To LAN Chile as CC-CZP 6/98, op by LADECO
G-BGJK	236	22032	2/81	3/81	British Airtours. To BA 9/83. Sold 4/94. To Transaero as YL-BAB 7/94.
G-BGJL	236	22033	4/81	4/81	British Airtours. Op by BA 9/83–84. W/o Manchester 22/8/85.
G-BGJM	236	22034	4/81	4/81	British Airtours. To BA 9/83. Sold 5/94. Repainted in Transaero c/s & leased back to EuroGatwick 5–6/95. Painted for Lithuanian A/l as LY-GBA 6/94, leased again to EuroGatwick 7/94. Stored then to Transaero as YL-BAC 3/95.
G-BKYA	236	23159	8/84	9/84	To BAR 5/93.

G-BKYB	236	23160	9/84	9/84	To BAR 6/93.
G-BKYC	236	23161	10/84	10/84	To EuroGatwick 3/97. Stored LGW 6/98. To Pegasus Aviation Inc. 10/98. To Aero Peru as OB-1711 10/98. To Access Air N624AC 5/99.
G-BKYD	236	23162	10/84	10/84	To BAR 10/93. Sold 4/95. To Cayman A/w as VR-CEF.
G-BKYE	236	23163	10/84	11/84	To BAR 1/93. To Comair as ZS-OLA 5/99.
G-BKYF	236	23164	10/84	11/84	To BAR 12/92, to EuroGatwick 3/97. To Pegasus Aviation Inc. as N925PG 11/98. To Aero Peru as OB-1712 11/98.
G-BKYG	236	23165	11/84	12/84	To BAR 2/93, to EuroGatwick. To Pegasus Aviation Inc. as N926PG 12/98. To Aero Peru as OB-1713 12/98. To Access Air as N625AC 5/99.
G-BKYH	236	23166	11/84	12/84	To BAR 12/92.
G-BKYI	236	23167	12/84	1/85	To BAR 3/97. To Comair as ZS-OLB 6/99.
G-BKYJ	236	23168	1/85	1/85	To BAR 5/93, to EuroGatwick 3/97. To Pegasus Aviation Inc. 10/98. To N927PG 3/99.
G-BKYK	236	23169	1/85	2/85	Christmas c/s 12/94–1/95. To BAR 3/97. Disp. 7/99.
G-BKYL	236	23170	2/85	2/85	To BAR 12/92, to EuroGatwick 3/97.
G-BKYM	236	23171	2/85	3/85	To BAR 3/93. Wfu 5/99. To Aeroliners Argentinas.
G-BKYN	236	23172	2/85	3/85	To BAR 3/93.
G-BKYO	236	23225	4/85	4/85	To BAR 11/92.
G-BKYP	236	23226	4/85	4/85	To BAR 11/92.

737-400s from BA orders

G-DOCA	436	25267	9/91	10/91	To EuroGatwick.
G-DOCB	436	25304	10/91	10/91	To EuroGatwick 3/99.
G-DOCC	436	25305	10/91	10/91	To EuroGatwick 3/99.
G-DOCD	436	25349	10/91	11/91	To EuroGatwick 4/99.
G-DOCE	436	25350	11/91	11/91	To EuroGatwick 4/99.
G-DOCF	436	25407	11/91	12/91	To EuroGatwick 10/98.
G-DOCG	436	25408	12/91	12/91	To EuroGatwick.
G-DOCH	436	25428	12/91	12/91	To EuroGatwick 7/98.
G-DOCI	436	25839	12/91	1/92	To EuroGatwick.
G-DOCJ	436	25840	12/91	1/92	To EuroGatwick.
G-DOCK	436	25841	2/92	2/92	To EuroGatwick 2/97.
G-DOCL	436	25842	2/92	3/92	To EuroGatwick 11/96.
G-DOCM	436	25843	3/92	3/92	To EuroGatwick 6/96.
G-DOCN	436	25848	10/92	10/92	To EuroGatwick 3/96.
G-DOCO	436	25849	10/92	10/92	To EuroGatwick '95.
G-DOCP	436	25850	10/92	11/92	To EuroGatwick '95.
G-DOCR	436	25851	10/92	11/92	To EuroGatwick 3/95.
G-DOCS	436	25852	10/92	12/92	To EuroGatwick 3/95.
G-DOCT	436	25853	12/92	12/92	To EuroGatwick.
G-DOCU	436	25854	12/92	1/93	To EuroGatwick.
G-DOCV	436	25855	1/93	1/93	To EuroGatwick.
G-DOCW	436	25856	1/93	2/93	To EuroGatwick.
G-DOCX	436	25857	3/93	4/93	To EuroGatwick.
G-DOCY	436	25844	7/93	9/93	Del as G-BVBY to Mojave for storage. To LHR 3/94, painted as TC-ALS for lease to Albatros Air but not delivered. Leased to Eurobelgian (EBA) as OO-LTQ 4/94–10/96. Entered service with BA as G-DOCY 10/96.
G-DOCZ	436	25858	8/93	10/93	Del as G-BVBZ to Mojave for storage. Leased to Air Europa as EC-657 then EC-FXJ 5/94–12/94. Entered BA service as G-DOCZ 1/95. To EuroGatwick 2/95.
G-GBTA	436	25859	9/93	11/93	Del as G-BVHA to Mojave for storage. To LHR 2/94, painted in BA c/s & entered service as G-GBTA (Guild of British Travel Agents). To EuroGatwick 12/94.
G-GBTB	436	25860	10/93	12/93	Del as G-BVHB to Mojave for storage. Leased to Eurobelgian (EBA) as OO-LTS 4/94–10/96. Entered service with BA 11/96 as G-GBTB.

737s from Dan-Air

G-BNNJ	3Q8	24068	11/88	11/92	EuroGatwick. Lse to Air Foyle 5/93 for Sunseeker Leisure flights, basic BA c/s with 'Sunjet' t/t. Ret BA 11/93 & stored. Lse to Excalibur as G-OCHA 4/94.
G-BOWR	3Q8	23401	3/86	11/92	EuroGatwick. Disp 4/93, to Southwest as N685SW 5/93.
G-SCUH	3Q8	23254	4/85	11/92	EuroGatwick. Disp 6/93, to Morris Air as N780MA 7/93.
G-BNNK	4Q8	24069	11/88	11/92	EuroGatwick. Disp 3/95, to GB A/w 4/95.
G-BNNL	4Q8	24070	1/89	11/92	EuroGatwick. Disp 1/95, to GB A/w 3/95.
G-BPNZ	4Q8	24332	5/90	11/92	EuroGatwick. Disp 5/95 as N191LF. To China Hainan A/l 7/95 as B-2960.
G-BSNV	4Q8	25168	1/92	11/92	EuroGatwick.
G-BSNW	4Q8	25169	2/92	11/92	EuroGatwick.
G-BVNM	4S3	24163	3/89	11/92	EuroGatwick.
G-BVNN	4S3	24164	3/89	11/92	EuroGatwick.
G-BVNO	4S3	24167	6/89	11/92	EuroGatwick.
G-TREN	4S3	24796	6/90	11/92	EuroGatwick. To GB A/w 3/97.

737-400s from an inherited Dan-Air order

G-BUHJ	4Q8	25164	3/93	3/93	EuroGatwick.
G-BUHK	4Q8	26289	6/93	6/93	EuroGatwick.
G-BUHL	4S3	25134	7/91	4/93	EuroGatwick. Disp 3/96 & to GB A/w 3/96.

BA Regional leased 737-300s

G-OAMS	37Q	28548	11/97	12/97	
G-ODUS	36Q	28659	4/97	4/98	ex-DBA D-ADBX.
G-OFRA	36Q	29327	4/98	5/98	
G-OHAJ	36Q	29141	5/98	6/98	
G-OMUC	36Q	29405	6/98	7/98	
G-XBHX	36N	28572	5/98	5/98	
G-XMAN	36N	28573	6/98	6/98	

737-200s leased from Transavia

PH-TVD	2K2C	20943		9/78	Lse in BA c/s. Ret Transavia 6/79.

PH-TVE	2K2C	20944		10/78	Lse in BA c/s. Ret Transavia 3/80.
PH-TVH	222	19955		11/78	Lse in Transavia c/s with 'BA on lease' titles. Painted BA c/s 2/79. Ret Transavia 3/80.
PH-TVI	222	19940		11/77	Lse in Transavia c/s with BA stickers. Ret 8/78. Lse again, full BA c/s, 1/79–3/80.

737-300s leased from Maersk Air

G-BOZA	3L9	23718		11/88	Ex-OY-MMN. Ret Maersk 3/92, dep LHR 4/92 as PH-OZA for lse to Air Holland.
G-BOZB	3L9	24219		9/88	Del new. Ret Maersk 3/92, dep LHR 5/92 as OY-MMO.
OY-MMP	3L9	24220		9/88	Del new. Regd G-CMMP 11/88. Ret Maersk 11/91, dep LHR 12/91 for lse to Germania as D-AGEI.
OY-MMR	3L9	24221		10/88	Del new. Regd G-CMMR 2/90. Ret Maersk 11/91. Lse to Germania as D-AGEJ 4/92.

Miscellaneous 737 leases

G-BHWE	204	22364		4/85	British Airtours. Lse fm Britannia A/w. Ret 3/87.
G-BKBT	2K2	20943		5/84	British Airtours. Lse fm Transavia. Ret 4/85.
G-BLEA	2K2	21397		5/84	British Airtours. Lse fm Transavia. Ret 3/85 as PH-TVP.
G-BMEC	2S3	21776		5/83	British Airtours. Lse fm Air Europe, AE c/s, BA t/t. Ret 4/84.
G-BMHG	2S3	21774		11/84	British Airtours. Lse fm Air Europe, AE c/s, KT t/t. Ret 4/85.
G-BMOR	2S3	21775		5/83	British Airtours. Lse fm Air Europe, AE c/s, KT t/t. Ret 4/84.
G-BMSM	2S3	22279		11/84	British Airtours. Lse fm Air Europe, AE c/s, KT t/t. Ret 4/85.
G-BRJP	2S3	22660		11/83	British Airtours. Lse fm Air Europe. Ret 4/85. British Airtours lse again 11/85-4/86.
G-DDDV	2S3	22633		11/84	British Airtours. Lse fm Air Europe. Ret 4/85. Lse again 11/85-4/86, 11/86-4/87 and 10/87. Sub-lse GB A/w 3/88 in their c/s but op by Caledonian. Ret 11/89.
EI-BTW	2Q8	21960		6/88	BA. Lse fm GPA. Repainted Caledonian c/s 4/89, i/s 5/89 as G-IBTW. Ret BA LGW 11/89, ret GPA 3/90.
G-IBTX	2M8	21736		11/90	GB A/w. Lse fm TEA UK. Ret to lessor 1/93. Sold to Europe Aero Service as F-GLXG 2/93.
G-IBTY	2E3	22703		12/88	BA. Lse fm GPA. Sub-lse to GB A/w. Ret lessor 3/92. To East-West A/l as VT-EWB 5/92.
EI-BTZ	2U4	22576		3/88	BA. Lse fm ILFC. White with BA titles. Regd G-IBTZ 12/88. To Caledonian 4/89. To GB A/w 2/90. Ret lessor 3/92. To East-West A/l as VT-EWC 5/92.
TF-ABL	330	23525		5/98	BA EuroGatwick. Lse fm Air Atlanta. White with BA titles. Ret 10/98.

Boeing 747

747 'Classics' (747-100/200)

G-AWNA	136	19761	3/70	4/70	To AAR 11/98. To Bruntingthorpe 11/98. Wfu & B/u.
G-AWNB	136	19762	5/70	5/70	To AAR 9/98. To Roswell 9/98. Wfu.
G-AWNC	136	19763	5/70	6/70	To European Aviation 11/98. Stored Chateauroux 11/98.
G-AWND	136	19764	1/71	2/71	Stranded at Kuwait during Iraqi invasion 2/8/90. Destroyed on the ground during the liberation of Kuwait 27/2/91.
G-AWNE	136	19765	2/71	3/71	
G-AWNF	136	19766	2/71	3/71	
G-AWNG	136	20269	7/71	9/71	To AAR 12/98. To Roswell 12/98. Wfu.
G-AWNH	136	20270	11/71	11/71	To AAR 6/99. To Albuquerque 6/99. Wfu.
G-AWNI	136	20271	12/71	1/72	To TWA as N17125 3/81. To Tower Air as N605FF. W/o JFK 20/12/95.
G-AWNJ	136	20272	3/72	3/72	To AAR 12/98. To Roswell 12/98. Wfu.
G-AWNK	136	20273	3/72	3/72	To TWA N17126 3/81.
G-AWNL	136	20284	4/72	4/72	To AAR 11/98. To Roswell 11/98. Wfu.
G-AWNM	136	20708	4/73	5/73	Last delivery in BOAC c/s.
G-AWNN	136	20809	9/73	11/73	To AAR 5/99. To Roswell 5/99. Wfu.
G-AWNO	136	20810	10/73	12/73	
G-AWNP	136	20952	9/74	11/74	
G-BBPU	136	20953	10/74	3/75	Initially stored at Wichita.
G-BDPV	136	21213	2/76	4/76	To AAR 6/99. To Roswell 6/99. Wfu.
G-BDXA	236	21238	9/76	7/77	First Rolls-Royce 747-200.
G-BDXB	236	21239	2/77	6/77	
G-BDXC	236	21240	4/77	6/77	
G-BDXD	236	21241	1/78	4/78	
G-BDXE	236	21350	3/78	3/78	
G-BDXF	236	21351	4/78	4/78	
G-BDXG	236	21536	6/78	6/78	
G-BDXH	236	21635	3/79	3/79	'Glider' incident 24/6/82 over Indonesia.
G-BDXI	236	21830	2/80	5/80	
G-BDXJ	236	21831	3/80	10/80	
G-BDXK	236	22303	1/81	3/83	Stored in USA before delivery.
G-BDXL	236	22305	2/81	2/84	Stored in USA before delivery. Entered service with British Airtours 3/84. Ret BA 11/84.
G-BDXM	236	23711	2/87	2/87	Combi. Entered service 3/87 as Combi, later cvtd to all-pax.
G-BDXN	236	23735	3/87	3/87	Combi. Entered service 4/87 as Combi, later cvtd to all-pax.
G-BDXO	236	23799	4/87	4/87	
G-BDXP	236	24088	2/88	2/88	Combi. Entered service 3/88 as Combi. Last Combi op 5/91.
G-KILO	236F	22306	9/80	10/80	To Cathay Pacific as VR-HVY 3/82.

Leased 747s

G-BDPZ	148	19745	3/71	3/76	Lse from Aer Lingus to 10/78. Lsd again 4/79–5/81.
G-BLVE	2B4B	21097	5/75	4/85	Combi. Lse from MEA. Sub-lse British Airtours 10/87. Ret MEA 5/90 as N202AE.
G-BLVF	2B4B	21098	6/75	11/85	Combi. Lse from MEA. Ret MEA 5/90 as N203AE.
G-BMGS	283B	20121	10/71	3/86	Ex-LN-AEO of SAS. Entered service British Airtours 5/86. With BA 10/87–5/89. Caledonian sub-lse 6/89–11/89, BA 11/89–1/90. Ret to lessor. To Virgin as G-VOYG. Wfu Kemble 11/98. B/u 1/99.

Ex-British Caledonian 747s

G-BJXN	230B	20527	2/72	4/88	From BCAL. Ex-Braniff N611BN 4/82. To Continental as N78019 5/90.
G-CITB	2D3B	22579	3/81	4/88	From BCAL. Ex-Alia JY-AFS 9/87. Sold to All Nippon 12/89 but leased back by BA until 11/90. To JA8192.
G-GLYN	211B	21516	5/78	4/88	From BCAL. Ex-Wardair C-GXRA 10/86. To Nora Leasing 2/91, lse to PAL as N207AE.
G-HUGE	2D3B	21252	10/76	4/88	Combi. From BCAL. Ex-Alia JY-AFB 3/85. Sub-lse to Caledonian 2/89. To Potomac Capital as N512DC 11/90. Converted to freighter. To Cargolux as LX-ZCV 11/91.

G-NIGB	211B	21517	4/79	4/88	From BCAL. Ex-Wardair C-GXRD 3/87. To Nora Leasing 2/91, lse to PAL as N208AE.

747-436

G-BNLA	436	23908	6/89	6/89	
G-BNLB	436	23909	7/89	7/89	
G-BNLC	436	23910	6/89	7/89	
G-BNLD	436	23911	8/89	9/89	
G-BNLE	436	24047	10/89	11/89	
G-BNLF	436	24048	2/90	2/90	
G-BNLG	436	24049	2/90	2/90	
G-BNLH	436	24050	3/90	3/90	
G-BNLI	436	24051	4/90	4/90	
G-BNLJ	436	24052	5/90	5/90	
G-BNLK	436	24053	5/90	5/90	
G-BNLL	436	24054	5/90	6/90	
G-BNLM	436	24055	6/90	6/90	
G-BNLN	436	24056	6/90	7/90	
G-BNLO	436	24057	10/90	10/90	
G-BNLP	436	24058	12/90	12/90	
G-BNLR	436	24447	12/90	1/91	
G-BNLS	436	24629	2/91	3/91	
G-BNLT	436	24630	2/91	3/91	
G-BNLU	436	25406	12/91	1/92	
G-BNLV	436	25427	1/92	2/92	
G-BNLW	436	25432	2/92	3/92	
G-BNLX	436	25435	3/92	4/92	
G-BNLY	436	27090	1/93	2/93	
G-BNLZ	436	27091	2/93	3/93	Entered service 21/3/93 with British Asia A/w titles & tail. Repainted BA c/s 10/96.
G-CIVA	436	27092	3/93	3/93	Repainted as British Asia A/w 6/95.
G-CIVB	436	25811	2/94	2/94	'International Children's Conference' titles & tail 9–11/95.
G-CIVC	436	25812	2/94	2/94	
G-CIVD	436	27349	11/94	12/94	
G-CIVE	436	27350	12/94	12/94	Repainted as British Asia A/w 2/96.
G-CIVF	436	25434	3/95	3/95	'Lite.'
G-CIVG	436	25813	4/95	4/95	'Lite.'
G-CIVH	436	25809	4/96	4/96	'Lite.'
G-CIVI	436	25814	4/96	5/96	'Lite.'
G-CIVJ	436	25817	1/97	2/97	
G-CIVK	436	25818	2/97	2/97	
G-CIVL	436	27478	3/97	3/97	
G-CIVM	436	28700	5/97	6/97	
G-CIVN	436	28848	9/97	9/97	
G-CIVO	436	28849	11/97	12/97	
G-CIVP	436	28850	2/98	2/98	
G-CIVR	436	25820	2/98	3/98	
G-CIVS	436	28851	3/98	3/98	
G-CIVT	436	25821	3/98	3/98	
G-CIVU	436	25810	4/98	4/98	
G-CIVV	436	25819	4/98	5/98	
G-CIVW	436	25822	5/98	5/98	
G-CIVX	436	28852	8/98	9/98	
G-CIVY	436	28853	9/98	10/98	
G-CIVZ	436	28854	10/98	11/98	50th 747-436
G-BYGA	436	28855	12/98	2/99	
G-BYGB	436	28856	1/99	2/99	
G-BYGC	436	25823	1/99	1/99	
G-BYGD	436	28857	1/99	1/99	
G-BYGE	436	28858	1/99	2/99	
G-BYGF	436	25824	2/99	2/99	
G-BYGG	436	28859	4/99	4/99	57th 747-436

Boeing 757

G-BIKA	236	22172	10/82	3/83	
G-BIKB	236	22173	12/82	1/83	
G-BIKC	236	22174	1/83	1/83	Red poppy tail c/s 10/96–1/97.
G-BIKD	236	22175	2/83	3/83	
G-BIKF	236	22177	4/83	4/83	Lse to Air Europe in BA c/s and AE titles 4/83–10/83.
G-BIKG	236	22178	8/83	8/83	
G-BIKH	236	22179	9/83	10/83	
G-BIKI	236	22180	10/83	11/83	
G-BIKJ	236	22181	12/83	1/84	
G-BIKK	236	22182	1/84	2/84	
G-BIKL	236	22183	2/84	2/84	
G-BIKM	236	22184	3/84	3/84	
G-BIKN	236	22186	1/85	1/85	
G-BIKO	236	22187	1/85	2/85	
G-BIKP	236	22188	2/85	3/85	
G-BIKR	236	22189	3/85	3/85	
G-BIKS	236	22190	5/85	5/85	
G-BIKT	236	23398	10/85	11/85	
G-BIKU	236	23399	10/85	11/85	
G-BIKV	236	23400	11/85	12/85	
G-BIKW	236	23492	2/86	3/86	

G-BIKX	236	23493	2/86	3/86	
G-BIKY	236	23533	3/86	3/86	
G-BIKZ	236	23532	5/86	5/86	
G-BMRA	236	23710	2/87	3/87	
G-BMRB	236	23975	9/87	9/87	
G-BMRC	236	24072	1/88	1/88	
G-BMRD	236	24073	2/88	2/88	
G-BMRE	236	24074	3/88	3/88	
G-BMRF	236	24101	4/88	5/88	
G-BMRG	236	24102	5/88	5/88	
G-BMRH	236	24266	1/89	2/89	
G-BMRI	236	24267	2/89	2/89	
G-BMRJ	236	24268	2/89	3/89	Del to Caledonian. Op by BA 11/89–3/90. Ret BA 11/90.
G-BPEA	236	24370	3/89	3/89	Del to Caledonian. Lse to North American A/l 1/90–3/90. Lse to El Al 3/90–4/90. Lse to Nationair 12/90–3/91. Op by BA Shuttle 11/91–3/92. Lse to Nationair 12/92–3/93. Lse to LAPA 12/93–3/94 & 12/94–3/95. Ret BA 11/95. To EuroGatwick 3/97.
G-BPEB	236	24371	4/89	4/89	Del to Caledonian. Lse to Nationair 12/90–4/91. Lse to Nationair 12/91–4/92. Ret BA 11/95. To EuroGatwick 3/97.
G-BPEC	236	24882	10/90	11/90	Del to Caledonian. Lse to Nationair 11/91–4/92. Lse to Nationair 10/92–2/93. Ret BA 10/95, used by BAR 1/95–10/98.
G-BPED	236	25059	4/91	4/91	
G-BPEE	236	25060	4/91	5/91	Del to Caledonian. Ret BA 11/94, used by BAR 1/95–10/97.
G-BPEF	236	24120	4/88	2/92	Ex-Air Europe G-BOHC. Entered svce with Caledonian 5/92. Op BA Shuttle in full Cale c/s 10/93–4/94. Ret BA 10/95. To EuroGatwick 3/97. To LHR by 1/99.
G-BPEH	236	24121	6/88	2/92	Ex-Air Europe G-BNSE. Entered svce with Caledonian 5/92. Ret to lessor then to Istanbul A/l as TC-AHA 4/95.
G-BPEI	236	25806	2/94	3/94	
G-BPEJ	236	25807	3/94	4/94	
G-BPEK	236	25808	3/95	3/95	
G-CPEL	236	24398	4/89	8/92	Ex-Air Europe G-BRJE. Del from storage at Gatwick as N602DF. I/s 10/92.
G-CPEM	236	28665	3/97	3/97	
G-CPEN	236	28666	4/97	4/97	To EuroGatwick 5/97. To LHR by 1/99.
G-CPEO	236	28667	6/97	7/97	Utopia launch Boeing Field 10/6/97 before first flight.
G-CPEP	2Y0	25268	10/91	4/97	Ex-C-GTSU Air Transat. Five year lease.
G-CPER	236	29113	12/97	12/97	To EuroGatwick 1/98. To LHR 3/99.
G-CPES	236	29114	2/98	3/98	To EuroGatwick 3/98. To LHR 6/99.
G-CPET	236	29115	4/98	5/98	To EuroGatwick 5/98. To LHR 5/99.
G-CPEU	236	29941	4/99	5/99	
G-CPEV	236	29943	5/99	6/99	
G-CPEW	236		(6/99)		Sold before delivery.
G-CPEX	236		(6/99)		Sold before delivery.
G-CPEY	236		(6/99)		Sold before delivery.
G-CPEZ	236		(7/99)		Sold before delivery.

Leased 757s

G-BKRM	236	22176	3/83	11/84	Ordered by BA as G-BIKF, sold to Air Europe before del. Lse by BA 11/84 AE c/s BA t/t, painted full BA c/s 8/85. Ret AE 4/86. Lsd again 11/86–4/87, AE c/s but BA t/t added 2/87.
G-DRJC	2T7	23895	5/87	4/88	Lsd from Monarch, full BA c/s. Ret 4/89.
G-OOOB	28A	23822	4/87	11/87	Lsd from Air 2000, their c/s plus BA titles. Ret 4/88.
G-BUDX	236	25592	4/92	5/92	Op by Caledonian on behalf of Ambassador A/l. Flown in Ambassador c/s and Caledonian titles. Last Caledonian op 5/93. To Sunways 4/95 SE-DSK.

Boeing 767

G-BNWA	336	24333	5/89	4/90	S/H.
G-BNWB	336	24334	11/89	2/90	S/H.
G-BNWC	336	24335	1/90	2/90	S/H.
G-BNWD	336	24336	1/90	2/90	S/H.
G-BNWE	336	24337	2/90	3/90	S/H.
G-BNWF	336	24338	5/90	6/90	First L/H 767. To S/H 3/95.
G-BNWG	336	24339	6/90	7/90	L/H. To S/H.
G-BNWH	336	24340	10/90	10/90	L/H. To BAR S96.
G-BNWI	336	24341	11/90	12/90	L/H. To S/H S95. To Gatwick 1/96.
G-BNWJ	336	24342	3/91	4/91	Stored Mojave 4/91. To LHR 10/91, stored. In svce 4/92 S/H.
G-BNWK	336	24343	4/91	4/91	S/H.
G-BNWL	336	25203	4/91	4/91	Stored Mojave 4/91. To LHR, entered svce with S/H 10/91.
G-BNWM	336	25204	6/91	6/91	L/H. To S/H S95. To Gatwick 1/96.
G-BNWN	336	25444	10/91	10/91	L/H. To BAR 3/93. To L/H 1/95, to S/H 3/97.
G-BNWO	336	25442	2/92	3/92	L/H. To BAR 3/93. To L/H 10/94. To Gatwick S96.
G-BNWP	336	25443	2/92	3/92	S/H. To L/H, returned to S/H.
G-BNWR	336	25732	3/92	3/92	L/H. To Gatwick 3/96.
G-BNWS	336	25826	1/93	2/93	L/H. To S/H 2/97.
G-BNWT	336	25828	1/93	2/93	S/H. To L/H, returned to S/H.
G-BNWU	336	25829	3/93	3/93	BAR. To Gatwick S96.
G-BNWV	336	27140	4/93	4/93	S/H.
G-BNWW	336	25831	12/93	2/94	S/H.
G-BNWX	336	25832	1/94	3/94	L/H. To S/H.
G-BNWY	336	25834	3/96	4/96	S/H.
G-BNWZ	336	25733	2/97	2/97	S/H.
G-BZHA	336	29230	5/98	5/98	S/H.
G-BZHB	336	29231	5/98	5/98	S/H.
G-BZHC	336	29232	6/98	6/98	S/H.
N652US	2B7	24765			US Air, in BA c/s '93–96.
N654US	2B7	25225			US Air, in BA c/s 5/93–2/96.
N655US	2B7	25257			US Air, in BA c/s 9/93–3/96.

Boeing 777

G-ZZZA	236A	27105	2/95	5/96	F/f 2/2/95 as N77779. Visited LHR 20–21/4/95.
G-ZZZB	236A	27106	4/95	3/97	F/f 11/4/95 as N77771, used for engine/ETOPS testing and as a testbed for uprated GE90-92B.
G-ZZZC	236A	27107	9/95	11/95	
G-ZZZD	236A	27108	11/95	12/95	
G-ZZZE	236A	27109	12/95	1/96	
G-VIIA	236B	27483	10/96	7/97	First 777IGW, f/f 7/10/96.
G-VIIB	236B	27484	12/96	5/97	
G-VIIC	236B	27485	1/97	2/97	
G-VIID	236B	27486	2/97	2/97	
G-VIIE	236B	27487	2/97	2/97	
G-VIIF	236B	27488	3/97	3/97	
G-VIIG	236B	27489	3/97	4/97	
G-VIIH	236B	27490	4/97	5/97	
G-RAES	236B	27491	5/97	6/97	Arr LHR 14/6 new c/s, i/s 15/6 to Paris Airshow.
G-VIIJ	236B	27492	12/97	12/97	
G-VIIK	236B	28840	1/98	2/98	
G-VIIL	236B	27493	2/98	3/98	
G-VIIM	236B	28841	3/98	3/98	
G-VIIN	236B	29319	8/98	8/98	
G-VIIO	236B	29320	1/99	1/99	AML two-class.
G-VIIP	236B	29321	1/99	2/99	AML two-class.
G-VIIR	236B	29322	3/99	3/99	AML two-class.
G-VIIS	236B	29323	3/99	4/99	
G-VIIT	236B	29962	5/99	5/99	
G-VIIU	236B	29963	5/99	5/99	
G-VIIV	236B	29964	6/99	6/99	
G-VIIW	236B			7/99	
G-VIIX	236B			8/99	
G-VIIY	236B			10/99	
G-YMMA	236ER			1/00	
G-YMMB	236ER			1/00	
G-YMMC	236ER			2/00	
G-YMMD	236ER			2/00	
G-YMME	236ER			3/00	
G-YMMF	236ER			5/00	
G-YMMG	236ER			12/00	
G-YMMH	236ER			1/01	
G-YMMI	236ER			2/01	
G-YMMJ	236ER			2/01	
G-YMMK	236ER			3/01	
G-YMML	236ER			4/01	
G-YMMM	236ER			5/01	
G-YMMN	236ER			1/02	
G-YMMO	236ER			3/02	
G-YMMP	236ER			4/02	

Airbus A319/320

G-BUSB	A320-110	0006	11/87	3/88	First flew as F-WWDD in BCAL c/s.
G-BUSC	A320-110	0008	12/87	6/88	First flew as F-WWDE in BCAL c/s.
G-BUSD	A320-110	0011	2/88	7/88	
G-BUSE	A320-110	0017	10/88	12/88	
G-BUSF	A320-110	0018	3/89	5/89	
G-BUSG	A320-210	0039	3/89	5/89	
G-BUSH	A320-210	0042	4/89	6/89	
G-BUSI	A320-210	0103	2/90	3/90	
G-BUSJ	A320-210	0109	/90	8/90	
G-BUSK	A320-210	0120	8/90	10/90	
G-EUPA	A319-131	1082		9/99	
G-EUPB	A319-131	1115			
G-EUPC	A319-131	1116			

(G-EUPA–Z = A319)
(G-EUOA–Z = A320)

Concorde

G-BOAA	102	206	11/75	1/76	Regd G-N94AA 1/79–7/80.
G-BOAB	102	208	5/76	9/76	Regd G-N94AB 1/79–9/80.
G-BOAC	102	204	2/75	2/76	Regd G-N81AC 1/79–8/80.
G-BOAD	102	210	8/76	12/76	Port side painted in Singapore Airlines c/s 1/79–11/80. Regd G-N94AD 1/79–6/80.
G-BOAE	102	212	3/77	7/77	Regd G-N94AE 1/79–7/80.
G-BOAF	102	216	4/79	6/80	Ex-G-BFKX. Del as G-N94AF, entered service as G-BOAF.
G-BOAG	102	214	4/78	2/80	Ex-G-BFKW. Re-regd G-BOAG 2/81. Stored '82–85 Re-entered service 26/4/85 LHR–JFK.
G-BBDG	100	202	2/74	84	Second production Concorde. Never entered service. Retired at Filton 12/81 and stored. Ownership transferred to BA.

INDIVIDUAL AIRCRAFT HISTORIES – TYPES NO LONGER OPERATED

Chapter five gives a brief history of aircraft types which have served British Airways but are now no longer operated. This appendix details the individual aircraft within those fleets giving first flight and delivery dates plus information about their use by the airline, and fate after leaving it.

Aircraft types no longer operated:
- Boeing 707
- BAC VC-10
- BAC One-Eleven
- HS-748 and BAe ATP
- HS Trident
- Lockheed TriStar
- McDonnell Douglas DC-10
- Vickers Viscount
- Vickers Vanguard / Merchantman

Format of tables: (example)

(1)	(2)	(3)	(4)	(5)	(6)
G-AXGW	336C	20374	2/70	3/70	To Alyemda as 7O-ACO 12/81.

(1) Aircraft registration
(2) Aircraft model number – i.e. Boeing 707-336C
(3) Constructor's number
(4) First flight – month/year
(5) Delivery to British Airways or predecessor (BEA, BOAC or subsidiary) – month/year
(6) Notes regarding the aircraft's service history with British Airways and its subsequent fate

Boeing 707

G-APFB	436	17703	5/59	5/60	Lse to Syrian Arab 3/74–2/75. To British Airtours 4/75.To Boeing at Kingman 11/76, stored then b/u.
G-APFC	436	17704	1/60	5/60	To Boeing at Wichita 5/75, b/u.
G-APFD	436	17705	3/60	4/60	BEA Airtours from 2/73 then British Airtours. Lse to Air Mauritius 10/77–4/79. To Boeing 11/79. To Commercial Air Transport Sales 11/79. To Air Transport Sales as N888NW 11/80. Stored at Fort Lauderdale until b/u 8/86.
G-APFF	436	17707	5/60	5/60	To British Airtours 5/74. To Boeing at Kingman 5/81, stored then b/u.
G-APFG	436	17708	5/60	6/60	BEA Airtours from 3/73 then British Airtours. Wfu at Stansted 11/80. To Aviation Traders for apprentice training 3/81. B/u 2/89, fuselage to Cardington for water-mist fire suppression trials.
G-APFH	436	17709	6/60	7/60	BEA Airtours from 1/72 then British Airtours. Damaged in a heavy landing at Heraklion 6/74, stored. Returned to LHR 4/75. To Boeing 5/75 at Wichita, to Marana and b/u.
G-APFI	436	17710	7/60	7/60	To British Airtours 2/75. To Boeing at Kingman 11/76, stored then b/u.
G-APFJ	436	17711	9/60	9/60	Lse to Malaysian A/l 5/74–4/75. To British Airtours 2/77. Flown to RAF Cosford 12/6/81 for Aerospace Museum. Preserved as part of BA Collection.
G-APFK	436	17712	9/60	9/60	BEA Airtours from 12/71 then British Airtours. W/o training at Prestwick 17/3/77.
G-APFL	436	17713	10/60	10/60	BEA Airtours from 12/72 then British Airtours. To Cargo Charter Co. as 9Q-CRW 4/80. To Coastal Airways 1/81 as 5X-CAU. Wfu Entebbe 1/83.
G-APFM	436	17714	10/60	11/60	To Boeing at Kingman 11/76, stored then b/u.
G-APFN	436	17715	10/60	11/60	To Boeing at Kingman 4/76, stored then b/u.
G-APFO	436	17716	10/60	12/60	BEA Airtours from 11/72 then British Airtours. To Boeing at Kingman 3/81, stored then b/u.
G-APFP	436	17717	11/60	12/60	To Boeing 10/75 & donated Franklin Institute Philadelphia. Displayed in BOAC colours. B/u 10/88.
G-ARRA	436	18411	1/62	2/62	To British Airtours 11/76. Wfu Stansted 11/80. To Europe Aero Service 3/81. To Coastal Airways as N4465D 8/83. W/o by fire at Perpignan 10/83.
G-ARRB	436	18412	1/63	2/63	To Boeing at Kingman 1/76, stored then b/u.
G-ARRC	436	18413	3/63	3/63	To British Airtours 12/76. Wfu Stansted 11/80. To Europe Aero Service 3/81. To Coastal Airways as N4465C 8/83. To Air Charter Service as 9Q-CTK '90. Wfu Kinshasa, b/u 4/95.

GARWD 465 18372 2/62 9/62 BEA Airtours from 1/73 then British Airtours. Sub-lse to Air Mauritius 4/79–4/81. To Boeing at Kingman 5/81, stored then b/u.

G-AYSL 321 17599 10/59 7/78 Lse by BA from Dan-Air to 10/78. Lse by British Airtours 5/79–10/79, stored Lasham. To International Air Leases as N80703 11/79. To Kivu Air Cargo 1/83, b/u Lasham 2/83.

G-ASZF 336C 18924 9/65 12/65 Freighter. Wfu LHR 3/82. To Air Supply Corp. 5/83. To RN Air Cargo as 5N-ARO 6/83. W/o by fire landing at Accra 25/9/83.

G-ASZG 336C 18925 11/65 12/65 Freighter. Wfu LHR by 3/82. To Air Supply Corp. 5/83. To Tratco as LX-FCV 12/83. Lse to Naganagani as XT-ABX 9/84. Stored Southend 5/92. To Omega Air 9/94. Lse to Brasair as EL-AKI 11/94. Regd PP-BRB 6/95. To BETA Cargo 10/96. Wfu Rio 4/98 & b/u.

GATWV 336C 19498 11/67 11/67 Freighter. Wfu LHR by 9/81. To Greyhound Guarantee 1/82. To Clipper International 1/82 lse to West African Air Cargo as 9G-ACX 2/82–4/86. To Aviation Consultants as N14A 5/86. Leases to St Lucia A/w and Seagreen Air Transport several times from 6/86. To Caribbean Air Transport. To Aero Zambia as 5Y-BNJ 9/98.

G-ATZD 365C 19590 11/67 5/69 To Tratco 5/83. To United African A/w as 5A-DJV 6/83. To ZAS as SU-DAI 11/86. To Okada Air as 5N-AOO 4/88. To Belgian International Cargo as OO-CDE 10/88. To Air Mercury Int'l Air Cargo 2/91. Stored 1/92. To Omega Air 6/92. Lse to Royal Jordanian as JY-AJM 7/92–4/97. To Argentine Air Force as LV-WXL 8/97.

G-AVPB 336C 19843 8/68 8/68 To British Airtours 4/81. Wfu LGW 10/83. To ZAS as SU-DAC 2/84. Stored Amsterdam 7/93–3/96. To Memphis Air as SU-PBA 3/96. W/o on take-off from Mombasa 10/3/98.

G-AWHU 379C 19821 5/68 6/68 To Air Supply Corp. 6/83. To 9Q-CKI 11/83. To Hang Kong Vietnam as VN-B3415 1/84. Regd VN-83415 10/86. To Equator Bank 8/89. Lse to DAS Air Cargo as 5X-JEF 8/90–1/91. Lse to Golden Star Cargo as ST-GLD 1–8/91. To RACE Cargo A/l as 9G-OLF 11/92. To Gemini A/l as 9G-ONE 11/92. To DAS Cargo as 5X-JEF 9/93.

G-AXGW 336C 20374 2/70 3/70 To Alyemda as 7O-ACO 12/81. Damaged Aden 8/85.

G-AXGX 336C 20375 3/70 3/70 Lse to State of Qatar 5/81. Bought 7/84, regd A7-AAC. Stored Southend 3/95 as VR-BZA. To Grumman Aerospace Corp. 5/96 for USAF E-8C J-Stars programme. To Lake Charles, Louisiana for storage/conversion.

GAXXY 336B 20456 2/71 2/71 To British Airtours 4/82. Wfu 3/84. To Maof A/l as 4X-BMC 7/84. To Omega Air as N343A 12/85. To Boeing 2/86, lse Transbrasil as PT-TCQ 2/86. Wfu Davis-Monthan, Arizona 5/88. B/u 4/93.

G-AXXZ 336B 20457 4/71 4/71 Lse to Zambia A/w 4/82. To Air Supply Corp. 6/83. Lse to West Coast A/l as 9G-ADB 8/83–10/83. To Benin Government as TY-BBR 11/83. W/o during aborted take-off at Sebha, Libya 13/6/85.

G-AYLT 336C 20517 5/71 5/71 To GKN-Sankey as 9Q-CLY 11/81. To ZAS as SU-DAD 1/85. To Air Hong Kong as VR-HKK 11/87. To Phoenix Aviation as 9G-TWO 10/92. Stored Southend 1/94–3/95. To Simba Air Cargo as 5Y-SIM 3/95.

British Aircraft Corporation VC-10

G-ARVB STV 805 12/62 2/65 Wfu and stored LHR 7/74. B/u 10/76.

G-ARVC STV 806 2/63 12/64 Lse Gulf Air 7/74, bought 10/75 & regd A40-VC. Stored Stansted 12/77. To Filton 3/78. Conv. to K2, to 101 Sqdn as ZA144 2/84.

G-ARVE STV 807 4/63 10/64 Wfu and stored LHR 10/74. B/u 10/76.

G-ARVF STV 808 7/63 9/64 To UAE Govt 7/74. To Saarbrucken 23/3/81 & taken to the Flugzeugmuseum, Hermeskeil, Germany. Preserved.

G-ARVG STV 809 10/63 6/64 Lse Gulf Air 6/74, bought 10/75 & regd A40-VG. Lse to BA 8/77 for s/h routes. Stored Stansted 12/77. To Filton 3/78. First VC-10 tanker conv. first flight 22/6/82 as ZA141. To 101 Sqdn 10/84.

G-ARVH STV 810 11/63 7/64 Wfu and stored LHR 10/74. B/u 10/76.

G-ARVI STV 811 12/63 4/64 Lse Gulf Air 3/74, bought 10/75 & regd A40-VI. Stored Stansted 12/77. To Filton by 3/78. Conv. K2, to 101 Sqdn as ZA142 4/84.

G-ARVJ STV 812 2/64 4/64 Lse Ruler of Qatar 10/75–4/81 Gulf Air c/s. Wfu and stored LHR. To RAF at Brize Norton 10/9/82, reduced slowly for spares. Serial ZD493 allocated but not worn.

G-ARVK STV 813 3/64 5/64 Lse Gulf Air 6/75, bought 10/75 & regd A40-VK. Stored Stansted 12/77. To Filton 3/78, conv. to K2 & f/f 12/82 as ZA143. To 101 Sqdn 9/83. Stored RAF St. Athan 10/98.

G-ARVL STV 814 6/64 6/64 Lse Gulf Air 4/74, bought 10/75 & regd A40-VL. Lse Air Ceylon 12/77–3/78. To Filton, conv. to K2, to 101 Sqdn as ZA140 7/83.

GARVM STV 815 7/64 7/64 Retained as Super VC-10 trainer. Tail painted BA c/s then a/c fully repainted 1976. To Cosford Aerospace Museum 22/10/79.

G-ASGA SUV 851 5/64 12/65 Wfu 3/81. To Prestwick then Abingdon 4/81 & stored by RAF as ZD230. To Filton 1/91, conv. to K4 & to 101 Sqdn 12/94.

G-ASGB SUV 852 9/64 4/65 Wfu 3/81. To Prestwick then Abingdon 4/81 & stored by RAF as ZD231. B/u 3/87.

G-ASGC SUV 853 1/65 3/65 Wfu LHR 10/79. To Duxford 15/4/80. Preserved.

G-ASGD SUV 854 2/65 3/65 Wfu LHR, to Prestwick 4/80, stored. To RAF as ZD232 5/81, to Brize Norton and used for ground training. Fuselage still intact but wings removed by 6/93.

G-ASGE	SUV	855	3/65	3/65	Wfu LHR, to Prestwick 5/80, stored. To RAF as ZD233 5/81, to Brize Norton by 8/81. B/u 1982 & fuselage to Catterick then Manston for fire/rescue training.
G-ASGF	SUV	856	3/65	4/65	Wfu LHR 3/81. To RAF at Brize Norton 4/81 as ZD234. B/u 1982, nose used for simulator.
G-ASGG	SUV	857	5/65	6/67	Wfu LHR 3/81. To Prestwick then Abingdon 4/81 & stored by RAF as ZD235. To Filton 7/91. Final K4, to 101 Sqdn 3/96.
G-ASGH	SUV	858	10/65	11/65	Wfu LHR 1/80. To Prestwick 4/80, stored. To Abingdon 4/81 & stored by RAF as ZD236. B/u 4/87.
G-ASGI	SUV	859	1/66	2/66	Wfu LHR, to Prestwick 4/80, stored. To Abingdon 5/81 & stored by RAF as ZD237. B/u 3/87.
G-ASGJ	SUV	860	2/67	3/67	Wfu LHR, to Prestwick 4/80, stored. To Abingdon 5/81 & stored by RAF as ZD238. B/u 4/87.
G-ASGK	SUV	861	9/67	10/67	Wfu LHR, to Prestwick 5/80, stored. To Abingdon 4/81 & stored by RAF as ZD239. B/u 4/87.
G-ASGL	SUV	862	12/67	1/68	Wfu LHR, to Prestwick 5/80, stored. To Abingdon 4/81 & stored by RAF as ZD240. To Filton 10/90, conv. K4, to 101 Sqdn 7/94.
GASGM	SUV	863	2/68	4/68	Wfu LHR, to Prestwick 5/80, stored. To Abingdon 4/81 & stored by RAF as ZD241. To Filton 8/91, conv. K4 & to 101 Sqdn 6/95.
G-ASGO	SUV	865	9/68	9/68	W/o by terrorist action at Amsterdam 4/3/74.
G-ASGP	SUV	866	11/68	12/68	Wfu LHR 3/81. To Abingdon 5/81 & stored by RAF as ZD242. To Filton 7/90, first K4, first flight 30/7/93. To 101 Sqdn 4/94.
G-ASGR	SUV	867	2/69	5/69	Wfu LHR, to Prestwick 5/80, stored. To Abingdon by 5/81 & stored by RAF as ZD243. B/u & fuselage to Filton 8/93.

British Aircraft Corporation One-Eleven

G-AVMH	510	136	2/68	6/69	Wfu Hurn 11/92. To European Avn 5/93, i/s 2/94. Wfu Hurn 10/98.
G-AVMI	510	137	5/68	4/69	Wfu Hurn 11/92. To European Avn. 5/93, i/s 2/94.
G-AVMJ	510	138	7/68	8/68	Wfu Hurn 1/92. To European Avn. 5/93. Stored Filton 5/93, dismantled & fuselage used as cabin crew trainer at Hurn.
G-AVMK	510	139	8/68	9/68	Wfu Hurn 12/92. To European Avn 5/93, i/s 4/94. Wfu Hurn 10/98.
G-AVML	510	140	8/68	10/68	Wfu Hurn 1/92. To European Avn. 5/93, i/s 4/95.
G-AVMM	510	141	9/68	10/68	Wfu Hurn 1/92. To European Avn. 5/93, i/s 9/98.
G-AVMN	510	142	10/68	11/68	Wfu Hurn 8/92. To European Avn. 5/93, i/s 7/94.
G-AVMO	510	143	10/68	11/68	Wfu Hurn 12/92. To BA Collection, Cosford Museum 22/3/93.
G-AVMP	510	144	11/68	12/68	Wfu Hurn 10/92. To European Avn. 5/93, i/s 4/95.
G-AVMR	510	145	11/68	5/70	Wfu Hurn 1/92. To European Avn. 5/93, stored Filton then Hurn.
G-AVMS	510	146	12/68	1/69	Wfu Hurn 1/93. To European Avn. 5/93, i/s 10/94.
G-AVMT	510	147	1/69	3/69	Wfu Hurn 10/92. To European Avn. 5/93, i/s 11/93.
G-AVMU	510	148	1/69	3/69	Wfu Hurn 10/92. To Duxford Avn. Society 4/3/93.
G-AVMV	510	149	3/69	4/69	Wfu Hurn 8/92. To European Avn. 5/93, stored Filton then Hurn.
G-AVMW	510	150	4/69	5/69	Wfu Hurn 12/92. To European Avn. 5/93, i/s 11/93.
G-AVMX	510	151	6/69	6/69	Wfu Hurn 1/92. To European Avn. 5/93, stored Filton then Hurn.
G-AVMY	510	152	7/69	7/69	Wfu Hurn 1/92. To European Avn. 5/93, i/s 6/95.
G-AVMZ	510	153	8/69	8/69	Wfu Hurn 11/91. To European Avn. 5/93, i/s 10/96.
G-AVGP	408	114	6/67	4/70	Ex-Cambrian. Wfu Hurn 11/88. To Birmingham European 6/90, Brymon European 10/92, Maersk Air 8/93 & painted BA c/s. To Nationwide as ZS-OAF 12/96.
G-AVOE	416	129	3/68	12/70	Ex-Cambrian. Wfu Cardiff 6/80, returned to BAe. To BAF/Air Manchester as G-SURE 4/82. To Britt A/w as N390BA 6/84. To Okada Air as 5N-AYS 9/87. Wfu & b/u by 10/92.
G-AVOF	416	131	1/68	12/69	Ex-Cambrian. Wfu Cardiff 12/80, returned to BAe. Stored Hurn. Lse BIA, BCAL, Dan-Air. To Britt A/w as N392BA 3/85. To Okada Air as 5N-AYT 5/87.
G-AWBL	416	132	4/68	2/71	Ex-Cambrian. Wfu Hurn 11/88. To Birmingham European 1/90, Brymon European 10/92, Maersk Air 8/93 & painted BA c/s. To Nationwide as ZS-NYZ 7/96.
G-BBME	401	066	4/66	7/73	Wfu Hurn 11/88. To Birmingham European 1/90, Brymon European 10/92, Maersk Air 8/93 & painted BA c/s. To Nationwide as ZS-OAG 1/97.
G-BBMF	401	074	6/66	12/73	Wfu Hurn 11/88. To Birmingham European 4/90, To Okada Air as 5N-EHI 8/91.
G-BBMG	408	115	5/68	9/73	Wfu Hurn 11/88. To Birmingham European 2/90, Brymon European 10/92, Maersk Air 8/93 & painted BA c/s. To Nationwide as ZS-OAH 4/97.
G-BGKE	539	263	1/80	3/80	Wfu Hurn 4/91. To GEC Ferranti Defence Systems 6/91. To Defence Research Agency as ZH763 3/94, now DERA.
G-BGKF	539	264	5/80	6/80	Wfu Hurn 4/91. To Okada Air as 5N-ORO 7/91.
G-BGKG	539	265	8/80	8/80	Wfu Hurn 4/91. To Okada Air as 5N-BIN 7/91.

Ex-British Caledonian One-Elevens

G-AWYR	501	174	3/69	4/88	Ex-BCAL. Lse Ryanair as EI-CID 6/93–3/94. Lse Maersk Air in BA c/s as G-AWYR 8/94, bought 9/95. Wfu 7/98. To Executive Air Services as 5N-ESA 12/98.
G-AWYS	501	175	4/69	4/88	Ex-BCAL. Lse Brymon European 3/93, to Maersk Air 8/93, painted BA c/s. Bought 9/95. To Executive Air Services as 5N-ESB 8/98.

G-AWYT	501	176	5/69	4/88	Ex-BCAL. Lse Ryanair as EI-CIE 6/93–1/94. To Express City as 9Q-CKY 10/94. Wfu Kinshasa by 2/98.
G-AWYU	501	177	6/69	4/88	Ex-BCAL. Lse Ryanair as EI-CIC 6/93–3/94. To Express City as 9Q-CKI 11/94. Wfu Kinshasa by 2/98.
G-AWYV	501	178	6/69	4/88	Ex-BCAL. Wfu Hurn. To European Avn. 7/94. Lse Maersk Air 4/96–4/98 & op in BA colours.
G-AXJK	501	191	8/69	4/88	Ex-BCAL. Lse Ryanair as EI-CIB 6/93–2/94. To Express City as 9Q-CKP 10/94. Wfu Kinshasa by 2/98.
G-AXJM	501	214	3/70	4/88	Ex-BCAL. To Oriental A/l as 5N-OAL 9/93. Wfu Lagos by 1/98.
G-AXLL	523	193	9/69	4/88	Ex-BCAL. Wfu Hurn 12/92. To European Avn. 12/94, i/s 7/95.
G-AYOP	530	233	3/71	4/88	Ex-BCAL. Wfu Hurn 12/92. To European Avn. 7/94, i/s 5/95.
G-AZMF	530	240	3/72	4/88	Ex-BCAL. Wfu Hurn 12/92. To European Avn. 9/94. i/s 1/95 in 48-seat VIP configuration. Note this a/c was also leased from BCAL 11/78–4/79.
G-AZPZ	515	229	12/70	4/88	Ex-BCAL. Wfu Lasham 7/93. To Oriental A/l as 5N-IMO 5/94.W/o Tamanrasset, Algeria 18/9/94.
G-BJRT	528	234	2/71	4/88	Ex-BCAL. To JARO Int'l as YR-JBA 10/93.
G-BJRU	528	238	2/72	4/88	Ex-BCAL. To JARO Int'l as YR-JBB 10/93.

Leased One-Elevens

A40-BU	432	157	11/68	8/77	Lse from Gulf Air until 11/77. To 5N-AXQ of Okada Air 10/90.
G-AXOX	432	121	8/68	11/86	Lse from Air UK until 4/87. To Okada Air as 5N-AXT 6/90. Damaged Jos, Nigeria 7/97 & wfu.
G-BFWN	537	261	9/78	10/78	Lse from Cyprus A/w until 4/80. Became 5B-DAJ with Cyprus. To Nationwide as ZS-NUJ 7/95.

Hawker Siddeley HS-748 and British Aerospace ATP

HS-748

G-ATMI	2A	1592	3/66	3/83	Lse fm Dan-Air 3/83, 10/83, 4/84, 5–6/84. To Janes Aviation 7/92, op by Emerald A/w fm 9/93 as a freighter.
G-ATMJ	2A	1593	4/66	3/82	Lse fm Dan-Air until 3/89. To Janes Aviation 7/92, op by Emerald A/w fm 9/93 as a freighter.
G-AZSU	2A	1612	4/67	3/82	Lse fm Dan-Air until 2/85. To Aberdeen A/w 3/90, Euroair 9/92, to Air Provence Int'l as F-GPDC 5/95.
G-BCDZ	2A	1662	4/69	5/82	Lse fm BAe until 11/82. To Calm Air Int'l as C-GSBF 10/84.
G-BCOE	2B	1736	6/75	7/75	Converted from -2A 6/85. To BAe 6/92, lse Air Nepal as 9N-ACN 3/93–3/94. Lse Impulse A/l as VH-IMI 10/94. Stored after conversion to freighter config. To Int'l Aviation 7/98.
G-BCOF	2B	1737	8/75	9/75	Converted from -2A 4/85. To BAe 1/92. Lse Impulse A/l as VH-IMK 11/94, freighter. To Int'l Aviation 1/98.
G-BFLL	2A	1658	10/68	4/82	Lse fm Dan-Air until 1/85 and 9–10/85, 1/86, 11/86–4/87, 10/87, 10–11/88. To Euroair 9/92, to Air Provence as F-GODD 7/95.
G-BGJV	2B	1768	6/79	1/85	Retd BAe 11/91. To Sri Lanka A/F as CR-834 12/91. Operated by Helitours as 4R-HVA, w/o in Sri Lanka 29/4/95.
G-BGMN	2A	1766	6/79	6/86	Lse fm Euroair until 4/89. Lse to JEA 12/89–9/91. To Airfast Services Indonesia PT as PK-OCH 7/92. To Emerald A/w as G-BGMN 10/98.
G-BGMO	2A	1767	8/79	6/86	Lse fm Euroair until 4/89. Lse to JEA 10/89–10/91. To Mt. Cook as ZK-MCB 12/93. To Emerald as G-BGMO 2/96.
G-BMFT	2A	1714	6/72	5/86	Lse fm Euroair until 7/86 & 4/87–4/89. Op by Scottish European, British Independant A/l, Aberdeen A/w and JEA '89-91. Lse Airfast Indonesia 11/93. To Emerald A/w 3/98 as freighter. Regd G-OPFW 7/98, painted in Parcelforce colours.
G-BOHY	2B	1784	3/81	3/88	Lse fm DLT to 10/91. Stored. To Necon Air as 9N-ADE 10/94.
G-BOHZ	2B	1785	4/81	3/88	Lse fm DLT to 12/91. Stored. To Executive Aerospace as ZS-NNW 12/94.
G-HDBA	2B	1798	11/84	12/84	To BAe 1/92. Lse Emirates as A6-GRM 4/92–1/93. Lse Nepal A/w as 9N-ACW 2/94. Damaged in Nepal 11/97 & wfu.
G-HDBB	2B	1799	11/84	12/84	To BAe 11/91. Lse Emirates as A6-ABM 4/92–1/93. To Nepal A/w as 9N-ACX 3/94. To International Air as VH-
G-HDBC	2B	1786	7/81	6/88	Lse fm DLT until 10/91. Stored. To Executive Aerospace as ZS-NWW 12/95.
G-HDBD	2B	1797	9/84	3/90	Lse fm BAe until 4/92. Op last BA 748 service Belfast–Glasgow 15/4/92. To Emerald A/w as G-EMRD 10/96.

BAe ATP

G-BTPA	ATP	2007	8/88	12/88	Ret BAe 6/98. To Air Europa Express as EC-GYE 10/98.
G-BTPC	ATP	2010	12/88	1/89	Ret BAe 8/98. To Air Europa Express as EC-GYF 10/98.
G-BTPD	ATP	2011	2/89	2/89	Ret BAe 8/98. To Air Europa Express as EC-GYR 11/98.
G-BTPE	ATP	2012	3/89	3/89	Ret BAe 10/98. To Air Europa Express as EC-GZH 12/98.
G-BTPF	ATP	2013	4/89	5/89	Ret BAe 12/98. To Air Europa Express 5/99.

G-BTPG	ATP	2014	5/89	5/89	Ret BAe 2/99. To Air Europa Express 4/99.
G-BTPH	ATP	2015	6/89	6/89	Ret BAe 2/99. To Air Europa Express.
G-BTPJ	ATP	2016	6/89	7/89	Ret BAe 2/99. To Air Europa Express.
G-BTPK	ATP	2041	9/91	11/91	Ret BAe 11/96. To Canarias Regional Air as EC-GLC 1/97. To Air Europa Express as EC-GSG 2/98.
G-BTPL	ATP	2042	10/91	11/91	Ret BAe 11/96. To Canarias Regional Air as EC-GLH 3/97. To Air Europa Express 3/99.
G-BTPM	ATP	2043	11/91	12/91	Ret BAe 12/96. To Canarias Regional Air as EC-GNI 4/97. To Air Europa Express as EC-GSH 2/98.
G-BTPN	ATP	2044	12/91	12/91	Ret BAe 1/97. To Canarias Regional Air as EC-GNJ 4/97. To Air Europa Express as EC-GSI 2/98.
G-BTPO	ATP	2051	7/92	7/92	Ret BAe 3/99. For British World as G-OBLUP 10/99.
G-BUWP	ATP	2053	9/92	8/93	Lse fm BAe, white c/s. Bought 6/94 & repainted. Ret BAe 4/99. For British World as G-OBWR 10/99
G-BRLY	ATP	2025	8/90	4/91	Lse fm BAe to 10/91, 3–6/92, 4/93–1/94, 8/94–11/94, 12/94–6/95. Lse to Manx 7/95 then British Regional. Used on some BA svcs. Ret BAe 1/99.

Hawker Siddeley Trident

G-ARPA	1C	2101	1/62	8/65	Wfu LHR 2/75. To Prestwick storage, b/u 4/76.
G-ARPB	1C	2102	5/62	12/67	Wfu LHR 3/75. To Prestwick storage then BAA fire training 1/78.
G-ARPC	1C	2103	8/62	9/64	Damaged by fire LHR 28/12/75. B/u 6/77.
G-ARPD	1C	2104	1/63	1/65	Wfu LHR 4/81. To CAA Fire School at Tees-Side 8/81.
G-ARPE	1C	2105	6/63	7/64	Wfu LHR 4/74. To Prestwick storage, b/u 5/76.
G-ARPF	1C	2106	10/63	3/64	Wfu LHR 3/75. To Prestwick storage, b/u 5/76.
G-ARPG	1C	2107	1/64	2/64	Wfu LHR 3/75. To Prestwick storage, b/u 5/76.
G-ARPH	1C	2108	3/64	3/64	Wfu LHR 4/81. To Cosford Museum 4/82. Preserved.
G-ARPJ	1C	2110	5/64	5/64	Wfu LHR 3/75. To Prestwick storage, b/u 5/76.
G-ARPK	1C	2111	6/64	6/64	To Manchester Airport Authority 3/82.
G-ARPL	1C	2112	7/64	8/64	To BAA Edinburgh Airport 3/82, b/u 3/96.
G-ARPM	1C	2113	9/64	10/64	Wfu LHR 3/75. To Prestwick storage, b/u 5/76.
G-ARPN	1C	2115	11/64	12/64	To BAA Aberdeen Airport 3/82, b/u 8/94.
G-ARPO	1C	2116	1/65	1/65	Wfu LHR 3/83. Last Trident One flight 12/12/83 to Tees-Side for CAA Fire school.
G-ARPP	1C	2117	2/65	2/65	Wfu Glasgow 2/83 & to Fire Service. Retained in good condition.
G-ARPR	1C	2119	4/65	4/65	Wfu LHR 3/81. To CAA Fire School at Tees-Side 9/81.
G-ARPU	1C	2122	8/65	8/65	Wfu LHR 11/74, b/u 11/75.
G-ARPW	1C	2123	10/65	10/65	Wfu LHR 5/81. To CAA Fire School at Tees-Side 3/82.
G-ARPX	1C	2124	5/66	5/66	Wfu LHR 10/82. To Air Service Training, Perth 11/82.
G-ARPZ	1C	2128	6/66	7/66	Wfu and to British Aerospace at Dunsfold 4/83.
G-AVFA	2E	2140	7/67	12/69	Wfu LHR 3/83, b/u 1/84.
G-AVFB	2E	2141	11/67	5/77	Ex-Cyprus A/w abandoned Nicosia. Arr LHR 5/77, overhauled & in service 12/77. To Duxford Aviation Soc. 6/82. Preserved.
G-AVFC	2E	2142	1/68	8/68	Wfu LHR 10/81, b/u 11/81.
G-AVFD	2E	2143	3/68	4/68	Wfu LHR 3/82, b/u 4/82.
G-AVFE	2E	2144	4/68	5/68	Wfu and to Belfast Airport Authority 2/85.
G-AVFF	2E	2145	5/68	5/68	Wfu LHR 11/84. To Southend 1/85, b/u.
G-AVFG	2E	2146	6/68	7/68	Wfu LHR 4/85, last T2 service Edinburgh-LHR 25/4/85. Used as ground trainer at LHR in new BA c/s fm 9/85. To fire service training LHR. Now in very poor condition.
G-AVFH	2E	2147	7/68	8/68	Wfu LHR 12/81, b/u 5/82. Fuselage to the Mosquito Museum at London Colney.
G-AVFI	2E	2148	8/68	11/68	Wfu LHR 9/81, b/u 5/82.
G-AVFJ	2E	2149	10/68	12/68	Wfu LHR 3/82. To CAA Fire School at Tees-Side 6/82.
G-AVFK	2E	2150	11/68	1/69	Wfu LHR 12/81, b/u 5/82. Fuselage to MoD, dark grey c/s. At RAF Shawbury '95 for training exercise. To RAF Valley 6/96.
G-AVFL	2E	2151	1/69	2/69	Wfu LHR 12/84. To Southend 1/85, b/u.
G-AVFM	2E	2152	3/69	4/69	Wfu LHR 11/83. To Brunel University, Bristol 1/84.
G-AVFN	2E	2153	5/69	5/69	Wfu LHR 12/84. To Southend 1/85, b/u.
G-AVFO	2E	2156	6/70	6/70	Wfu LHR 1/85. To Southend 2/85, b/u.
G-AZXM	2E	2154	8/69	6/72	Ex-Cyprus A/w. Wfu LHR 1/85. To Southend 2/85, b/u.
G-ASWU	1E	2114	11/64	5/77	Ex-Cyprus A/w abandoned Nicosia. Arr LHR 5/77, overhauled & entered service 12/77. Wfu LHR 8/80, b/u 5/81.
G-AVYB	1E	2136	2/68	12/71	Ex-Northeast/BAS. Wfu LHR 8/80, b/u 5/81, fuselage to MoD.
G-AVYC	1E	2137	10/67	4/69	Ex-Northeast/BAS. Wfu LHR 7/80, b/u 5/81.
G-AVYD	1E	2138	2/69	4/69	Ex-Northeast/BAS. Skidded off runway & w/o Bilbao 15/9/75.
G-AVYE	1E	2139	4/68	1/72	Ex-Northeast/BAS. Wfu LHR 9/80. To Science Museum store at Wroughton 4/81. B/u 6/89, fuselage to BAe at Hatfield.
G-AWYZ	3B	2301	12/69	3/72	Wfu LHR 10/83, b/u 6/84.
G-AWZA	3B	2302	3/70	5/71	Wfu LHR 10/82, b/u 1/84.

G-AWZB	3B	2303	8/70	2/71	Wfu LHR 11/83, b/u 6/84.
G-AWZC	3B	2304	12/70	2/71	Wfu LHR 10/84. To Air Charter Service as 9Q-CTM 11/84.
G-AWZD	3B	2305	3/71	3/71	Wfu LHR 2/85. To Air Charter Service as 9Q-CTI 8/85.
G-AWZE	3B	2306	3/71	4/71	Wfu LHR 5/83. Used as ground trainer then b/u 6/84.
G-AWZF	3B	2307	4/71	5/71	Wfu LHR 1/85. To Air Charter Service as 9Q-CTZ 2/85.
G-AWZG	3B	2308	6/71	6/71	Wfu LHR 5/85. To Air Charter Service as 9Q-CTD 9/85.
G-AWZH	3B	2309	7/71	7/71	Wfu LHR 9/85, b/u by 6/86.
G-AWZI	3B	2310	8/71	8/71	Wfu LHR 5/85, b/u 6/87, fuselage to Surrey Fire Brigade at Reigate.
G-AWZJ	3B	2311	9/71	9/71	Wfu LHR 12/85. To Prestwick 2/86 for emergency training.
G-AWZK	3B	2312	10/71	10/71	Wfu LHR 11/85. Re-painted into new BA 'Landor' scheme 6/86, used as ground trainer at LHR with shortened wings. Maintained by the Trident Preservation Society.
G-AWZL	3B	2313	11/71	11/71	Wfu LHR 11/83. Used as ground trainer then b/u 6/86.
G-AWZM	3B	2314	12/71	12/71	Wfu LHR 12/85. To Science Museum store at Wroughton 2/86.
G-AWZN	3B	2315	1/72	1/72	Wfu LHR 12/85. To College of Aeronautics, Cranfield 3/86 for cabin evacuation trials. B/u 11/95.
G-AWZO	3B	2316	2/72	2/72	Wfu LHR after last sched T3 svce 31/12/85. To BAe at Hatfield 4/86.
G-AWZP	3B	2317	3/72	3/72	Wfu LHR 10/85, b/u 6/86, nose to Manchester Museum of Science & Industry.
G-AWZR	3B	2318	4/72	4/72	Wfu LHR 9/85. To CAA fire school at Tees-Side 3/86.
G-AWZS	3B	2319	4/72	5/72	Wfu LHR 9/85. To CAA fire school at Tees-Side 3/86.
G-AWZT	3B	2320	5/72	6/72	W/o near Zagreb 10/9/76 after collision with Inex-Adria DC-9.
G-AWZU	3B	2321	6/72	7/72	Wfu LHR 31/12/85, last T3 in service along with G-AWZO. To Stansted 3/86 for emergency training.
G-AWZV	3B	2322	8/72	8/72	Wfu LHR 12/85. To Air Charter Service as 9Q-CTZ 5/86.
G-AWZW	3B	2323	11/72	11/72	Wfu LHR 10/83, b/u 6/84.
G-AWZX	3B	2324	1/73	3/73	Wfu LGW 10/84 & to BAA for emergency service training.
G-AWZZ	3B	2326	4/73	4/73	Wfu Birmingham 11/84 & to Airport Fire Service.
G-AYVF	3B	2325	3/73	3/73	Wfu LHR 2/84, b/u 6/84.

Lockheed L-1011 TriStar

G-BBAE	1	1083	8/74	10/74	Lse British Airtours 4/85. T/f to Caledonian 3/88. Lse to Worldways as C-FCXB 11/88–4/89 & 12/89–4/90. Converted to Series-100 6/90.
G-BBAF	1	1093	10/74	11/74	Last BA service 11/90. Conv. to Series-100 then to Caledonian 4/91. Lse to Aer Lingus 6/96–9/96 & 5/97–10/97.
G-BBAG	1	1094	10/74	11/74	Wfu 2/91. Stored Mojave 6/91. To Cathay Pacific as VR-HMW 3/93, op by Dragonair. To Air Transat as C-GTSX 10/95.
G-BBAH	1	1101	1/75	1/75	To Caledonian 5/90. Converted to Series-100 5/91.
G-BBAI	1	1102	1/75	2/75	To British Airtours 4/85. Returned 11/87. To Caledonian 3/88. Lse to Worldways as C-FCXJ 12/88–4/89 and 12/89–4/90.
G-BBAJ	1	1106	2/75	3/75	Long-haul use by 10/78. Op by British Airtours 4/82–11/86. To British Airtours 5/87. T/f to Caledonian 3/88. Converted to Series-100 12/89.
G-BEAK	1	1132	1/76	1/76	Conv. to Series-50 1985. Op by British Airtours 4/87–11/87. Wfu 3/91. To Mojave 6/91, stored. To American International A/w as N110CK 5/96. At Oscoda, Michigan 9/97 stored.
G-BEAL	1	1145	11/76	12/76	Long-haul by mid-77. Lse to British Airtours 4/83–3/84. Converted to Series-50 1985. Lse to British Airtours 5/87, t/f Caledonian 3/88. Ret BA 4/89. Lse to Caledonian 11/89–1/90 and 3/90–10/92. Stored LHR. Lse to Caledonian 7-10/93. Stored Roswell, New Mexico 11/93–5/94. Lse to Air Ops as SE-DPM. To Caledonian 5/96 as G-CEAP. Wfu LGW 11/97.To Classic A/w as G-IOIT 5/98. Wfu Stansted.
G-BEAM	1	1146	1/77	2/77	Lse to British Airtours 4/82–11/84. Conv. to Series-50 1985. Lse to British Airtours 3/85–10/86 & 4/87–3/88. Wfu 3/91, to Mojave 5/91, stored. To American International A/w as N112CK 7/96. At Oscoda, Michigan 9/97, stored.
G-BFCA	500	1157	10/78	4/80	To RAF as ZD948 3/83, stored LHR. Entered service 6/83 in ex-BA colours. To 216 Sqdn 11/84. Converted to KC1.
G-BFCB	500	1159	1/79	7/79	To RAF 3/83, leased back. Lse to British Airtours 5/83–11/83. Ret. to RAF as ZD949. Conv. to K1 & to 216 Sqdn 8/86.
G-BFCC	500	1164	4/79	4/79	To RAF as ZD950 2/83. To Cambridge 6/83. First flight as a tanker 7/85. To 216 Sqdn. TriStar KC1.
G-BFCD	500	1165	5/79	5/79	To RAF as ZD951 3/83, stored LHR. Lse to BA 10–11/83 as G-BFCD for Royal tour. To Cambridge 1/84. First flight as K1 3/86, to 216 Sqdn.
G-BFCE	500	1168	7/79	7/79	To RAF as ZD952 3/83, stored LHR. Entered service 7/83 in ex-BA colours. Lse to British Airtours 6/85–9/85 as G-BFCE. To Cambridge 9/85. Conv. to KC1 & to 216 Sqdn.
G-BFCF	500	1174	4/80	5/80	To RAF as ZD953 2/83, to Cambridge 2/83. First flight as tanker 10/85. To 216 Sqdn. TriStar KC1.
G-BGBB	200	1178	2/80	3/80	Wfu LHR 5/91. To Mojave 6/91, stored. Ret to LHR 8/91, lse Air Lanka as 4R-ULN 9/91–9/94. To American International A/w as N105CK 12/94. Converted to freighter.

G-BGBC	200	1182	4/80	4/80	Wfu LHR 10/91. To Mojave 1/92, stored. To American International A/w as N107CK 8/96. Converted to freighter.
G-BHBL	200	1193	9/80	9/80	Wfu 5/91, stored LGW. Back in service 8/91-10/91. To Mojave 11/91, stored. To American International A/w as N104CK 9/94. Converted to freighter.
G-BHBM	200	1198	11/80	11/80	Wfu 11/91, stored Cambridge. Lse to Kuwait A/w 6/92–10/92. Stored Cambridge. To American International A/w as N102CK 7/94. First freighter conversion, first flight 8/95.
G-BHBN	200	1204	2/81	4/81	Wfu 5/91 LGW. To Mojave 6/91, stored. To American International A/w as N108CK 12/96. Passenger config.
G-BHBO	200	1205	3/81	4/81	Wfu 3/91 LGW. To Mojave 6/91, stored. To American International A/w as N109CK 12/96. Passenger config.
G-BHBP	200	1211	5/81	5/81	Lse to British Airtours 5/81–3/82 & 5/85–10/85. Wfu 5/91, to Mojave, stored. Lse to Air Lanka as 4R-ULM 8/91–11/94. Stored Cambridge. To American International A/w as N106CK 7/95. Converted to freighter.
G-BHBR	200	1212	5/81	5/81	Lse to British Airtours 5/81–12/81 & 5/85–9/85. Wfu 11/91, stored Cambridge. Lse to Kuwait A/w 6/92–10/92. Stored Cambridge. To American International A/w N103CK 7/94, delivered as a freighter 1/96.

Leased TriStars

N323EA	1	1045	9/73	10/78	Lse from Eastern Airlines. Returned ex-LHR 2/80. To Cathay Pacific as VR-HOG 12/88.
G-BLUS	500	1235	7/82	4/85	Lse from Air Lanka. Returned to Hong Kong 3/88 as 4R-ULA.
G-BLUT	500	1236	8/82	4/85	Lse from Air Lanka. Returned at Hong Kong 3/88 as 4R-ULB.

McDonnell Douglas DC-10
Ex-British Caledonian DC-10s

G-BEBL	30	46949	4/88	Del new to BCAL 3/77. Wfu 12/98. For Gemini Air Cargo.
G-BEBM	30	46921	4/88	Del new to BCAL 2/77. Wfu 10/98. To Naples 12/98 for freighter conversion.
G-BHDH	30	47816	4/88	Del new to BCAL 4/80. Lsd Caledonian 5/93–10/95. Op by AML 3/98-3/99. Wfu 3/99.
G-BHDI	30	47831	4/88	Del new to BCAL 7/80. Stored 4–9/93. Op by AML 3/98–2/99. Wfu 2/99.
G-BHDJ	30	47840	4/88	Del new to BCAL 10/80. Wfu 3/99. For Gemini Air Cargo.
G-DCIO	30	48277	4/88	Del new to BCAL 4/81. Wfu 3/99.
G-MULL	30	47888	4/88	Ex-YA-LAS Ariana Afghan Airlines, bought by BCAL 3/85. Wfu 3/99.
G-NIUK	30	46932	4/88	Ex-9Q-CLT Air Zaire, bought by BCAL 6/85. Lse to Kuwait A/l 5–8/92. Stored 8/92–10/93. Used for Gatwick-Faro 10/93–3/94. To Caledonian 10/94. Op by Caledonian for BA 4/95–3/97. Op by AML 3/97-3/99. Wfu 3/99. For Gemini Air Cargo.

ANZ / BA Interchange 1975–79

ZK-NZL	30	47846	To American N136AA 10/81. W/o during aborted take-off at Dallas-Fort Worth 5/88.
ZK-NZM	30	47847	To American N137AA 7/82.
ZK-NZN	30	47848	To Western A/L N821L 4/81. American N144AA 2/85.
ZK-NZP	30	46910	W/o Mt Erebus, Antarctica 28/11/79.
ZK-NZQ	30	46911	To American N138AA 9/82. To Continental as N14074.
ZK-NZR	30	47849	To UTA F-GDJK 12/82. To AOM as F-GNDC.
ZK-NZS	30	46954	To LAN Chile CC-CJS 6/82. SAS SE-DFH 8/86. AOM F-ODLY.
ZK-NZT	30	46950	To LAN Chile CC-CJT 6/82. American N164AA 6/86.

Vickers Viscount

G-AMOG	701	7	2/53	3/53	Op by Cambrian for BOAC/BA from Prestwick 4/72 to 31/3/76.To BA Collection, Cosford Museum 4/76.
G-AMON	701	27	1/54	3/54	Op by Cambrian for BOAC/BA from Prestwick 6/73 to 31/3/76.Wfu at Southend 6/76, b/u 5/79.
G-AOJB	802	151	9/56	2/57	Ex-Scottish A/w. Wfu 4/76 Liverpool, to Fire Service 10/76. B/u.
G-AOJC	802	152	11/56	1/57	Ex-Scottish A/w. Wfu Cardiff 10/75, pres Wales A/C Museum. B/u 2/96 after Museum closed.
G-AOJD	802	153	11/56	1/57	Ex-Channel Islands. Wfu Jersey 3/76, to Fire Service 9/76.
G-AOJE	802	154	1/57	1/57	Ex-Scottish A/w. Wfu Cardiff 3/80. To BAF & b/u 8/81.
G-AOJF	802	155	1/57	2/57	Ex-Scottish A/w. Wfu Cardiff 2/80. B/u 8/81.
G-AOHG	802	156	2/57	2/57	Ex-Channel Islands. Wfu Cardiff 4/75. B/u 10/75.
G-AOHH	802	157	2/57	3/57	Ex-Scottish A/w. Wfu Leeds-Bradford 11/75. B/u 1976.
G-AOHJ	802	159	3/57	3/57	Ex-Channel Islands. Wfu Newcastle 4/76. B/u 7/76.
G-AOHK	802	160	3/57	4/57	Ex-Channel Islands. Wfu Leeds-Bradford 4/76. B/u, forward-fuselage plus part of 'OHO to a Jersey hotel.
G-AOHL	802	161	3/57	4/57	Ex-Scottish A/w. Wfu Cardiff 4/80. To BAF, wfu Southend 2/81. Fuselage used as cabin crew trainer.

G-AOHM	802	162	5/57	6/57	Ex-Channel Islands. Wfu Cardiff 5/80. To BAF 2/81. Parcelforce freighter 7/96. Stored Southend 1/98. To Airwing 2000 Ltd ex-Southend 5/99.
G-AOHN	802	163	4/57	5/57	Ex-Channel Islands. Wfu Cardiff 8/75. B/u.
G-AOHO	802	164	4/57	5/57	Ex-Channel Islands. Wfu Jersey 3/76. B/u, fuselage to Hotel de France with parts from 'OHK.
G-AOHR	802	166	5/57	6/57	Ex-Channel Islands. Wfu Cardiff 8/75. B/u 6/76.
G-AOHS	802	167	6/57	6/57	Ex-Scottish A/w. Wfu Cardiff 6/75. B/u.
G-AOHT	802	168	6/57	7/57	Ex-Channel Islands. Wfu Cardiff 4/80. To BAF 7/81. Lse Skybus as ZK-SKY 9-12/81. To Polar A/w 3/83, Euroair 5/84, BAF 8/85. Wfu Southend 7/87 & b/u 3/91.
G-AOHV	802	170	7/57	7/57	Ex-Channel Islands. Wfu Cardiff 3/80. To BAF 1/81, Polar A/w 3/83, Alexandra Avn as G-BLNB 6/84, BAF 8/85. Parcelforce freighter as G-OPFI 3/94. Stored Southend 1/98. To Airwing 2000 Ltd ex-Southend 5/99.
G-AOHW	802	253	7/57	8/57	Ex-Channel Islands. Wfu Newcastle 11/75. To Fire Service 5/76.
G-AORD	802	171	8/57	9/57	Ex-Channel Islands. Wfu Birmingham 12/75. To Airport Fire Service 1976, b/u.
G-AOYG	806	256	10/57	3/58	Ex-Cambrian. Wfu Cardiff 4/82. To BAF 1/84. Wfu Southend 12/92, b/u 1/94.
G-AOYH	806	311	10/57	12/57	Ex-Northeast. To BAF 3/82. To North Cariboo Air as C-GWPY 7/83. To Euroair as G-BNAA 3/85. To BAF 8/85. Wfu Southend 5/87 & b/u.
G-AOYI	806	257	11/57	1/58	Ex-Cambrian. Wfu Cardiff 4/80. To BAF 7/81, London European A/w as G-LOND 2/85. To Caicos Int'l A/w 3/86 & lse to BAF. Wfu Southend, b/u 2/93.
G-AOYJ	806	259	12/57	1/58	Ex-Cambrian. Wfu Cardiff 3/81. To BAF 4/81. Regd G-BLOA 8/84. Wfu Southend 5/93 & b/u 8/96.
G-AOYL	806	261	1/58	2/58	Ex-Northeast. Wfu Cardiff 5/82. To BAF 1/84. Wfu Southend & b/u 2/93.
G-AOYM	806	262	2/58	3/58	Ex-Cambrian. Wfu Cardiff 5/82. To BAF 2/84. To L.A.Canarias as EC-DYC 10/85. Wfu Tenerife 5/89 & stored.
G-AOYN	806	263	3/58	3/58	Ex-Cambrian. Wfu Cardiff 4/80. To BAF 2/81. Parcelforce freighter as G-OPAS 10/94. Wfu Southend 6/96, b/u.
G-AOYO	806	264	3/58	4/58	Ex-Northeast. Wfu Cardiff 4/82. To BAF 1/84. To L.A.Canarias as EC-DXU 9/85. Wfu Tenerife 5/89 & stored.
G-AOYP	806	265	5/58	5/58	Ex-Cambrian. To BAF 4/81. Parcelforce freighter as G-PFBT 3/94. To Heli-Jet Aviation 5/97, based Lanseria, S.Africa.
G-AOYR	806	266	3/58	4/58	Ex-Northeast. Wfu Cardiff 3/82. To BAF 1/84. Wfu Southend 4/94, b/u 6/96.
G-AOYS	806	267	5/58	6/58	Ex-Cambrian. Wfu Cardiff 4/80. To BAF 5/81. B/u Southend 2/85.
G-APEX	806	381	6/58	6/58	Ex-Northeast. Wfu Cardiff 4/80. To BAF 3/81. Wfu Southend 3/84, b/u by 1994.
G-APEY	806	382	7/58	7/58	Ex-Northeast. Wfu 3/81, to BAF 4/81. To Heli-Jet Aviation 6/97 & based Lanseria, S.Africa.
G-APIM	806	412	6/58	6/58	Ex-Cambrian. Wfu Cardiff 4/82. To BAF 1/84. Damaged at Southend 1/88, Wfu & to Brooklands Museum. Preserved.

Leased Viscounts

G-AVJB	815	375	8/59	76	Op by BMA for BA from Prestwick 3-6/76. To Intra A/w, BAF, Baltic Aviation as SE-IVY 11/86. Wfu 12/87. Preserved at Hillerstorf in Sweden.
G-BAPE	814	341	1/59	3/76	Op by BMA for BA from Prestwick until 3/77. To Intra A/w, Express Air Services, Southern Int'l, Royal American as N145RA 6/82, Viscount Unlimited 2/88. Wfu and Stored Tucson.
G-BAPG	814	344	3/59	3/76	Op by BMA for BA from Prestwick until 3/77. To Intra A/w, Southern Int'l, Baltic A/l. Wfu Southend 6/92, b/u 6/97.

Vickers Vanguard / Merchantman

G-APEG	953C	710	5/61	5/61	To ABC 12/79. Wfu East Midlands 6/83 & b/u.
G-APEI	953	712	7/61	7/61	To Merpati 3/75 as PK-MVD. Wfu Jakarta by 1/81 & b/u.
G-APEJ	953C	713	8/61	8/61	To ABC 11/79. Wfu East Midlands 12/92 & b/u. Nose preserved at Brooklands.
G-APEK	953C	714	8/61	9/61	To ABC 11/79. Wfu Perpignan, stored minus engines.
G-APEL	953C	715	9/61	10/61	Stored Prestwick 8/75–7/76. To Europe Aero Service as F-BYCF 8/76. To Air Gabon as TR-LZA 1/80. To Inter Cargo Service as F-GEJF 1987. W/o Toulouse 1/88.
G-APEM	953C	716	10/61	11/61	To Europe Aero Service as F-BYCE 9/76. To ABC 7/87. Wfu East Midlands 1/94 & b/u.
G-APEO	953C	718	11/61	11/61	Stored Prestwick 4/75–10/76. Wfu LHR 10/76, b/u 8/77.
G-APEP	953C	719	11/61	12/61	To ABC 11/79. Wfu and preserved at Brooklands 10/96.
G-APER	953	720	12/61	1/62	Wfu LHR 6/74, b/u 6/75.
G-APES	953C	721	1/62	1/62	Stored Prestwick 5/75–8/76. To ABC 11/76. Wfu East Midlands 2/95. B/u.
G-APET	953C	722	2/62	2/62	To ABC 11/79. Wfu East Midlands 7/91. To airport fire service & b/u.
G-APEU	953	723	3/62	3/62	Wfu LHR 6/74, b/u 6/75.

'WORLD IMAGE' TAIL DESIGNS

Design name – Description – Artist – Aircraft carrying the design

Animals and Trees

Kg' oocoan hee naka hiian thee e. An oil painting in the style of ancient cave paintings, depicting seven wild jackals resting under the trees of an oasis representing the creatures & plants of the Kalahari Desert. From Cgoise Ntcoxo, of the Ncoakhoe tribe, Kalahari Desert, Botswana.

G-BGDT	B737-236	
G-BNLZ	B747-436	
G-CPEL	B757-236	
G-DOCD	B737-436	
G-VIIK	B777-236	
G-BXAS	RJ-100	Cityflyer
G-EMBD	EMB-145	British Regional
ZS-SBR	B737-244	Comair

Avignon

The final one of four DBA-designs, this painting, *The men who sold the world for fun*, from Berlin artist Jim Avignon depicts in strong colours distorted two-dimensional figures under the night sky of Berlin. DBA's 737s are the only BA-liveried aircraft to carry individual names.

D-ADBA	B737-3L9	*Metropolis*
D-ADBB	B737-3L9	*Kosmopolit* – ret to lessor 4/99
D-ADBD	B737-3L9	*Papageno* – ret to lessor 3/99
D-ADBI	B737-3L9	*Phantasia*
D-ADBQ	B737-31S	*Paradiesvogel*
D-ADBT	B737-31S	*Phantasia*
D-ADBU	B737-31S	*Metropolis*

Bauhaus

A ceramic panel of bold, brightly-coloured geometric shapes created by Antje Bruggemann, a German artist. This is the only one of the four DBA designs to appear on non-DBA aircraft and is often referred to as *Sterntaler* or 'Fairytale'.

G-BGDE	B737-236	
G-BPET	B757-236	
G-BUSG	A320	
G-EMBB	EMB-145	British Regional
G-MSKM	Canadair RJ	Maersk

G-OFRA	B737-36Q	BA Regional
D-ADBE	B737-3L9	*Sterntaler* – ret to lessor 10/98
D-ADBK	B737-31S	*Aurora*
D-ADBL	B737-31S	*Himmelsturmer*
D-ADBR	B737-31S	*Sternschnuppe*
D-ADBS	B737-31S	*Rheingold*
D-ADBV	B737-31S	*Sterntaler*
D-ADBW	B737-31S	*Wolkenreiter*
ZS-NNG	B737-236	Comair

Bavaria

DBA's four designs represent the artwork, culture and traditions found in different regions of Germany. *Bavaria* illustrates the quill embroidery used to decorate leather goods in southern Germany and incorporates symbols which represent loyalty, good luck and fertility, such as the Edelweiss Alpine flower. Herbert Rieger is the artist.

D-ADBC	B737-3L9	*Enzian*
D-ADBF	B737-3L9	*Windrose* – ret to lessor 10/98
D-ADBG	B737-3L9	*Edelweiss*
D-ADBH	B737-3L9	*Bavaria*

Blue Poole

Seagull and dolphin pattern from Sally Tuffin, a ceramic artist with Poole Pottery in Dorset, created using the technique of brush stroke painting over a matt glaze.

G-BDXD	B747-236	
G-BIKA	B757-236	
G-BKYB	B737-236	
G-CPEM	B757-236	
G-DOCC	B737-436	
G-MAUD	ATP	British Regional
G-MSKA	B737-5L9	Maersk
G-TREN	B737-4S3	GB Airways
ZS-NNH	B737-236	Comair

Calligraphy

Gottfried Pott, a professor of calligraphy and script, created this DBA-only design using ancient Gothic script as a tribute to Johannes Gutenberg, the pioneering fifteenth century printer.

D-ADBM	B737-31S	*Schnifttanz*
D-ADBN	B737-31S	*Wolkenschreiber*
D-ADBO	B737-31S	*Himmelsbrief*
D-ADBP	B737-31S	*Federtraum*

APPENDIX THREE

Chatham Dockyard or Union Flag

This stylised British Union Jack flag is derived from an Admiral's Original Flag Loft design held in the Historic Royal Dockyard, Chatham, Kent.

All Concordes plus an increasing number of the subsonic fleet.

Chelsea Rose

Winning design from a joint BA/*Sunday Times* competition for art students. Pierce Casey, an Irish student of textile printing at the University of East London, created the layered red rose. Originally a one-off, this design has now been adopted by many more aircraft. Also known as *English Rose*.

G-BDXK	B747-236	
G-BIKB	B757-236	
G-BMRD	B757-236	
G-BNLA	B747-436	
G-BNLL	B747-436	
G-BNWB	B767-336	
G-BNWE	B767-236	
G-BNWR	B767-336 – now Union Flag	
G-BYGA	B747-436	
G-BYGC	B747-436	
G-BYGF	B747-436	
G-DOCG	B737-436	
G-VIIO	B777-236	
G-VIIS	B777-236	
G-BNNL	B737-4Q8	GB Airways
G-BRYI	DHC-8	Brymon
G-BZAV	RJ-100	Cityflyer
G-MAJL	Jetstream 41	British Regional
G-MSKN	Canadair RJ	Maersk Air
N-495MC	B747-400F	Atlas Air

Cockerel of Lowicz

Kogutki Lowickie. Symmetrical Polish folk art images which include a cockerel, peacocks and flowers, cut out from paper using sheep shears. Creator Danuta Wojda also produced *Mazowieckie Kwiatki* (Flower from Mazowsze), a similar design now flying on GB Airways 737 G-OGBC.

G-BGDG	B737-236 – ret to lessor 4/98	
G-BNLT	B747-436	
G-BPED	B757-236	
G-BUSB	A320	
G-DOCF	B737-436	
G-BNMT	SD-3-60	Loganair
G-BRYW	DHC-8	Brymon
G-OGBC	B737-34S	GB Airways – *Flowers of Mazowsze*
G-EMBC	EMB-145	British Regional
ZS-SBO	B737-244	Comair

Colour Down the Side

An abstract 'light and landscape' painting of strong, vertical and horizontal colours inspired by the Cornish home of artist Terry Frost and painted in 1968.

G-BRYT   DHC-8   Brymon

(PHOTO: ROBBIE SHAW)

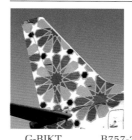

Crossing Borders

A decorative Egyptian scroll painted by Cairo-born Chant Avedissian who has used traditional Pharaonic colours to portray symmetrical patterns incorporating ancient symbols and folk images of travel and good luck.

G-BIKT	B757-236	
G-DOCT	B737-436	
G-MEDD	A320	British Mediterranean
G-MSKO	Canadair RJ	Maersk Air
G-OGBE	B737-3L9	GB Airways

Delftblue Daybreak

A blue and white Delft ceramics design featuring traditional Dutch national motifs, from Hugo Kaagman, a former Amsterdam graffiti artist.

G-BGDF	B737-236	
G-BIKX	B757-236	
G-BNLD	B747-436	
G-BNWA	B767-336	
G-BZHB	B767-336	
G-CIVC	B747-436	
G-CIVN	B747-436	
G-CIVT	B747-436	
G-RAES	B777-236	
G-VIIU	B777-236	
G-BXAR	RJ-100	Cityflyer
G-MSKE	B737-5L9	Maersk Air
G-BNMW	SD-3-60	Loganair
G-OHAJ	B737-36Q	BA Regional
PH-KJG	Jetstream 31	Base
ZS-NOV	B727-230	Comair

Dove

Colum, a Celtic illuminated manuscript design inspired by books such as the ninth century *Book of Kells*, evoking the memory of the founder of this Irish artform, Columcille or St Columba. Timothy O'Neill, calligrapher, Dublin.

G-BGDR	B737-236	
G-BNLC	B747-436	
G-BNWK	B767-336	
G-BNWT	B767-336	
G-BNWV	B767-336	
G-BYGB	B747-436	
G-CIVP	B747-436	
G-CPEP	B757-2Y0	
G-DOCX	B737-436	
G-VIIP	B777-236	
G-BJOP	Islander	Loganair
G-BNMU	SD-3-60	Loganair
G-BRYV	DHC-8	Brymon

(continued)

G-BYTP	ATR-72	Cityflyer
G-BZAU	RJ-100	Cityflyer
G-EMBA	EMB-145	British Regional
G-MAJC	Jetstream 41	British Regional
G-MSKB	B737-5L9	Maersk Air
G-OGBB	B737-34S	GB Airways
G-OMUC	B737-36Q	BA Regional
OY-SVO	Jetstream 31	Sun-Air
OY-SVT	ATP	Sun-Air
(OYSVZ)	Jetstream 31	Sun-Air
ZS-NZV	B727-230	Comair

Flower Field

Blomsterang. A Swedish design for a large glass bowl incorporating folk motifs of bold, simple hearts and flowers. From Ulrica Hydman-Vallien.

G-BDXG	B747-236	
G-BMRI	B757-236	
G-BNWU	B767-336	
G-DOCE	B737-436	
G-EMBH	EMB-145	British Regional
OY-SVJ	Jetstream 31	Sun-Air
ZS-NOU	B727-230	Comair

Golden Khokhloma

A patterned design from Russia depicting fruit and flowers in scarlet, black and gold lacquers. This 300-year-old folk-art technique from the mid-Volga region is used to decorate wooden table utensils known as Khokhloma-ware. The creator of this design is Taisia Akimovna Belyantzeva from the village of Semenov. The design is also know as Kudrina from Semenov.

G-BIKH	B757-236	
G-BNWJ	B767-336	
G-XMAN	B737-36N	BA Regional

Grand Union

Adult section winner in a BA/*Sunday Times* competition. Christine Bass, a graphic artist from Buckinghamshire, produced a brightly coloured rose design using the 200-year-old style of art found on the narrowboats of the Grand Union Canal.

G-BMRJ	B757-236	
G-BRYP	DHC-8	Brymon
G-DOCH	B737-436	
G-EMBF	EMB-145	British Regional
(GMSKP)	Canadair RJ	Maersk Air
G-XBHX	B737-36N	BA Regional

Louvre Pyramid

Air Liberté scheme unveiled in October 1998. Depicts innovation combined with tradition in the form of the futuristic Louvre Pyramid in front of France's national museum and art gallery which was formerly a royal palace.

F-GPZA	MD-83	Air Liberté

(Photo: SPA Photography)

Mountain of the Birds

Benyhone. Woven tartan plaid inspired by the colours of the Scottish landscape from Peter MacDonald, a traditional Scottish hand-weaver.

G-BGDL	B737-236	
G-BIKL	B757-236	
G-BIKO	B757-236	
G-BNLI	B747-436	
G-BNWF	B767-336	
G-BNWT	B767-336	
G-BUSE	A320	
G-BVNO	B737-4S3	
G-CIVO	B747-436	
G-CIVW	B747-436	
G-CIVZ	B747-436	
G-DOCA	B737-436	
G-DOCJ	B737-436	
G-DOCV	B737-436	
G-VIIJ	B777-236	
G-VIIR	B777-236	
G-BLDV	Islander	Loganair
G-BPFN	SD-3-60	Loganair
G-BRYU	DHC-8	Brymon
G-BWTM	ATR-72	Cityflyer
G-GNTE	Saab 340B	British Regional
G-GNTZ	BAe 146	British Regional
G-LGNA	Saab 340B	Loganair
OY-SVI	ATP	Sun-Air
ZS-OBO	B727-230	Comair

Nalanji Dreaming

One of three Australian images, *Nalanji Dreaming* (Our Place) is an Aboriginal design depicting flowers and sea creatures. It is also one of two images borrowed from partner airline Qantas, whose 747-336 VH-EBU flies with this design covering its entire fuselage.

G-BMRH	B757-236
G-BNLN	B747-436

Ndebele

Murals in bright colours and geometric patterns as used by the Ndebele people of the Mpumalanga district of Southern Africa to decorate the outside walls of their houses. Two similar designs from twin-sisters Emmly and Martha Masanabo are in use.

G-BGDA	B737-236		(Martha)
G-BIKC	B757-236		(Emmly)
G-BIKW	B757-236		(Martha)
G-BNLJ	B747-436		(Martha)
G-BNLM	B747-436		(Martha)
G-BNLO	B747-436		(Emmly)
G-BNWD	B767-336		(Emmly)
G-DOCL	B737-436		(Martha)
G-DOCU	B737-436		(Martha)
G-MAJB	Jetstream 41	British Regional	
G-MSKJ	Jetstream 41	Maersk Air	(Martha)

G-MSKL	Canadair RJ	Maersk Air	(Emmly)
G-OGBD	B737-300	GB Airways	(Martha)
OY-SVS	Jetstream 41	Sun-Air	
ZS-SBN	B737-244	Comair	

Paithani

A traditional Sari weave from Paithan, Maharashtra, reflecting 2,000 years of the Indian cloth-weaving craft. The Paithani sari is woven from pure silk and gold. This design came from Meera Mehta, a Mumbai textiles designer.

G-BDXO	B747-236	
G-BMRA	B757-236	
G-EMBI	EMB-145	British Regional

Rendezvous

A poem in the form of a Chinese scroll describing the boiling of water for a traditional tea ceremony. Created by Yip Man-Yam, a calligrapher from Hong Kong. One aircraft, 757 G-BMRG, has the image applied over a cream-coloured tail.

G-BGJE	B737-236	
G-BIKI	B757-236	
G-BIKN	B757-236	
G-BMRE	B757-236	
G-BMRG	B757-236	
G-BNLR	B747-436	
G-BNWC	B767-336	
G-BNWP	B767-336	
G-BYGD	B747-436	
G-BYGE	B747-436	
G-BYGG	B747-436	
G-CIVV	B747-436	
G-CPEU	B757-236	
G-CPEV	B757-236	
G-DOCM	B737-436	
G-DOCW	B737-436	
G-VIIT	B777-236	
G-ZZZC	B777-236A	
G-BRYY	DHC-8	Brymon
G-MANO	ATP	British Regional
G-MEDB	A320	British Mediterranean
G-OAMS	B737-37Q	BA Regional
OY-SVP	Jetstream 31	Sun-Air
OY-SVR	Jetstream 31	Sun-Air

Rights of Man

Air Liberté scheme unveiled in October 1998. Part of the French Declaration of *The Rights of Man*, 1789, by Olivier Vinet: 'Mankind is born free, lives free and has equal rights.'

F-GFZB	MD-83	Air Liberté
F-GIOG	Fokker 100	Air Liberté
F-GIOI	Fokker 100	Air Liberté
F-GHEB	MD-83	Air Liberté
F-GPVA	DC-10	Air Liberté
F-GRML	MD-83	Air Liberté

Water Dreaming

A 'dreamings' painting made up from complex dot-matrix patterns rich in sacred symbols, as used by Aboriginal people to depict their origins and ceremonial beliefs. From Clifford Possum Tjapaltjarri of the Anmatyerre people, Northern Territory of Australia.

G-BKYE	B737-236	
G-BMRF	B757-236	
G-BNLK	B747-436	
G-BUSJ	A320	
G-EMBG	EMB-145	British Regional

Waves and Cranes

Nami Tsuru. A symbolic painting created using the ancient Japanese art-form of Nihon-ga with ink and pigments applied to hand-made paper or silk to depict cranes flying serenely over waves. From Matazo Kayama, Japan.

G-BGDJ	B737-236	
G-BKYP	B737-236	
G-BPEC	B757-236	
G-BUSK	A320	
G-BZHC	B767-336	
G-CIVM	B747-436	
G-CIVR	B747-436	
G-CIVX	B747-436 – now Union Flag	
G-VIIM	B777-236	
G-BVTJ	ATR-72	Cityflyer
G-ODUS	B737-36Q	BA Regional
G-OGBA	B737-4S3	GB Airways
ZS-NLN	B737-2L9	Comair

Waves of the City

A modern abstract oil painting from Jenifer Kobylarz of New York who has used 'sinuous organic lines' and vivid colours to convey an impression of frozen motion.

G-BIKJ	B757-236	
G-BNLV	B747-436	
G-BNLX	B747-336	
G-BNWG	B767-336	
G-BNWH	B767-336	BA Regional
G-DOCR	B737-436	
G-VIIA	B777-236	
G-BNNK	B737-4Q8	GB Airways
G-BRYS	DHC-8	Brymon
G-BZAT	RJ-100	Cityflyer
G-EMBE	EMB-145	British Regional
G-MSKC	B737-5L9	Maersk Air
OY-SVF	Jetstream 31	Sun-Air

Whale Rider

A painted wood carving featuring the bold forms and shapes found in traditional Pacific Northwest art. Joe David of the Tla o Qui Aht people from this remote region of Canada incorporated his own tribal style to depict a whaling tradition.

G-BGDO	B737-236	
G-BNLG	B747-436	
G-CIVS	B747-436	
G-CIVY	B747-436	
G-CPEO	B757-236	

G-VIIN	B777-236	
G-BXTN	ATR-72	Cityflyer
G-MEDA	A320	British Mediterranean
G-MSKD	B737-5L9	Maersk Air

Chelsea Rose
BA/*Sunday Times* competition winner. See earlier listing.

Wings
Vinger. Simple but bold abstract shapes in red, white, yellow and blue represent seagulls over the islands of Denmark. Per Arnoldi, Danish artist.

G-BNLH	B747-436	
G-BUSI	A320 – now Union Flag	
G-BZHA	B767-336	
G-CIVU	B747-436	
G-CPER	B757-236	
G-CPES	B757-236	
G-DOCB	B737-436	
G-VIIL	B777-236	
G-BUHL	B737-4S3	GB Airways
G-MAJK	Jetstream 41	British Regional
G-MSKK	Canadair RJ	Maersk Air
OY-SVU	ATP	Sun-Air
OY-SVW	Jetstream 41	Sun-Air

Grand Union
BA/*Sunday Times* competition winner. See earlier listing.

Wunala Dreaming
Kangaroo Dreaming, an Aboriginal design which for several years has decorated Qantas 747-438 VH-OJB and which, along with *Nalanji Dreaming* has been adopted to celebrate the BA/Qantas partnership.

G-BIKF	B757-236
G-BNLS	B747-436

Images of Romania
Primavera or *Spring.* A hand embroidered Romanian floral tablecloth design decorated with red, black and blue flowers. This was the winning entry in BA's 'design a tail-fin' competition for the airline's employees and was submitted by Morag Dumitru, Cabin Crew member.

G-BIKY	B757-236

Youm al-Suq
A modern, brightly coloured abstract inspired by traditional Saudi Arabian arts and crafts depicting the vibrant life of an Arab market day. Shadia Alem.

G-GBTA	B737-436

(PHOTO: ROBBIE SHAW)

Olympic
With the British Olympic Association 'lion' logo on the fin and 'Teaming Up For Britain' titles, this design promotes the British teams which are preparing to enter the Sydney 2000 Olympic Games and their sponsorship by BA.

G-BKYG	B737-236	Returned to lessor 10/98
G-BMRC	B757-236	
G-BUSC	A320	

Special schemes

To commemorate or promote special occasions and events, to recognise worthy groups or individuals and competition winners.

British Blend
Winning entry from the children's category in a BA/*Sunday Times* competition. This symbolic cartoon depiction of *Britain in a teacup* featuring an English rose, Irish harp, Scottish thistle and Welsh dragon was designed by 12-year-old Simon Baldwin from Middlesborough. An Airbus A320 carried this design from December 1997 to June 1998.

G-BUSI	A320	Replaced with *Wings* design June 1998

Poppy
For Remembrance Day, 11 November 1997, a 737-236 flew from its Gatwick-base with 'Pause To Remember' titles and a large red poppy emblem on the tail. During October 1998 another Gatwick aircraft received a similar scheme.

G-BKYG	B737-236	Replaced with Olympic scheme December 1997
G-BVNM	B737-4S3	

ABREVIATIONS AND TERMINOLOGY

ABC	Air Bridge Carriers, became just ABC then Hunting Cargo Airlines
A/l	Airline
AML	Airline Management Limited
ANZ	Air New Zealand
AOC	Air Operators Certificate
APU	Auxiliary Power Unit
ATEL	Aviation Traders (Engineering) Limited
A/w	Airways
BAC	British Aircraft Corporation
BAH	British Airways Helicopters
BAe	British Aerospace
BAR	British Airways Regional
BCAL	British Caledonian Airways
BEAH	BEA Helicopters
BIH	British International Helicopters
BMA	British Midland Airways
B-Med	British Mediterranean Airways
B/u	Broken up
CAA	Civil Aviation Authority
Canx	Cancelled
CAT 3A	Autoland capability in conditions of very restricted, vertical and horizontal visibility. Limits defined by aircraft type.
CDG	Charles de Gaulle Airport, Paris
Combi	Airliner capable of carrying a mix of both passengers and cargo in the cabin
Conv	Converted
CRT	Cathode-ray tube – screen for displaying aircraft instrumentation
C/s	Colour-scheme
Davis-Monthan	Davis-Monthan Air Force Base, Arizona. Site of the US military's Aerospace Maintenance and Regeneration Centre (AMARC)
DBA	Deutsche BA
Del	Delivered
DERA	Defence Evaluation and Research Agency
Disp	Disposed of – either sold or returned to owner
Dry lease	Lease of an aircraft without any operating crew
EOG	BA European Operations at Gatwick (also EuroGatwick)
ER	Extended-range
ETOPS	Extended-range Twin-jet Operations
EuroGatwick	BA European Operations at Gatwick (also EOG)
FF	First flight
GB A/w	GB Airways
GE	General Electric
GPA	Guinness Peat Aviation
HKG	Hong Kong Airport

ICAO Chapter Three	International Civil Aviation Organisation, Annex 16, Chapter Three – defines current internationally-agreed noise certification standards
IGS	BA Internal German Services
IGW	Increased Gross Weight
ILFC	International Lease Finance Corporation
Int'l	International
I/s	In-service date
IT	Inclusive Tour
JFK	JF Kennedy International Airport, New York
J-STARS	Joint Surveillance Target Attack Radar System
Landor	Landor Associates (American designers of BA's 1984 corporate identity)
LCD	Liquid-crystal display
LGW	Gatwick Airport
LHR	Heathrow Airport
L/H	Long-haul services of British Airways
Lite	Version of the 747-400 which operates to lower certificated weights
LOT	LOT Polish Airlines
Lse	Lease/leased
MEA	Middle East Airlines
MoD	Ministry of Defence
Op	Operated
P&W	Pratt & Whitney
Pres	Preserved
Regd	Registered
Ret	Returned
SAS	Scandinavian Airlines System
S/H	Short-haul services of British Airways
Shuttle 'back-ups'	Additional flights to honour seat guarantee on UK domestic Shuttle routes
Speedmarque	BA corporate symbol introduced with 1997 'Utopia' livery change
Speedbird	BOAC corporate symbol adopted by BA and used until 1984
Speedwing	Red stripe along fuselage of BA airliners introduced with 1984 'Landor' livery
Sqdn	Squadron
STOL	Short take-off and landing
STV	Standard VC-10
SUV	Super VC-10
TAT	TAT European Airlines
T/f	Transferred
Wet lease	Lease of an airliner including its operating crew
Utopia	Code-name for BA corporate identity introduced in 1997
Wfu	Withdrawn from operational use prior to sale or disposal
W/o	Written-off

BIBLIOGRAPHY

Air-Britain (Historians) Limited – monthly *Air-Britain News* and Boeing 707, One-Eleven, HS-748, Vickers Viscount and Vanguard monographs
A History of British Airways Helicopters and its Predecessors Since 1947, Phil Lo Bao
An Illustrated History of British European Airways, Phil Lo Bao
Air Transport World magazine articles
Australian Aviation – monthly magazine and *Legends of the Air 3 – Viscount, Comet & Concorde, The International Directory of Civil Aircraft*

Aviation Letter
British Airways the Path to Profitability, Alison Corke
Britsh Airways News
Flight International magazine articles and surveys
Hawker Siddeley Trident, Max Kingsley-Jones
Lockheed TriStar, Philip J. Birtles
The Aviation Hobby Shop – *Jet Airliner Production List, Turbo Prop Airliner Production List*
The Concorde Story, Christopher Orlebar
The Spirit of Dan-Air, Graham M. Simons

INDEX